IMAGES
of America

PHIPPSBURG

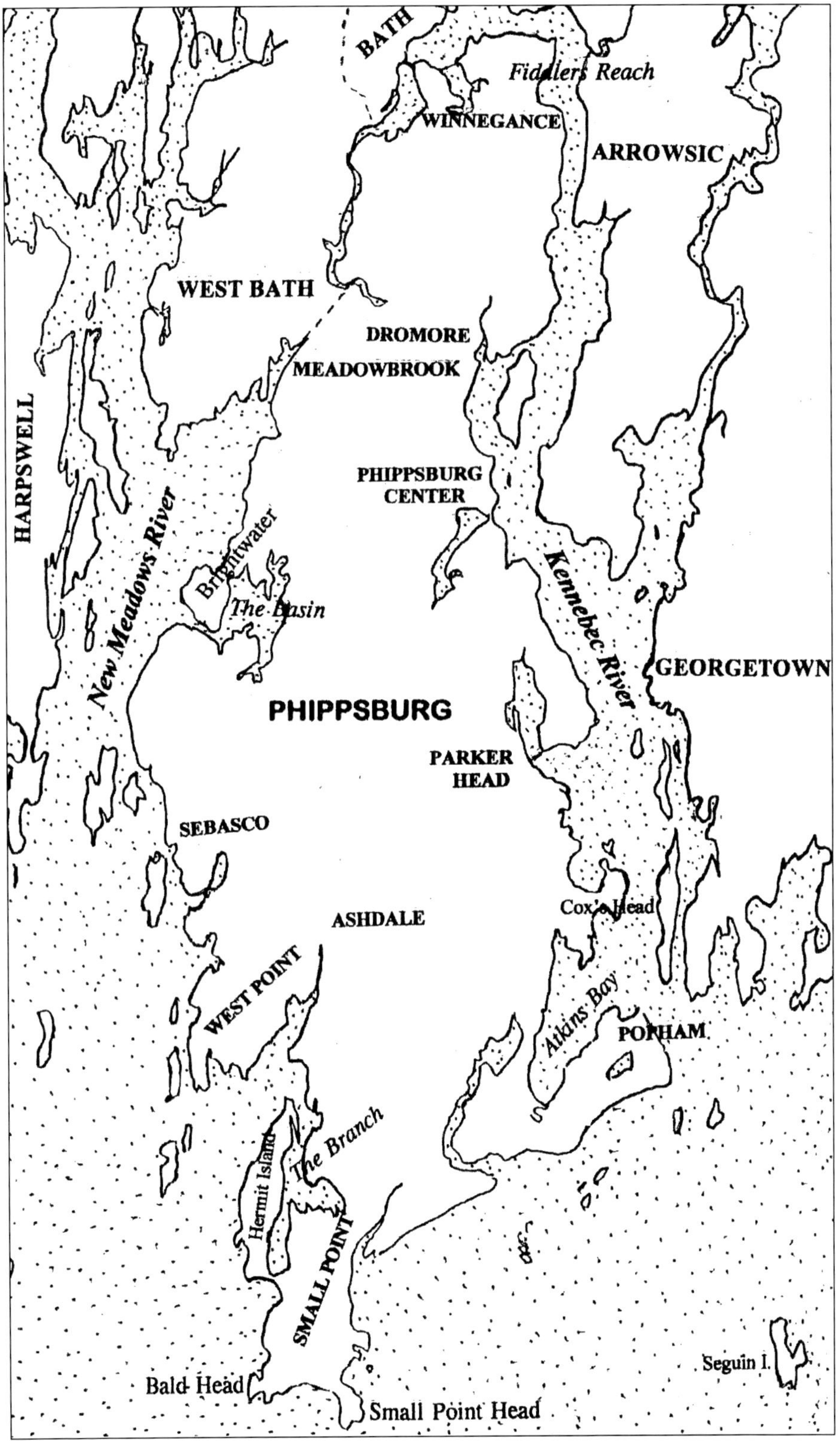
BATH
Fiddlers Reach
WINNEGANCE
ARROWSIC
WEST BATH
DROMORE
MEADOWBROOK
HARPSWELL
PHIPPSBURG CENTER
New Meadows River
Brightwater
The Basin
Kennebec River
GEORGETOWN
PHIPPSBURG
PARKER HEAD
SEBASCO
Cox's Head
ASHDALE
WEST POINT
Atkins Bay
POPHAM
The Branch
Hermit Island
SMALL POINT
Seguin I.
Bald Head
Small Point Head

IMAGES
of America

PHIPPSBURG

Elin B. Dozois

ARCADIA
PUBLISHING

ISBN 978-0-7385-0095-9

Published by Arcadia Publishing
Charleston, South Carolina

Printed in the United States of America

Library of Congress Catalog Card Number: 99-62769

For all general information contact Arcadia Publishing at:
Telephone 843-853-2070
Fax 843-853-0044
E-mail sales@arcadiapublishing.com
For customer service and orders:
Toll-Free 1-888-313-2665

Visit us on the Internet at www.arcadiapublishing.com

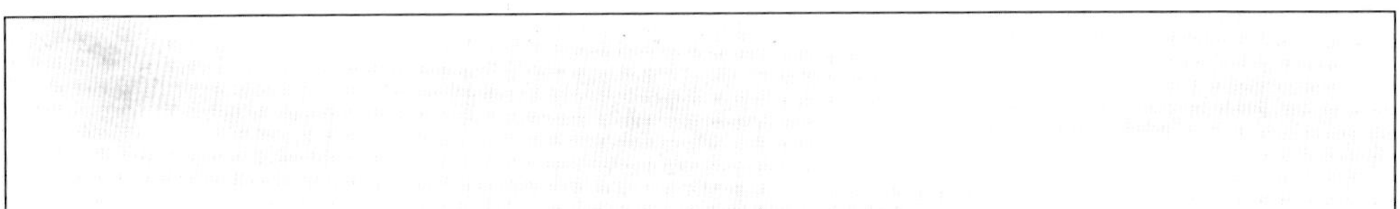

This monument on Sabino Hill in Popham was erected in August 1907 by the Maine Historical Society and is inscribed as follows: "The First English Colony on the Shores of New England was Founded Here August 20th, 1607, under George Popham." Reportedly, about 200 guests showed up on August 29, 1907, for the unveiling of the tablet, which was followed by a 17-gun salute.

Contents

ACKNOWLEDGMENTS

Many friends and neighbors have generously loaned or given their photographs, postcards, and other images, as well as their knowledge and memories, for inclusion in this book. They are as follows: Joyce Bibber (4, 15t, 15b, 16t); Carol Doughty (27b, 28b, 29b, 32t, 39b, 62t, 83t, 91b, 110b, 116b, 117b, 120b, 121t, 124b, 125t, 125b, 126t, 126b, 128t); Jean Flink (38t, 41t, 49b, 50t, 50b, 52t, 86b, 92b, 100b, 103t, 103b, 113t, 114t, 123t, 123b, 127b); June Gilliam (23b, 25t, 25b, 27t, 60b, 74t, 77b, 119t); William S. Gilman (13b, 24t, 24b, 26t, 28t, 29t, 31t, 31b, 32b, 40t, 40b, 42t, 43b, 45t, 51t, 52b, 59b, 60t, 63t, 68t, 70t, 70b, 71t, 71b, 80b, 81t, 84t, 84b, 85t, 89b, 101t, 101b, 102, 104t, 104b, 106b, 116t, 119b, 122b); Ada Haggett (11b, 12b, 13t, 16b, 50b, 81b, 87, 88t, 88b, 89t, 99, 100t); Arlene Hamel (53, 54t, 54b, 55b, 105t); Tom Hinkle (118b, 121b, 122t); Cynthia Hunt (47b, 76t, 76b); Fred and Mary Libby (17t, 17b, 18b, 35b, 36t, 43t, 57b, 58t, 68b); Lloyd Lowell (18t, 58b, 59t, 69t, 69b, 93b); Jane McLanathan (34t, 35t, 120t); Gary and Michelle Morong and Gola Davis (10b, 30t, 30b, 45b, 46t, 46b, 47t, 74b, 75t, 75b, 77t, 78b, 79t, 79b, 80t, 85b, 86t, 90t, 90b, 91t, 108b, 109t, 109b); Alice and Lester Munsey (8, 11t, 62b, 82b, 107); Laura Nickerson (14t, 14b, 33, 37, 39t, 41b, 55t, 56b, 57t, 64t, 65t, 65b, 66t, 66b, 78t, 108t, 113b, 115t, 117t, 118t, 124t, 128b); Everett Perkins (5); Don and Kathy Rankin (19t, 19b, 20t, 20b, 82t, 93t, 95t, 95b, 96, 97t, 97b, 127t); and Margaret Wyman (26b, 38b, 44b, 60b, 61, 62t, 72t, 72b, 73t, 73b).

In addition, photographs were borrowed from the Albert F. Totman Library (22b, 44t, 56t, 92t, 94b), the Phippsburg Congregational Church (48, 49t, 51b), the Phippsburg Historical Society (9, 10t, 67, 39t), and the Maine Historic Preservation Commission (12t, 23t, 63b, 64b, 111, 112t, 112b, 114b). I sincerely thank all those who were so willing to share their pictures and give of their time. I also thank Marylee Dodge for giving me permission to use the images of the moving of the "Spite House," and Ceres McCourt Houston for making available her schoolroom picture (39t).

I especially want to thank Joyce K. Bibber for all her assistance, advice, encouragement, and prodding. Without her help, the task of completing this book would have been much more difficult and much less enjoyable!

Introduction

The town of Phippsburg is a peninsula reaching into the Atlantic Ocean between the mouth of the Kennebec River and the inlet known as the New Meadows River. It is comprised of various areas or villages, from Winnegance and Dromore at the north end to Ashdale and Small Point to the south. Most are on the water, with Meadowbrook, Sebasco, and West Point to the west, on the New Meadows, and Phippsburg Center, Parker Head, and Popham to the east on the Kennebec River. In addition, there are several islands of various sizes.

Phippsburg is the site of the first attempt to establish an English settlement on the north Atlantic coast. In August of 1607, under the leadership of George Popham, Englishmen arrived in what is now Atkins Bay and erected a fortification. Harsh conditions during their first (and only) winter in this area led them to return home, but not before building the pinnace *Virginia*, the first English ship to be constructed in North America. Those men thus began what would become a major industry of the area from the 18th into the 20th century: shipbuilding.

Numerous further attempts to settle the area were given up because of Native-American attacks, but in 1716 a settlement and fortification called Augusta was established at Small Point. The population of the area eventually grew, and farms were developed along the Kennebec and on the western side of town. In 1738 most of the territory that would become Phippsburg was made a part of the town of Georgetown, However, in 1814, six years before Maine became a state, the separate town of Phippsburg was incorporated.

Phippsburg's history and development were greatly influenced by the geographical features of the area. As was typical in early settlements, nearly everyone farmed; however, the rough and ledge-covered landscape was such that many sought other means of livelihood. Encouraged by sheltered coves and bays, all with easy access to the Atlantic Ocean, men took to the sea to fish. Some of those inlets could be dammed to provide sites for tidal mills (in which local trees were turned to lumber) and, later, for ice ponds. The town's location on a major river encouraged development of commerce and shipbuilding, with local fish, ice, and lumber being shipped all over the world, often in Phippsburg-built ships. The mouth of a river needed defensive fortifications, which were constructed from colonial years onward and manned during all wars. In time the presence of rugged scenery and long stretches of beach encouraged the development of resorts. Many of the early occupations are now only memories, but fishing and some boatbuilding are still done, while summers bring seasonal visitors to resorts, individual cottages, and the beaches.

The difficulty of traveling over Phippsburg's ledges and bogs contributed to the establishment of individual communities within the town. Each of these villages had its own school, and often separate churches, post offices, stores, and social organizations as well. Though this individualism is still evident today, it began to fade somewhat with improved roads and automobiles making easier trips northward to Bath and was further lessened with the establishment of the new consolidated school that opened in 1958.

This book in no way attempts to tell the entirety of Phippsburg's unique history. Rather, it attempts to show, through the use of pictorial images, some of the changes in the area as it grew and developed into what we know as Phippsburg today. Coverage of the different areas has depended upon availability of pictures; but the collected photographs offer glimpses of life from the time of early photography into the 1960s.

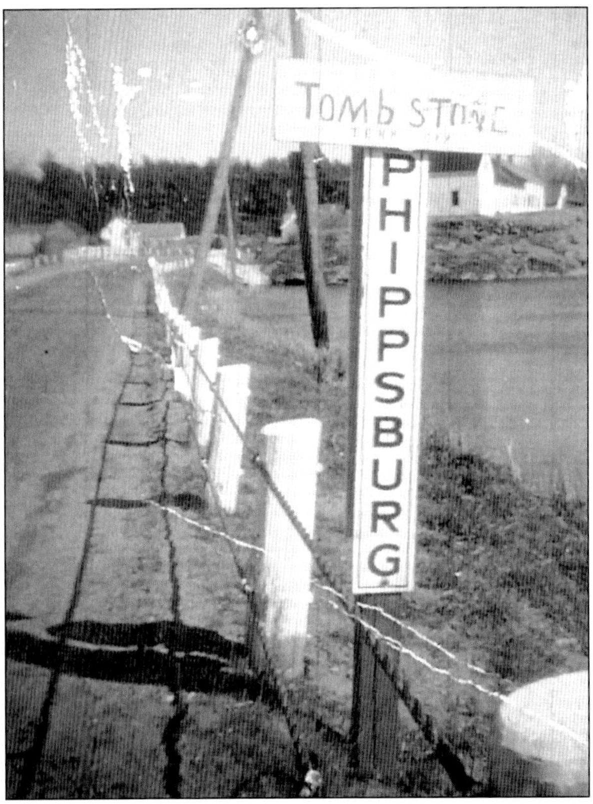

Beyond the Phippsburg town line sign was the settlement of Winnegance. Some jokester had added his own sign to the official one, much to the dismay of local authorities, c. 1950.

One

Our Town

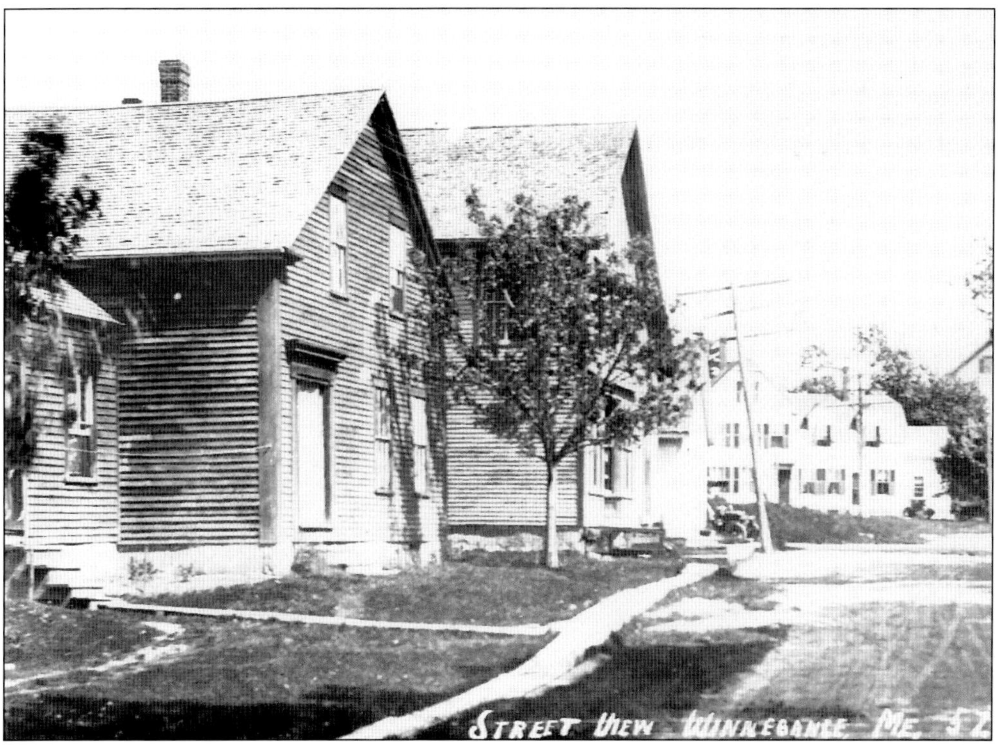

Phippsburg is made up of various communities. Winnegance, the site of a shipyard and early tidal lumber mills, was located across Winnegance Creek from Bath. This street view of Winnegance was taken in the early 1900s. Of the two buildings on the left, the first is now gone and the second is a furniture store. Straight ahead, the Manson-Ricker house and trees hide part of the Richard Morse homestead on the hill.

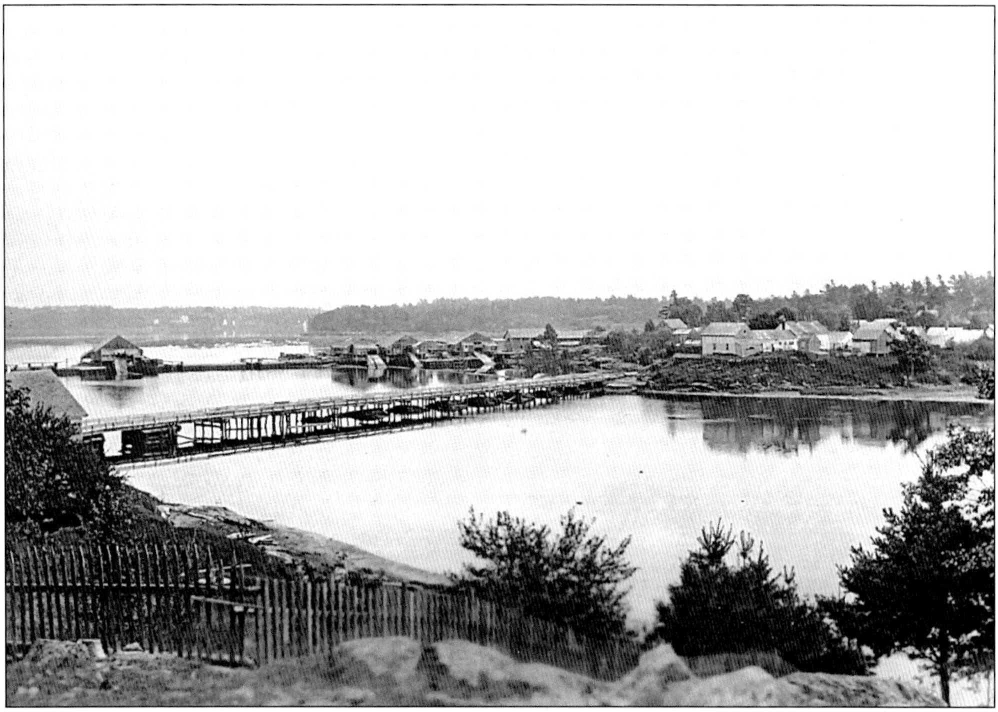

Winnegance, as seen from the Bath side of Winnegance Lake, was reached by a bridge until 1932, when a causeway replaced it. Beyond the bridge were several of the tidal mills that operated in Winnegance Bay throughout the 19th century.

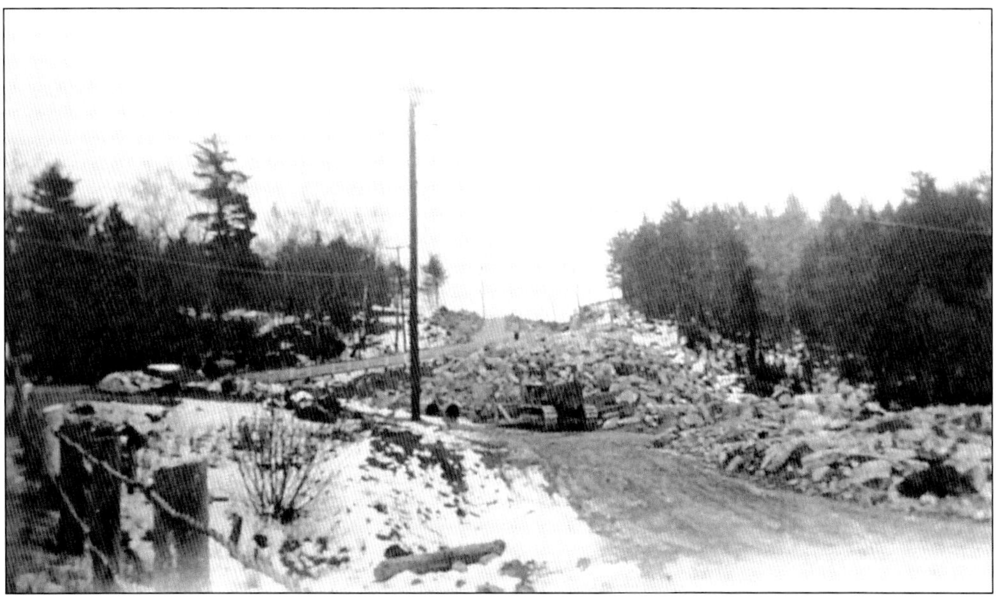

On the road south, Pitch Pine Hill in the Winnegance section of town was rocky, steep, and winding. Many stories have been told of drivers trying with difficulty to maneuver this stretch of road, particularly in the wintertime. The new road was under construction in 1954.

Road Commissioner Ralph Doughty made friends with a fawn that came to investigate road construction on the Clifford Road, *c*. 1960.

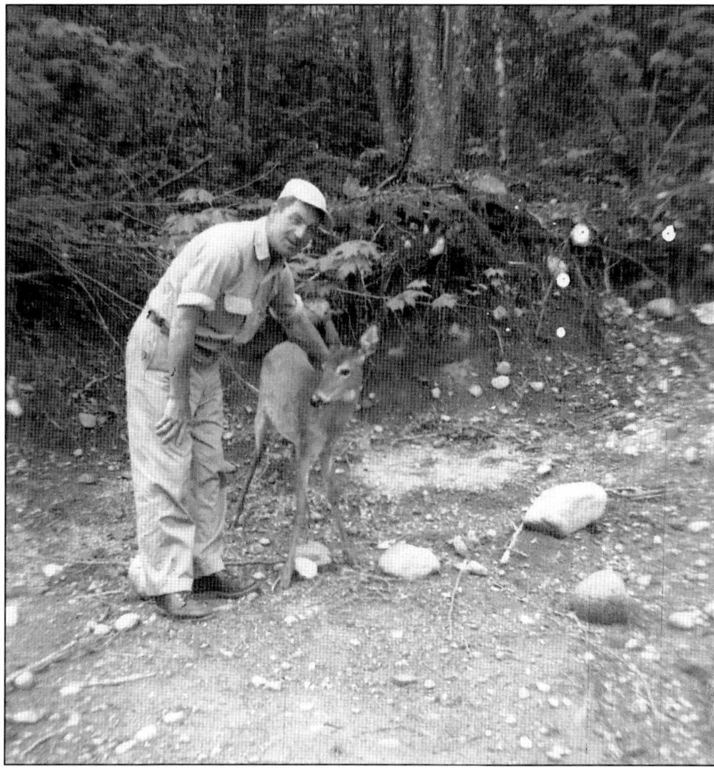

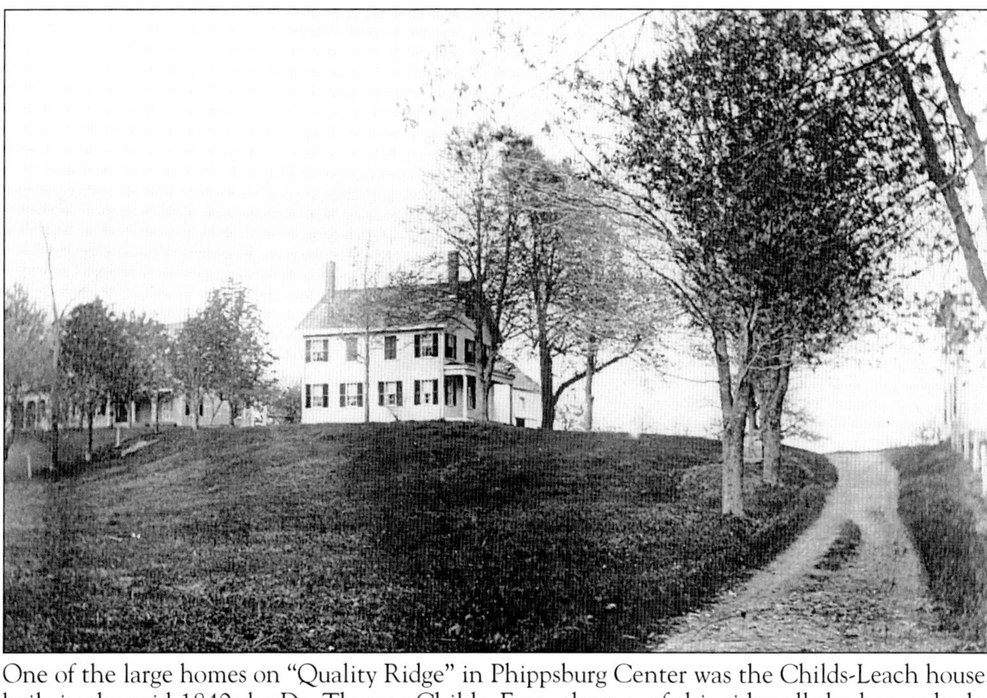

One of the large homes on "Quality Ridge" in Phippsburg Center was the Childs-Leach house, built in the mid-1840s by Dr. Thomas Childs. From the top of this ridge all the homes had a grand view of the Kennebec River and beyond. Both the Childs-Leach house and its neighbor to the north were destroyed by fire after 1960.

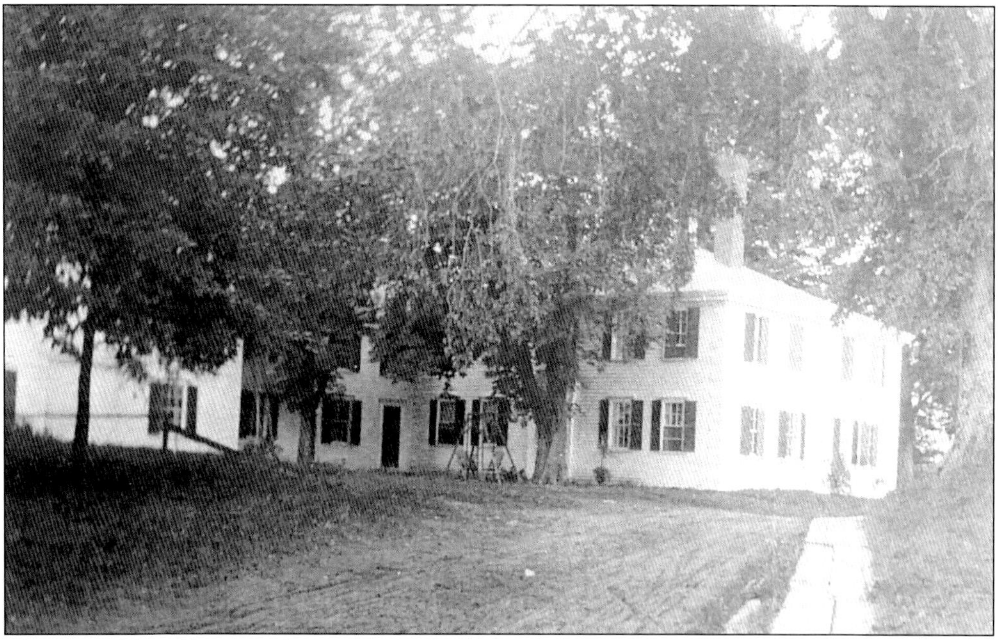

The McCobb-Hill-Minott house was built in 1773–74 on the Parker Head Road at Phippsburg Center. It was the home of Charles V. Minott Jr., who owned the nearby Minott Shipyard. Wooden sidewalks ran along the road before it was tarred in the late 1940s.

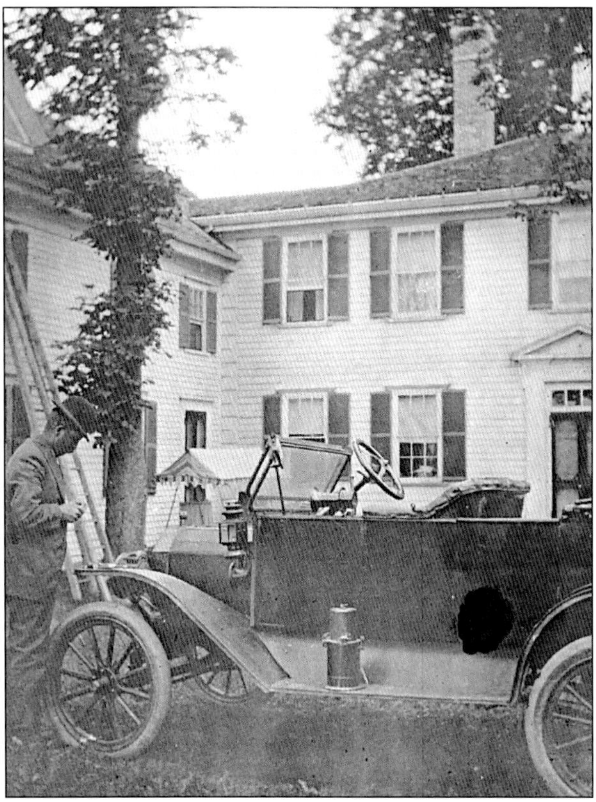

Charles V. Minott Jr. poses c. 1912 in front of the Minott home with his first car. Mr. Minott not only built and owned large vessels but was a storekeeper, postmaster, and sometime selectman as well.

This striking couple are Lottie and Henry Minott, standing by the Minott house on Church Lane. The picture was taken a few years after their 1907 marriage.

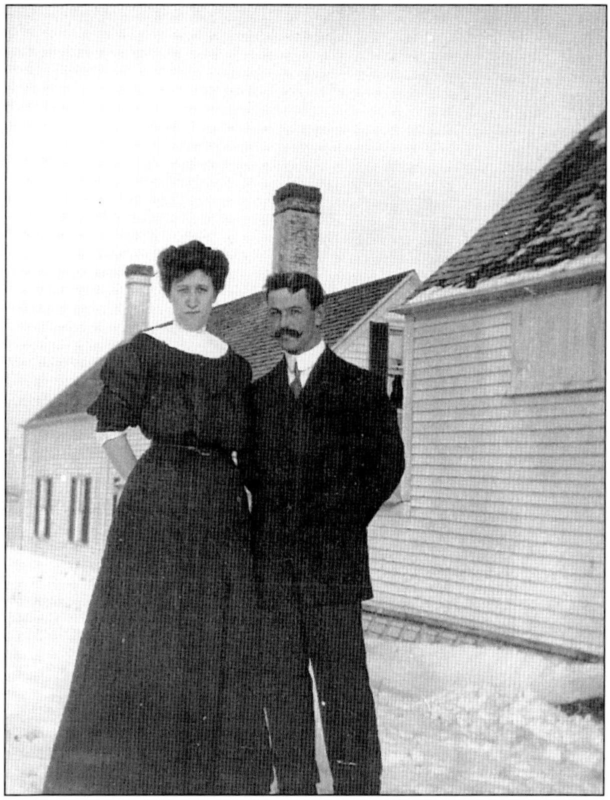

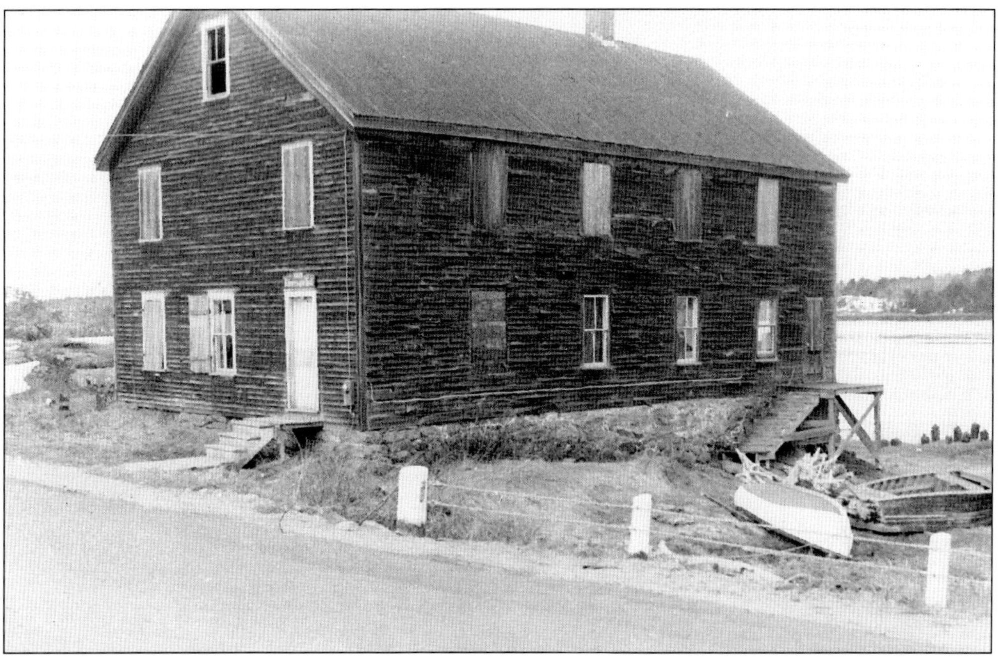

The old boardinghouse near Drummond Ice Pond, built in the 1880s, was later known as Riverside Hall and was home to various community groups. When it was torn down, its timbers were used for framing the Sportsmen's Club, which was built on Pitch Pine Hill in 1962.

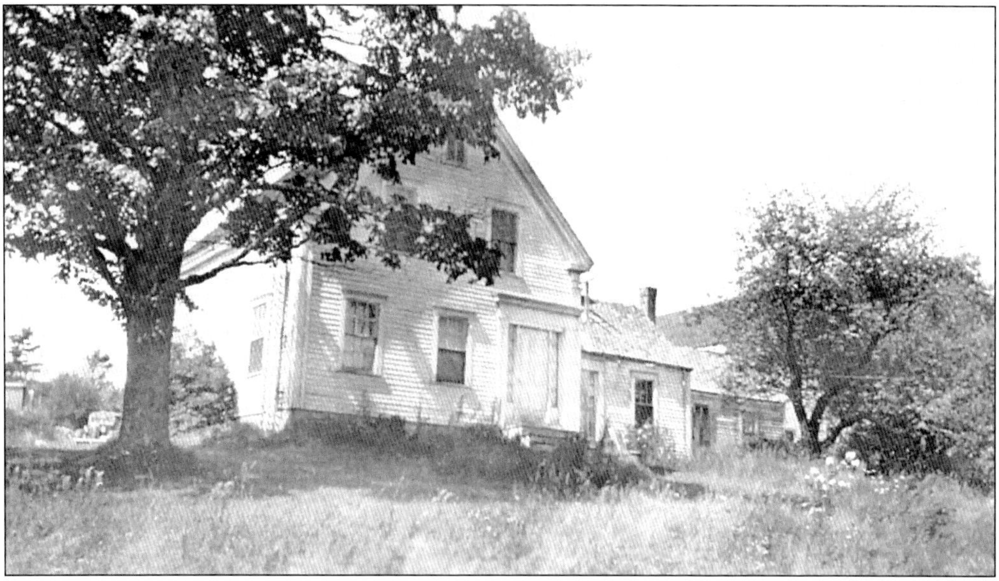

The Scott Campbell homestead, which in the summer of 1942 overlooked Center Pond from the west, was razed in the late 1960s.

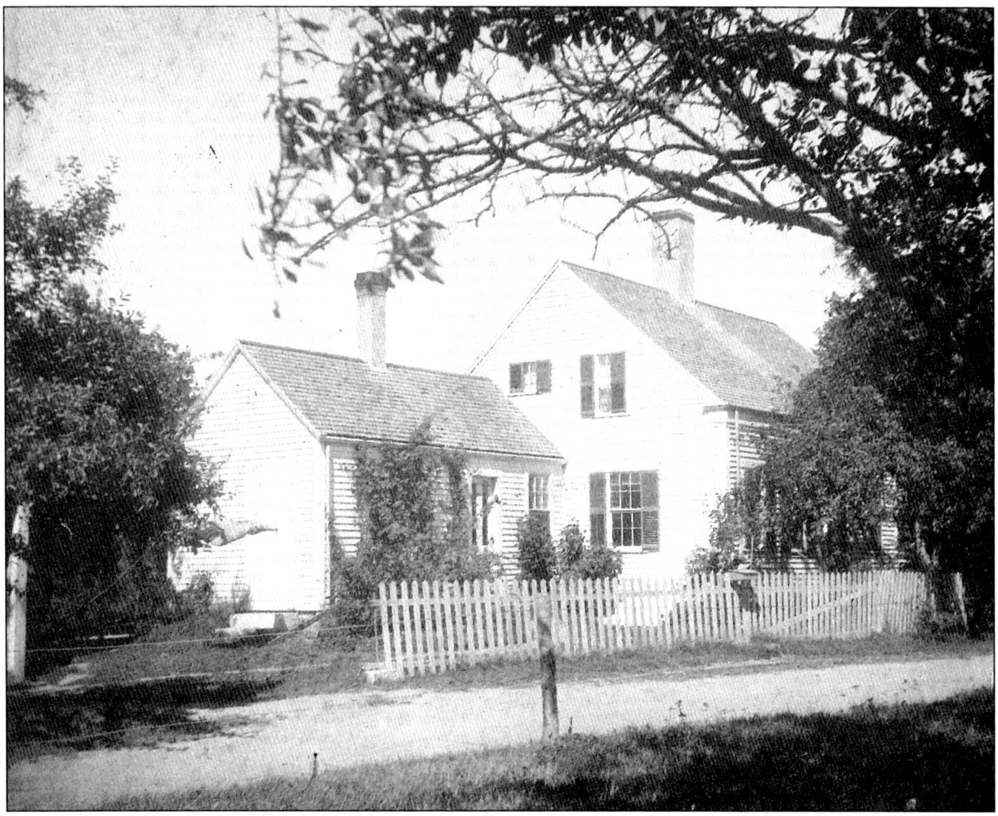

The Jewell-Malcolm house, shown here *c.* 1920, also overlooked the Center Pond. Until relocated in 1935, the road on the west side of the pond ran close to the front of the house.

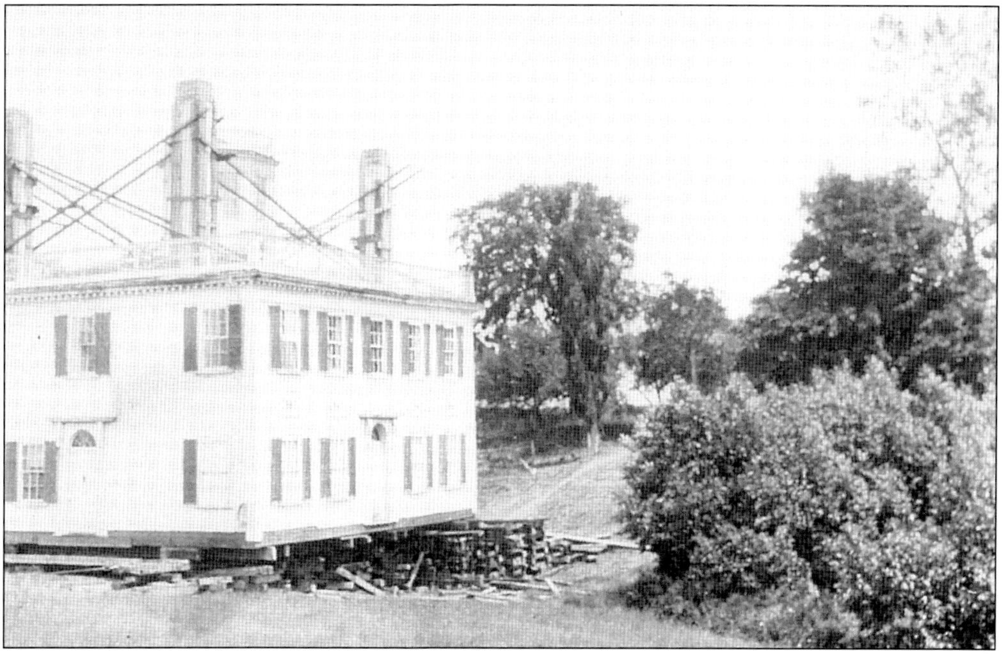

The Spite House was built overlooking the Center Pond in 1806 by Thomas McCobb. With its four chimneys, elaborate doorways, circular stairway, and richly carved woodwork inside and out, it was meant to be far grander than the McCobb house, which had been inherited by Thomas's stepmother. In 1925, the entire house was moved to Rockport. The photograph above shows the house immediately prior to its move. In the photograph below, the house has been loaded onto a lighter, after being pulled by oxen across the road to the old Minott Shipyard.

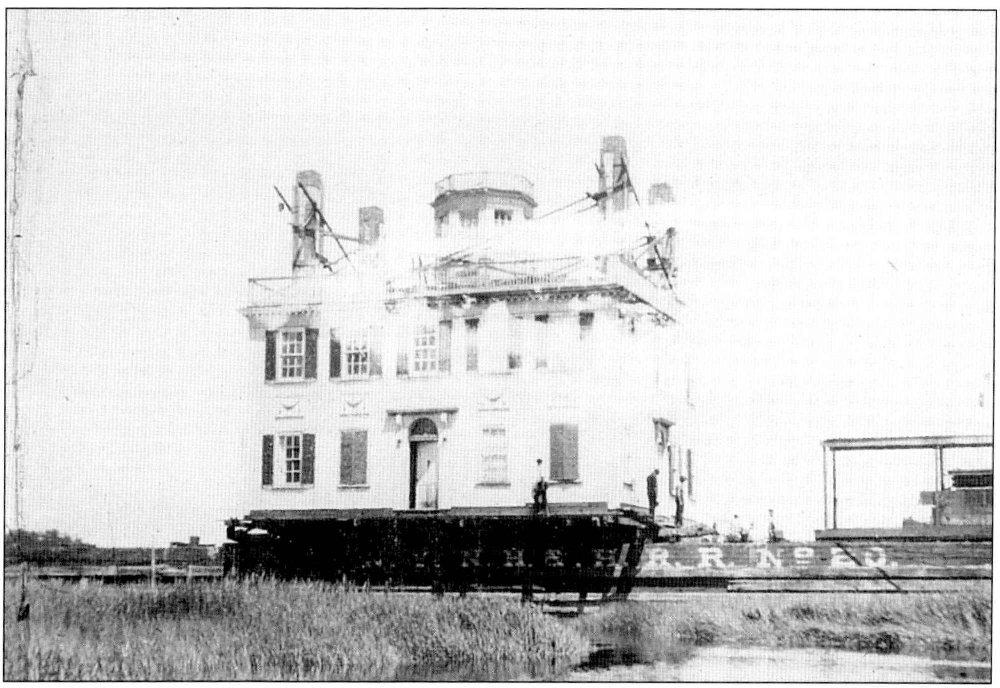

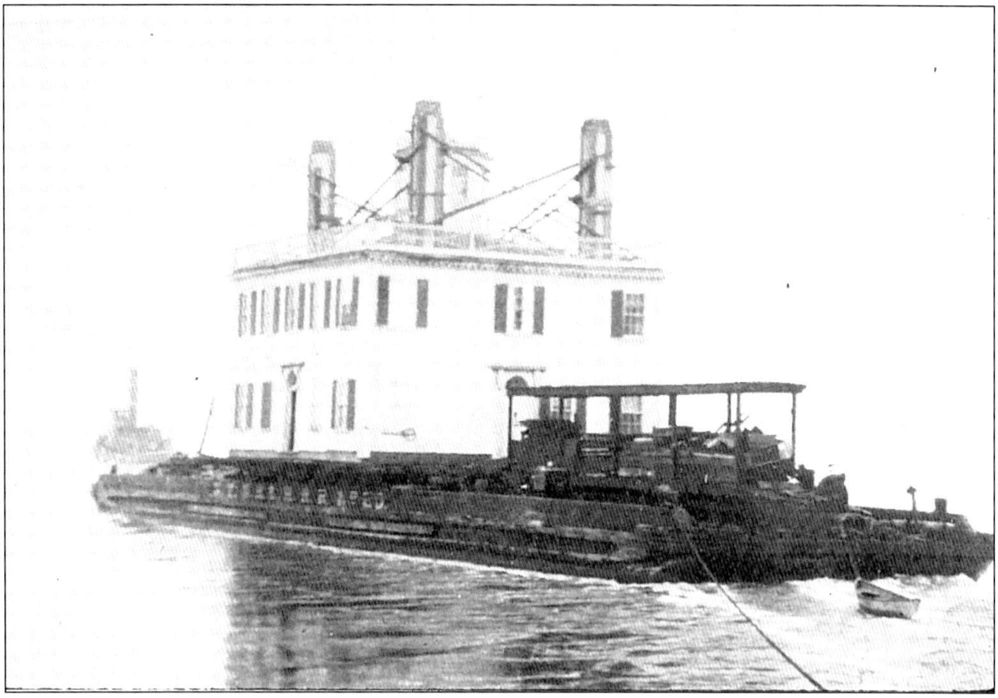

The Spite House made an impressive sight as it floated away on a barge furnished by the New York, New Haven, & Hartford Railroad. It was taken downriver and then east along the coast to Rockport.

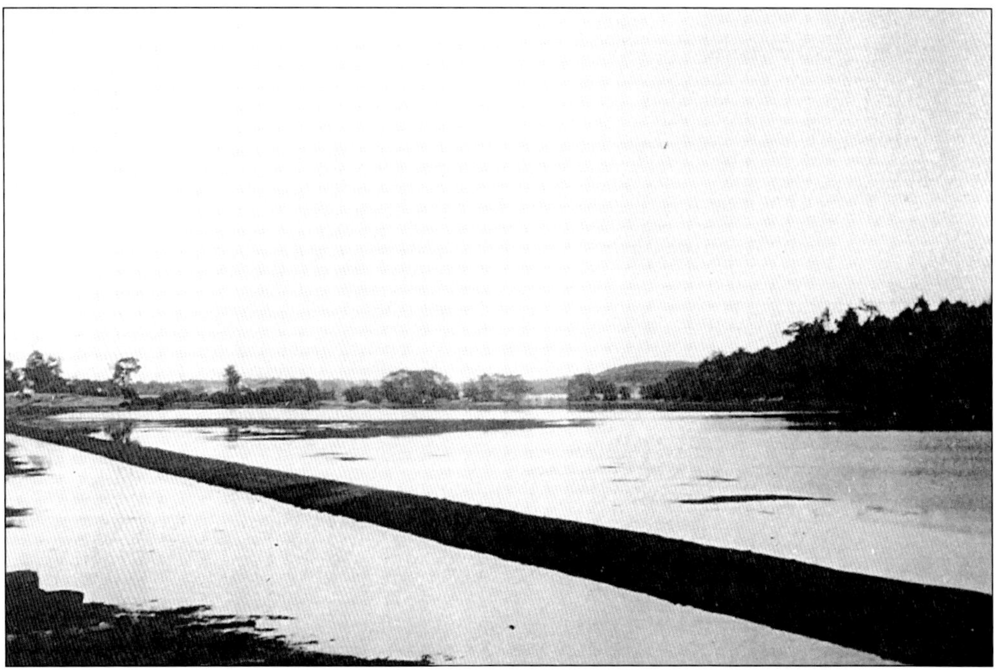

In 1882 the town voted to discontinue a portion of road at the Center, allowing for the building of the dam that formed the Center Pond (sometimes referred to as Minott Pond). This picture of the old road was taken in 1928, when the pond was drained to allow for repairs to the dam.

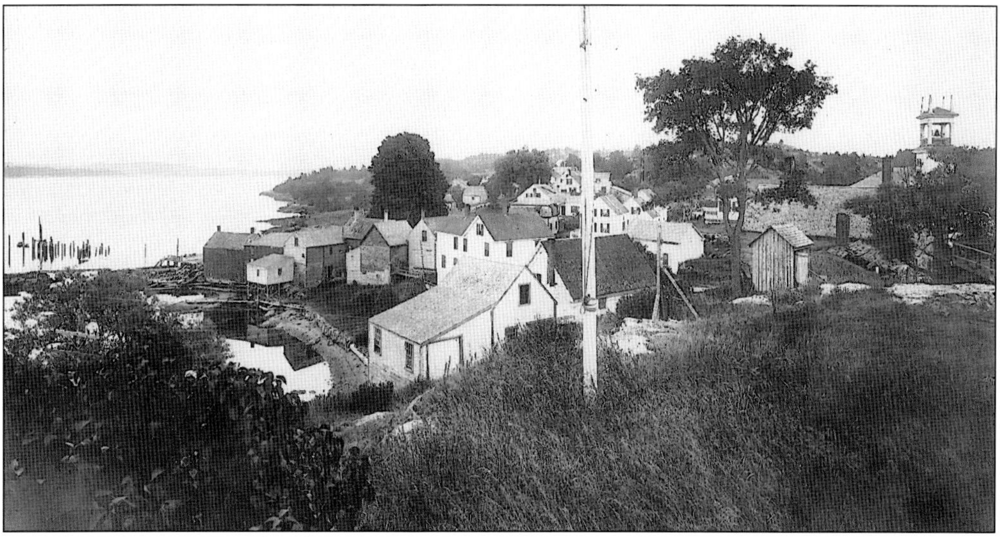

Lizzie Harrington's boardinghouse is the two-and-a-half-story white building in the center of this photograph of Parker Head Village before the fire of 1917. The Harrington's store is the last building on the left beyond what was Ed Wyman's house and outbuildings and Duley's Store. The steeple of the Parker Head Church (1846) can be seen at the right.

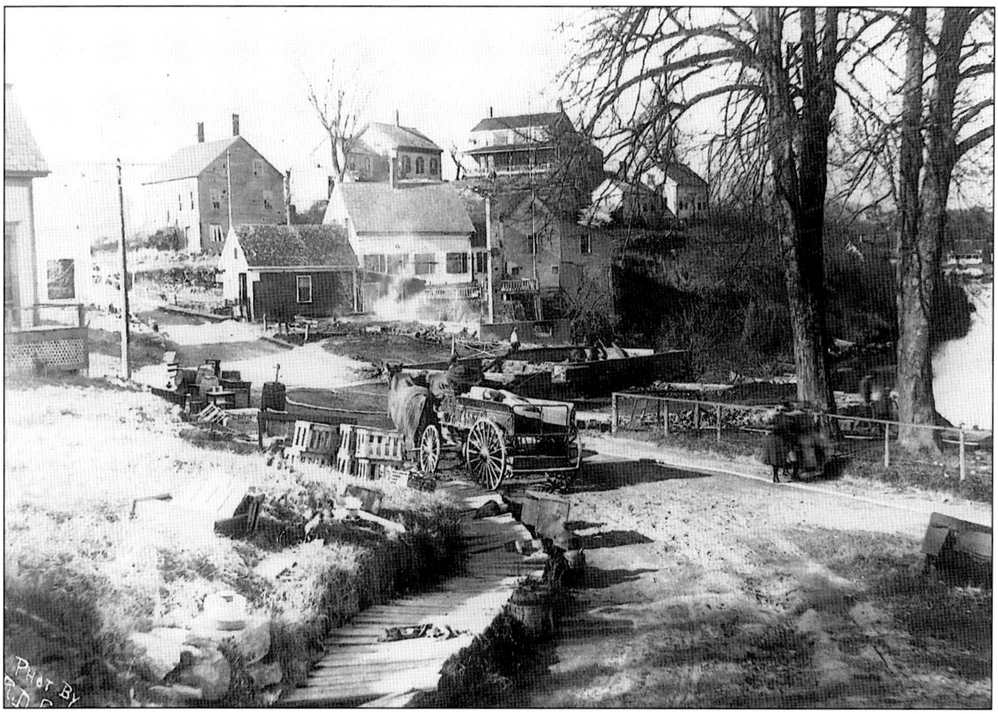

In 1917 a major fire destroyed three establishments in Parker Head Village. Foundations and smoldering embers marked all that remained of Lizzie Harrington's boardinghouse, Duley's Store and home, and the Ed Wyman homestead. To the left of the fire remains, the Parker Head Post Office survived. The horse-drawn vehicle has been identified as the fire truck. The crates and barrels on the opposite side of the road were presumably removed from the burning buildings. The wooden sidewalks were clearly in need of repair.

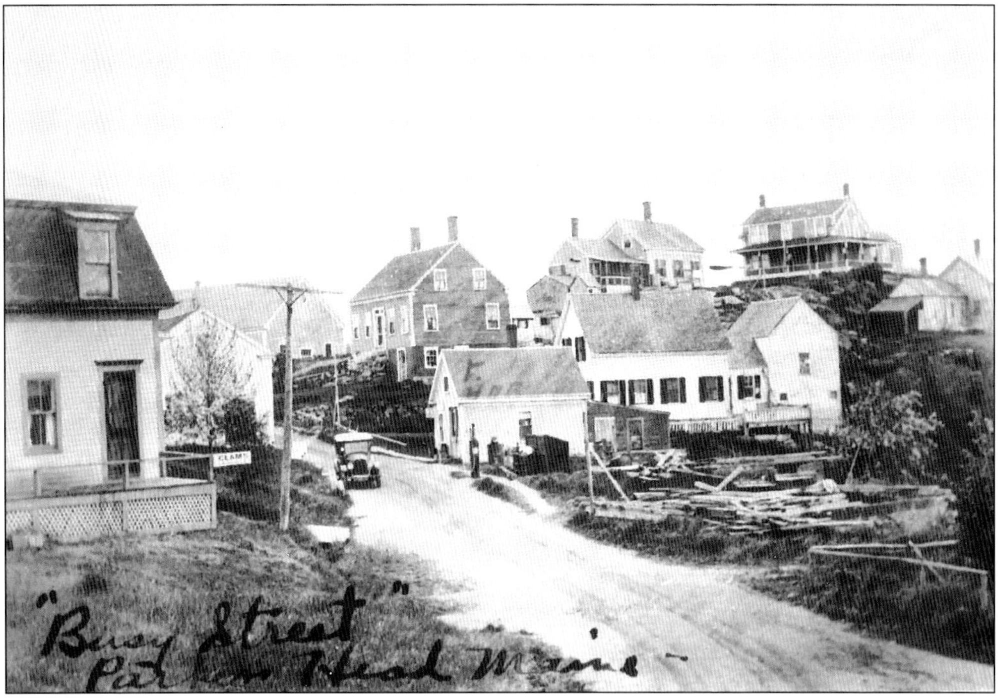

A postcard labeled " 'Busy Street,' Parker Head, Maine," shows reconstruction beginning after the fire of 1917, with the house on the left offering "Clams for sale" and a gas pump added beside the post office. "Busyness" is restricted to a car moving past the vestry. The dance hall can be seen beyond the vestry.

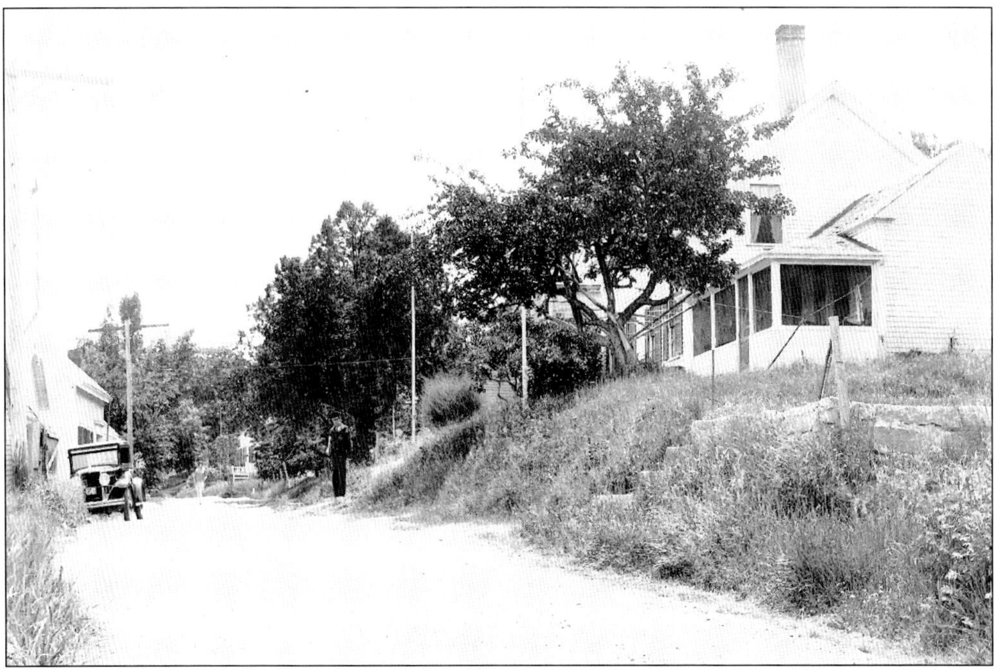

Standing in front of the Harrington homestead in Parker Head is Fred Harrington. Across the road is his new 1931 auto.

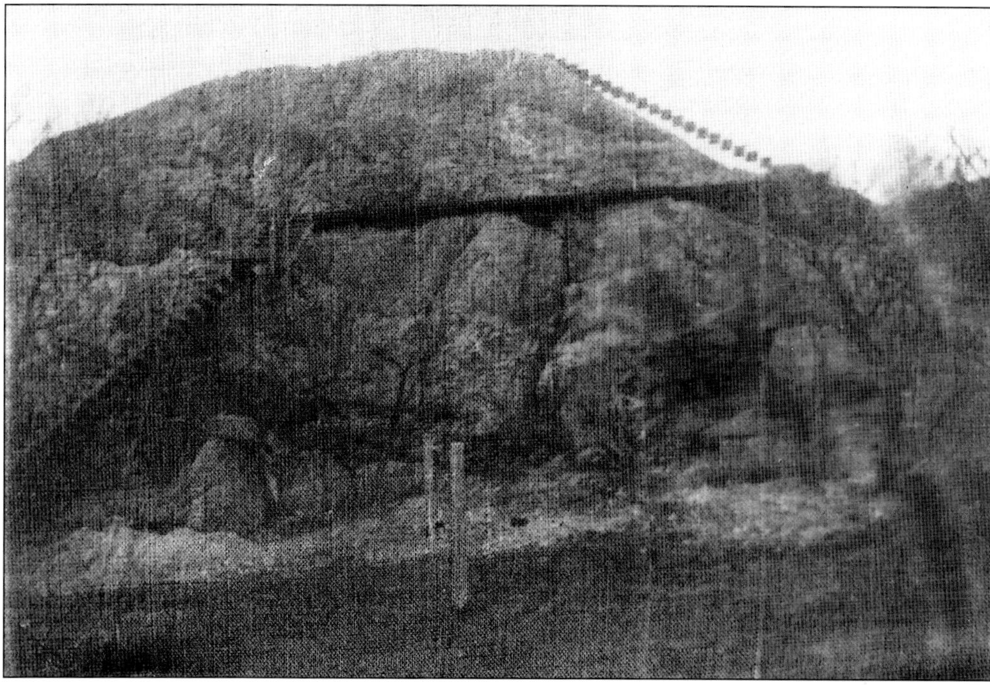

The original of this very early picture believed to be of Cox's Head was printed in blue on white fabric. Steps lead from left to right, then back to the top of the massive landform.

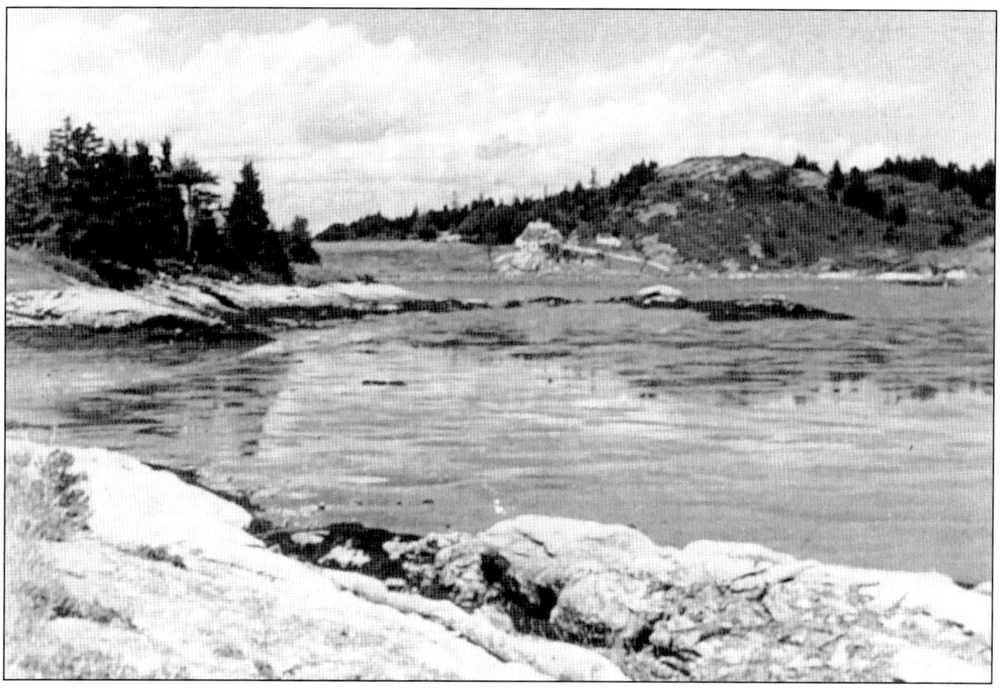

Cox's Head and the Thomas Perkins homestead were photographed from the entrance to Porterfield Creek in September 1945. The flagpole atop the Head was said to have been used for signaling colliers entering the river when the coaling station needed replenishing. Cox's Head was garrisoned during the American Revolution and the War of 1812.

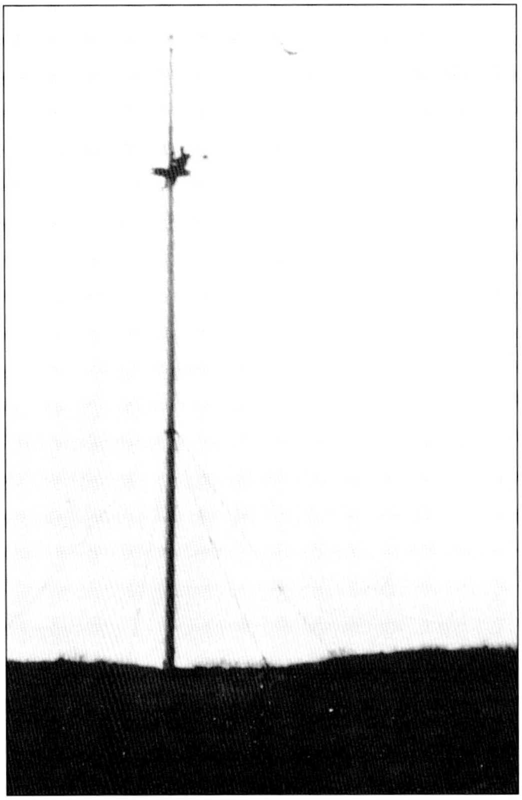

A signalman sits on the crossarms high up the flagpole at the top of Cox's Head.

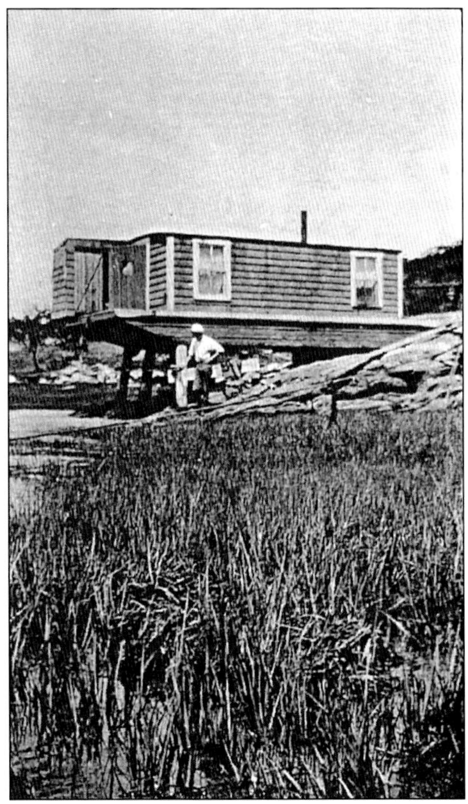

This barge was propped up on the Atkins Bay side of Cox's Head in 1923. Is it a cottage? A bathhouse? A fishhouse? The curtains and stack would indicate a residence of some sort. Where it came from and where it went is a mystery.

Everett Perkins of Cox's Head and Everett, MA, began painting after his retirement from the police force in 1965 and has been referred to as "our own Grandma Moses." Most of his paintings show remembered scenes from Cox's Head and Popham.

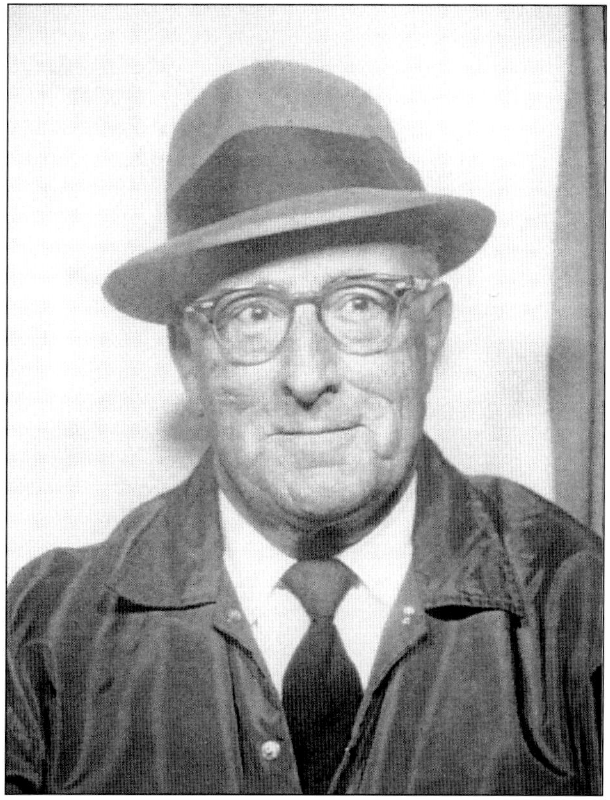

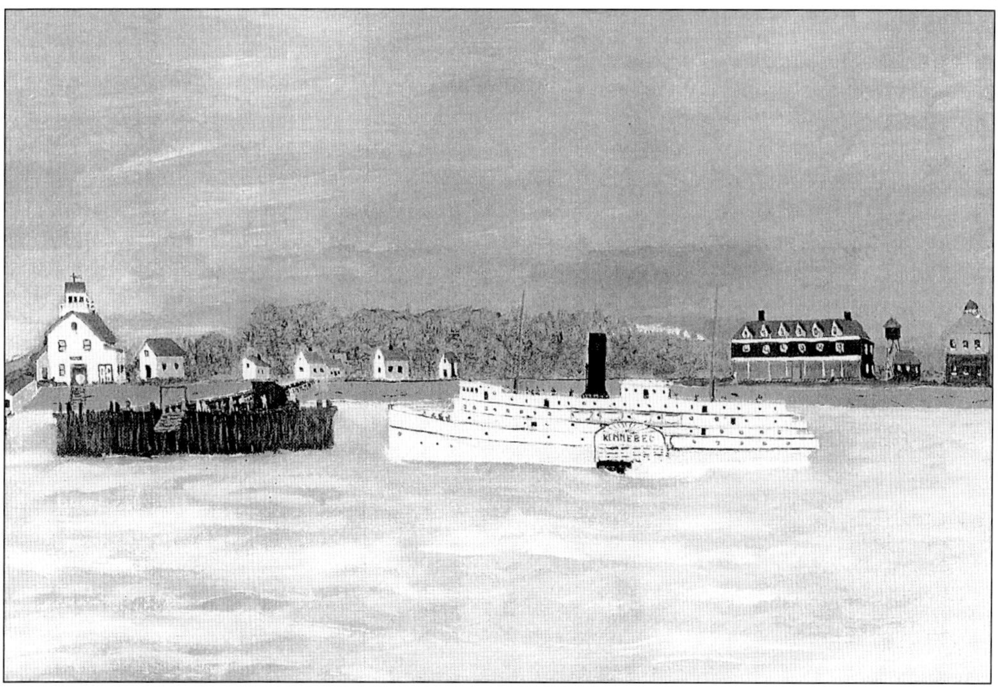

In this oil painting by Everett Perkins, the *Kennebec* was approaching the steamboat wharf between the Popham Life Saving Station and the Riverside Hotel.

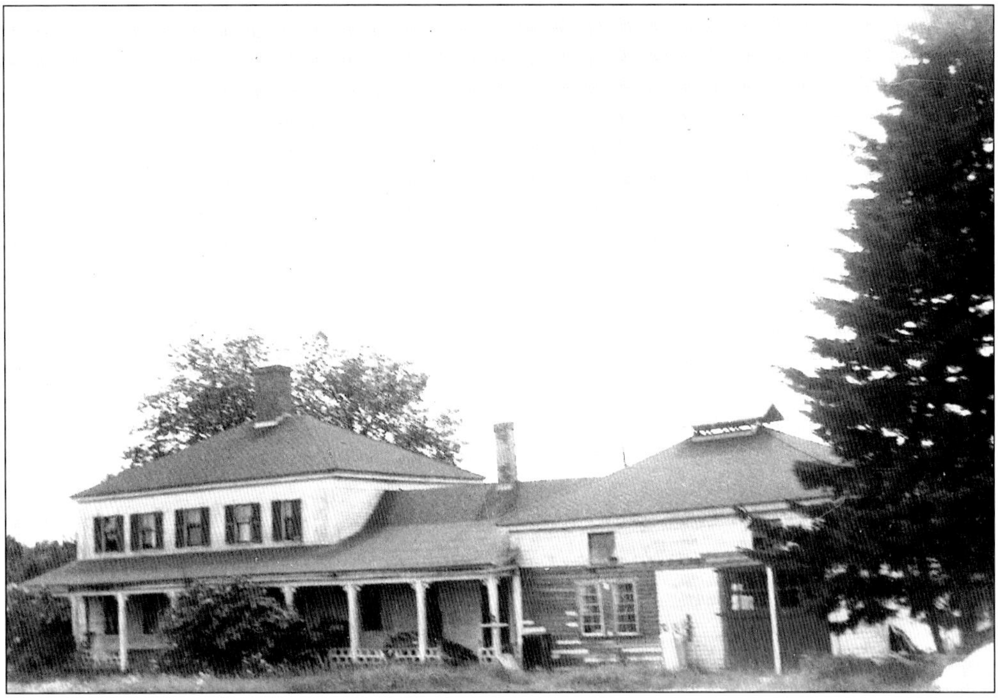

This early-19th-century center-chimney house, originally a Percy homestead, later became known as the Malcolm Place and then as the Thomas Place. It was located on top of the hill between Cox's Head and the Popham Road. The farm burned in October 1961.

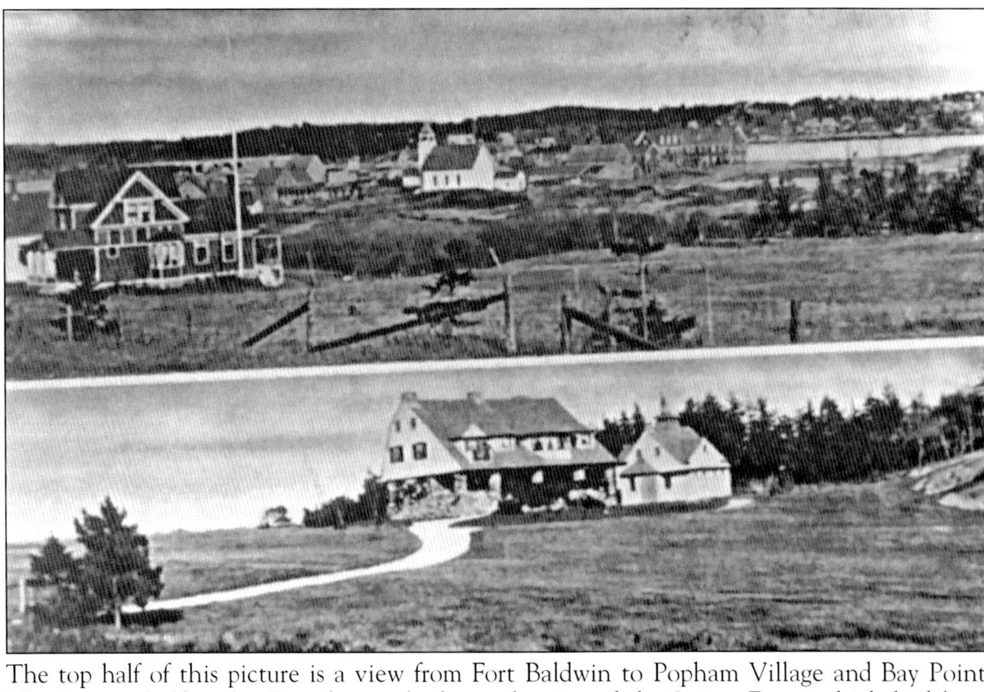

The top half of this picture is a view from Fort Baldwin to Popham Village and Bay Point. The bottom half is the Stonehouse, built on the site of the Irving Farm, which had been razed in 1891.

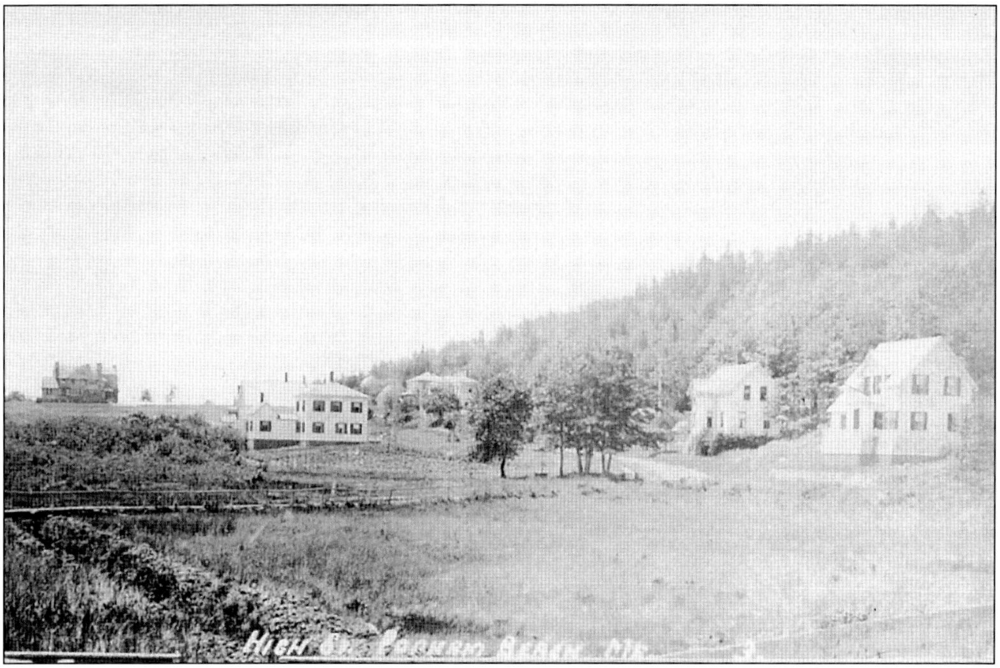

From left to right on High Street, Popham Beach, are the Stonehouse, the Herbert Sprague homestead (with the roof of the school visible beyond), Llewellyn Oliver's home, and the Captain James Perkins' house.

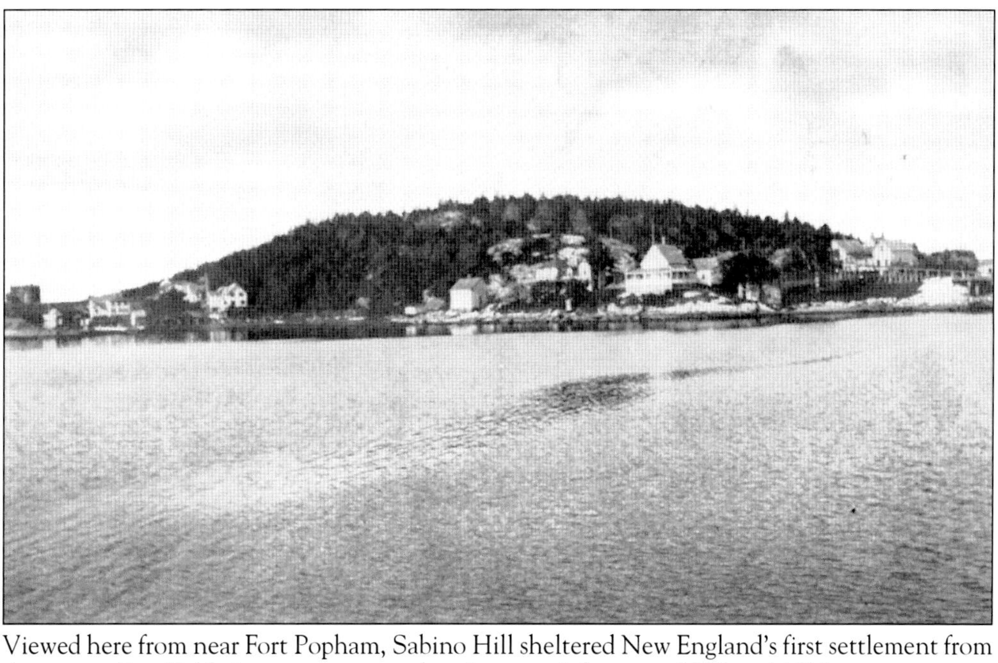

Viewed here from near Fort Popham, Sabino Hill sheltered New England's first settlement from the ocean. Fort Baldwin was constructed on its summit between 1905 and 1912.

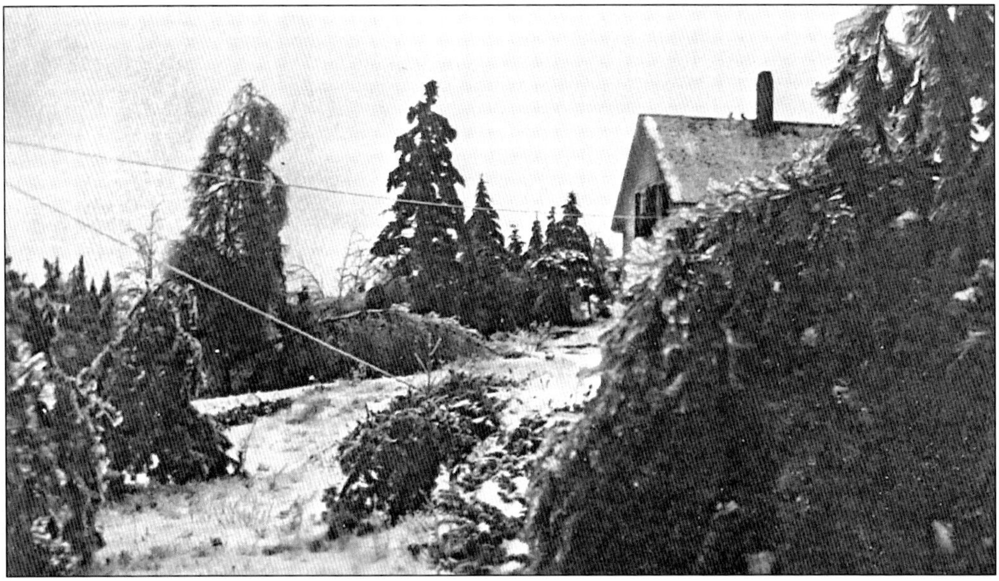

Downed telephone wires (electricity had not as yet reached the area) and snow-laden trees near the Gilman home on the Small Point Road were a result of the ice storm of 1926.

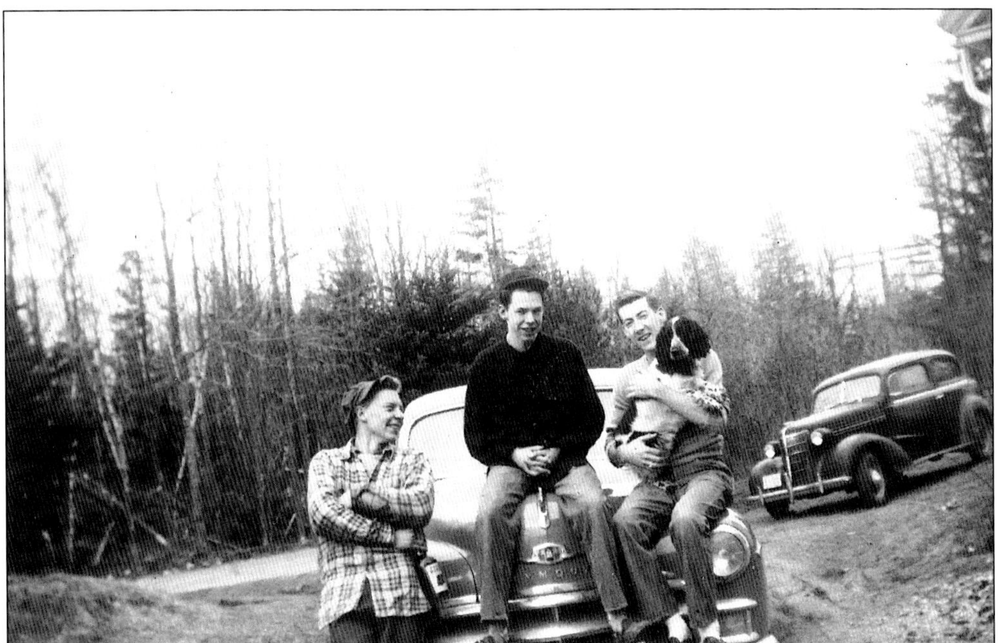

Maurice Blair, William S. Gilman, and Swanton H. Wyman Jr. pose on the hood of Stan Gilman's 1950 Plymouth. In the background is Junior's 1938 Chevrolet. The picture was taken at the Wyman home on the Small Point Road.

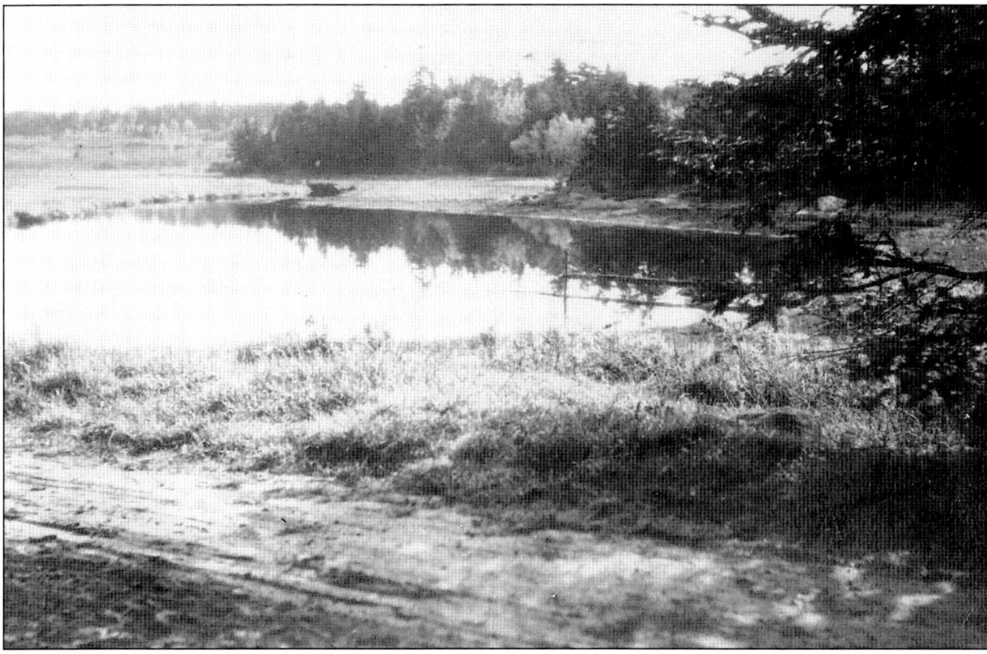

South of Morse's Mountain, the Small Point Road divides a portion of The Branch on the west from this former ice pond on the east.

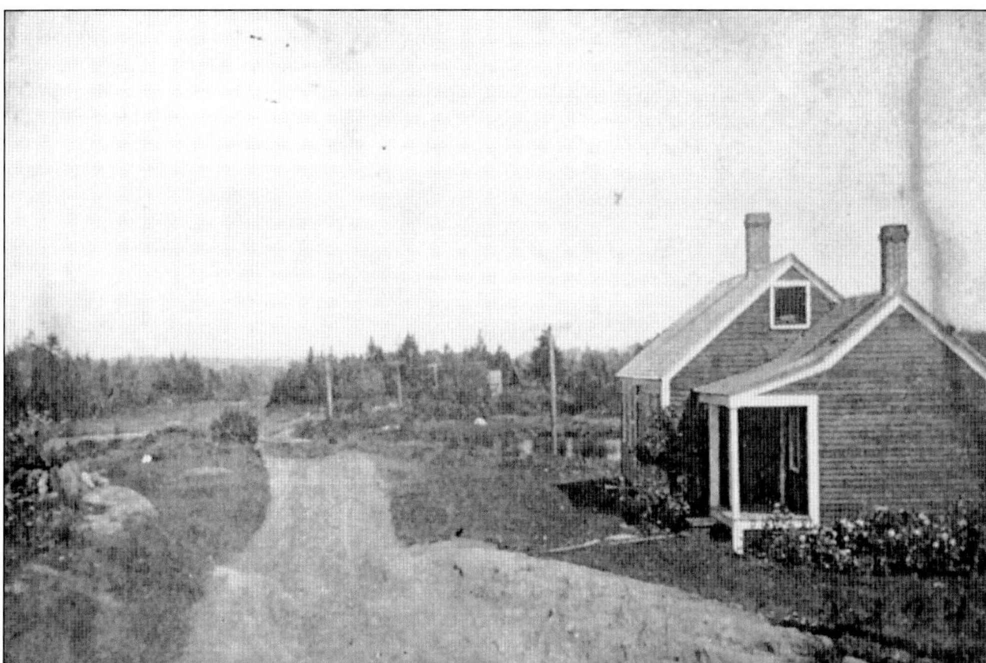

The same pond can be seen on the right, beyond the Sylvester-Dearborn house, moved here by oxen from Morse's Mountain.

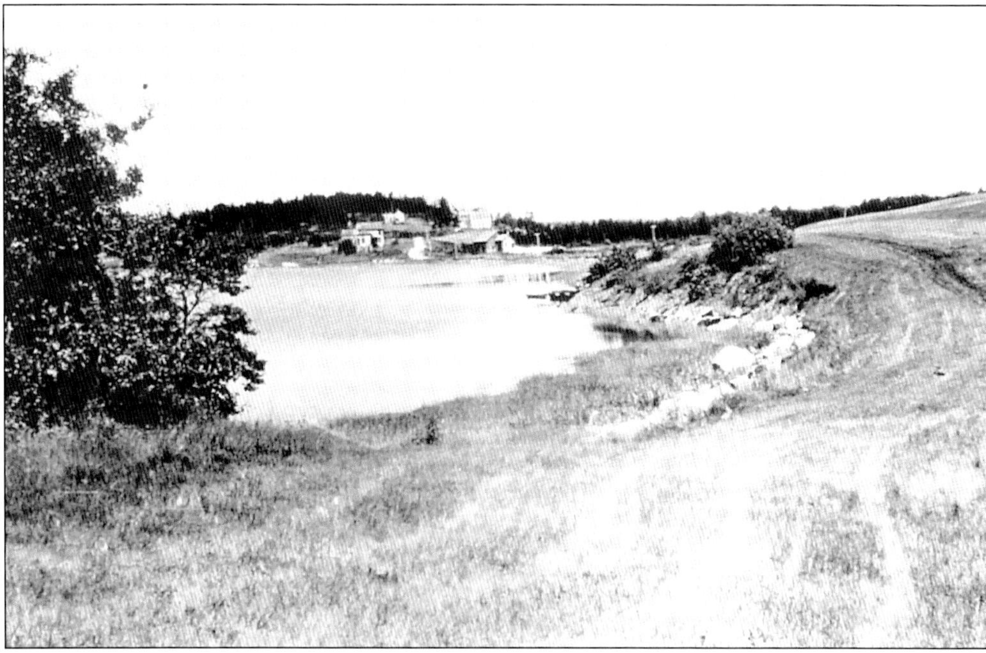

The field in the foreground was the site of the Sprague homestead of 1778. Across The Branch were homes belonging to the Charles Pyes, the Spragues, and the Thompsons.

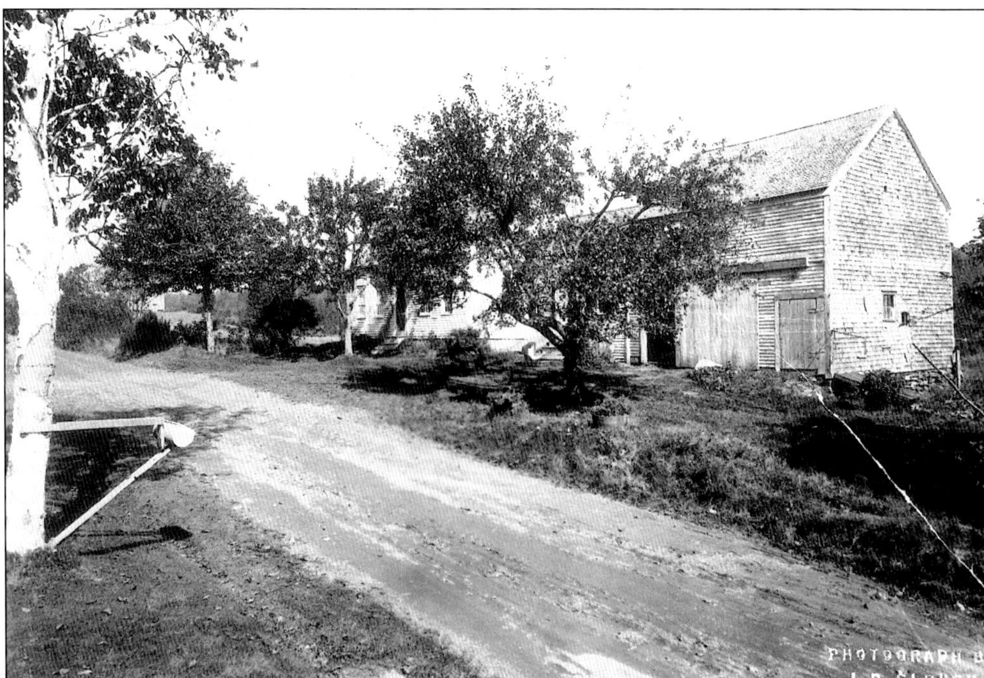

The Miles Webber house at Small Point was originally owned by the Wildes family. It was moved by a team of oxen from the Wildes' field when the road was built in its present location.

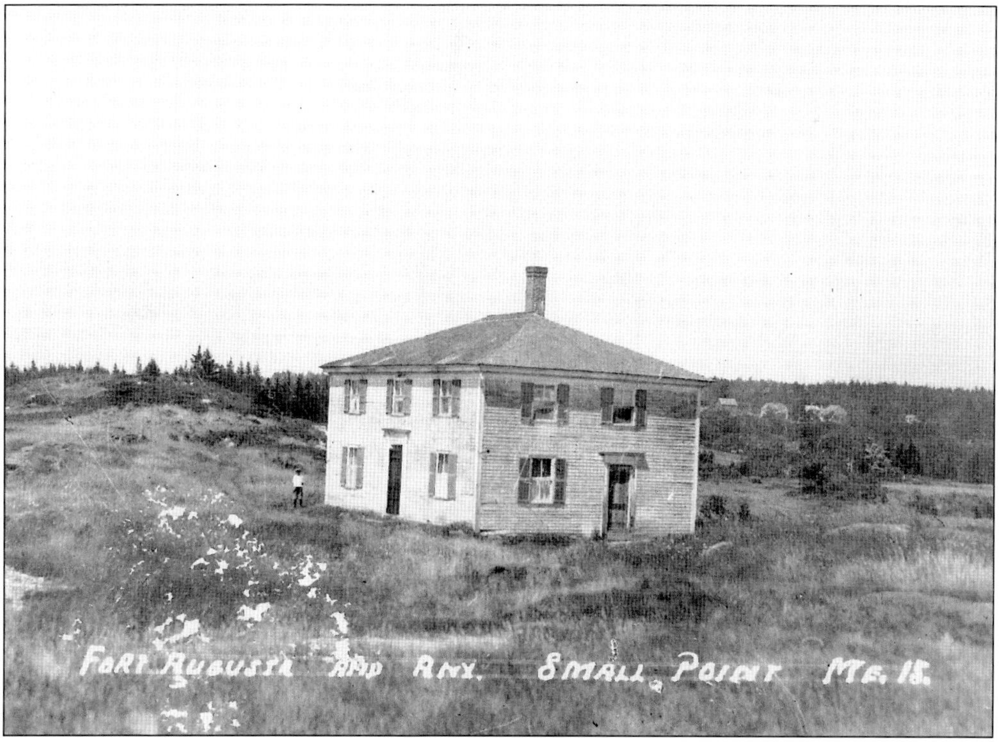

"The Square House" (*c.* 1790), sometimes referred to as the cottage or annex to the Alliquippa Hotel on Small Point Harbor, was home to the Lowell family. It was located just south of old Fort Augusta.

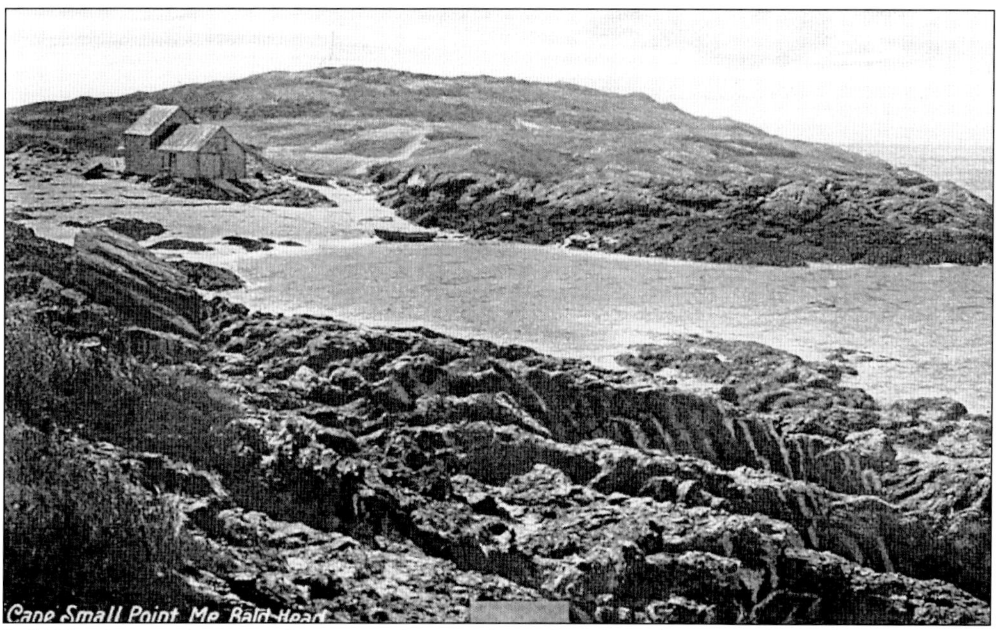

Bald Head is a rocky point that protrudes into Casco Bay from the west side of Small Point. The fishhouse of Lemuel Wallace, nestled in a sheltered cove here, was eventually abandoned and fell down in the 1930s or 1940s.

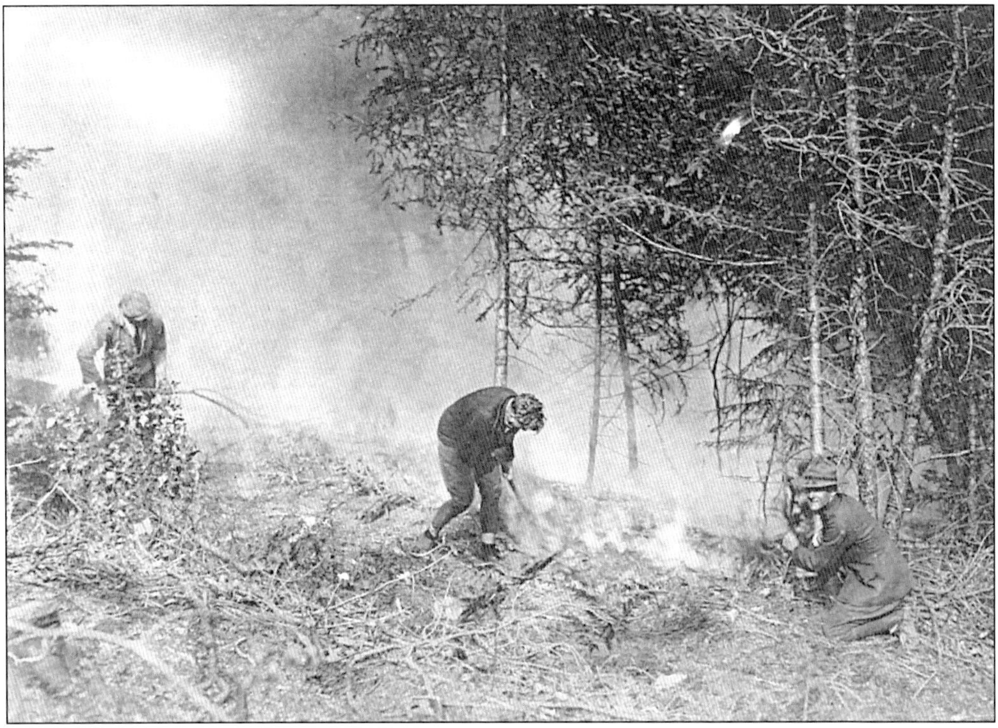

Phippsburg has had its share of fires over the years. In 1913, and again in 1927, fires burned a large portion of the town. Stanwood Gilman (center) and William H. Gilman (right), along with an unidentified man, fought a forest fire in Ashdale in 1927.

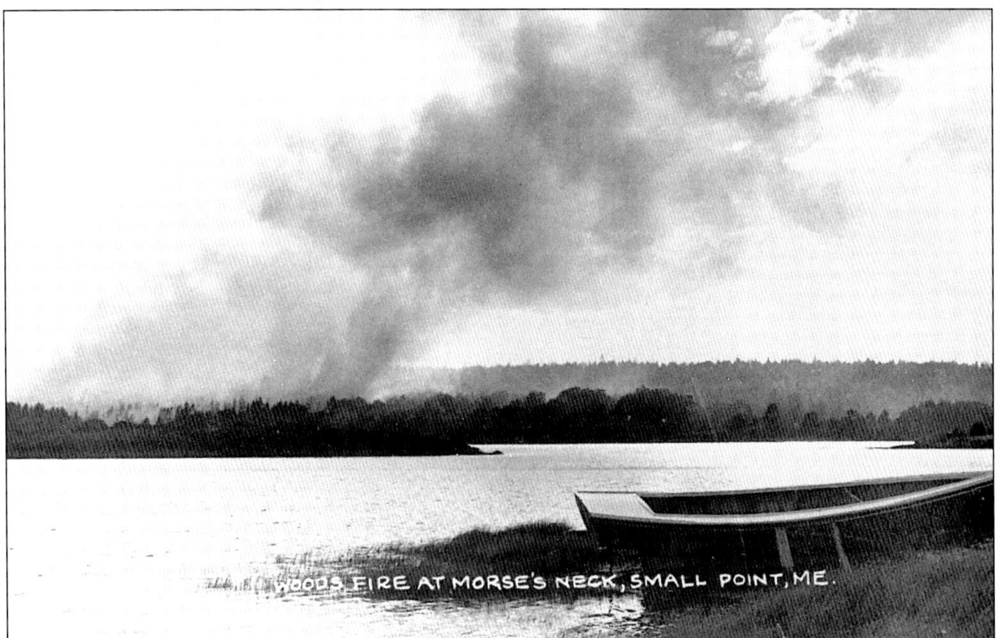

A forest fire on Morse's Neck, believed to be in the late 1930s, was photographed across a portion of The Branch. Morse's Neck later became known as Hermit Island.

Elisha Totman of the Small Point Road went out for a ride about 1910.

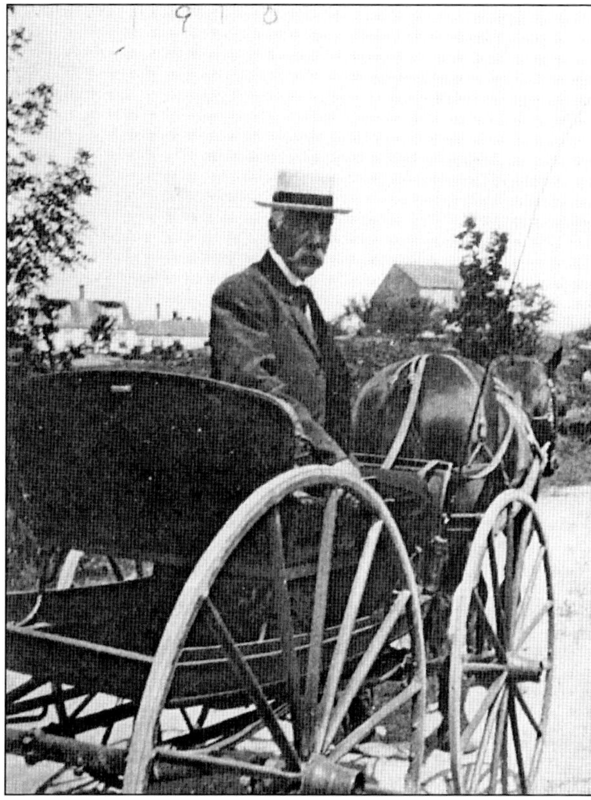

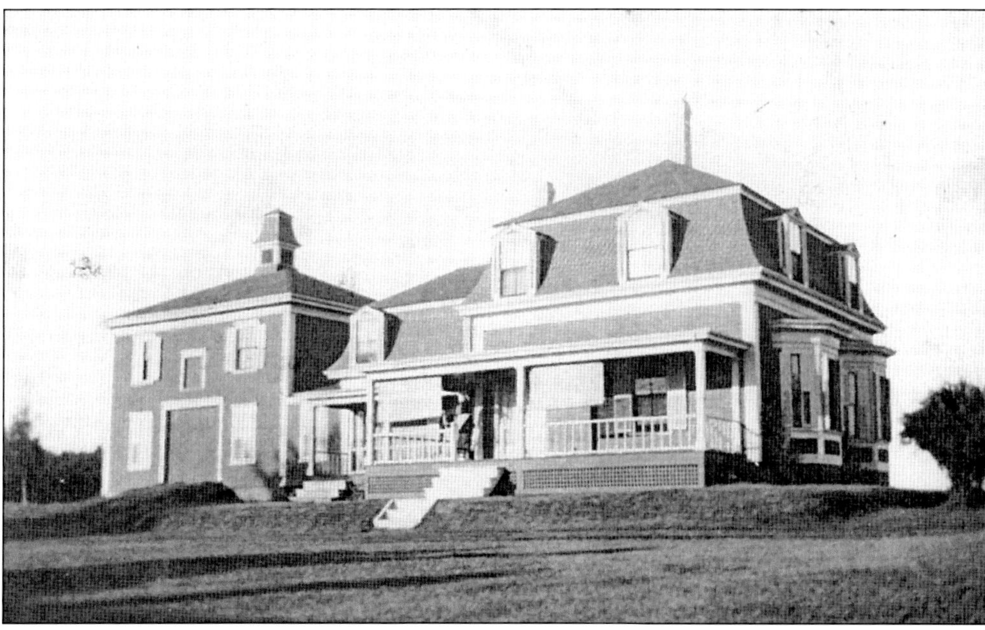

The Butler homestead in Sebasco, aptly called "The Anchorage," was the home of Captain William Butler. It stood on the hill overlooking the mouth of the New Meadows River, and its cupola was reportedly used as a landmark by mariners.

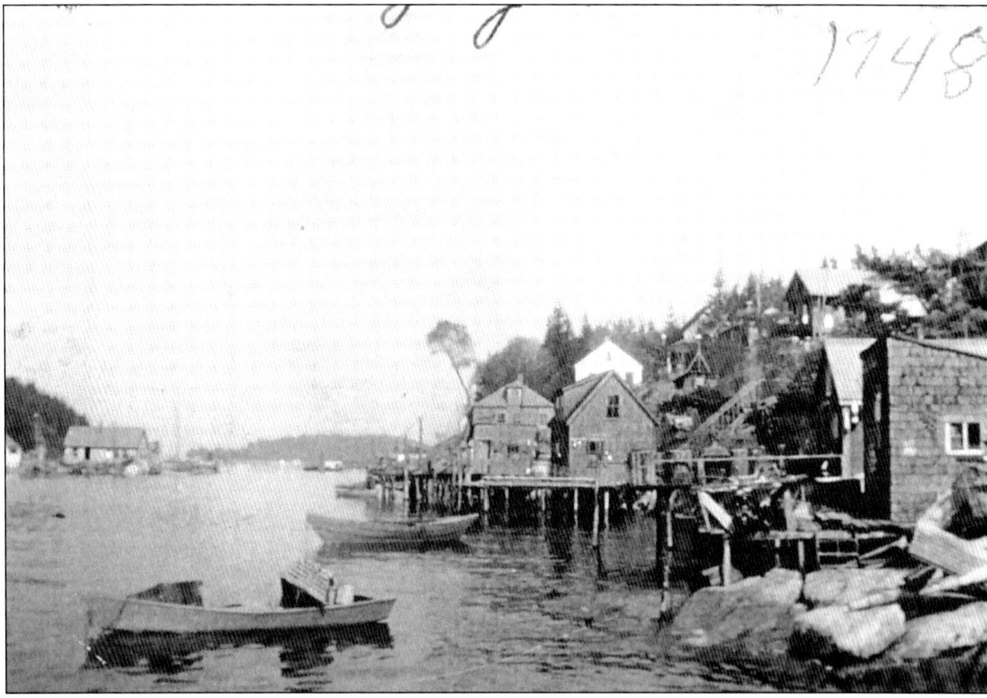

This 1948 view of the coastline on Carrying Place Cove as seen from the West Point Store wharf includes several fishhouses and boats.

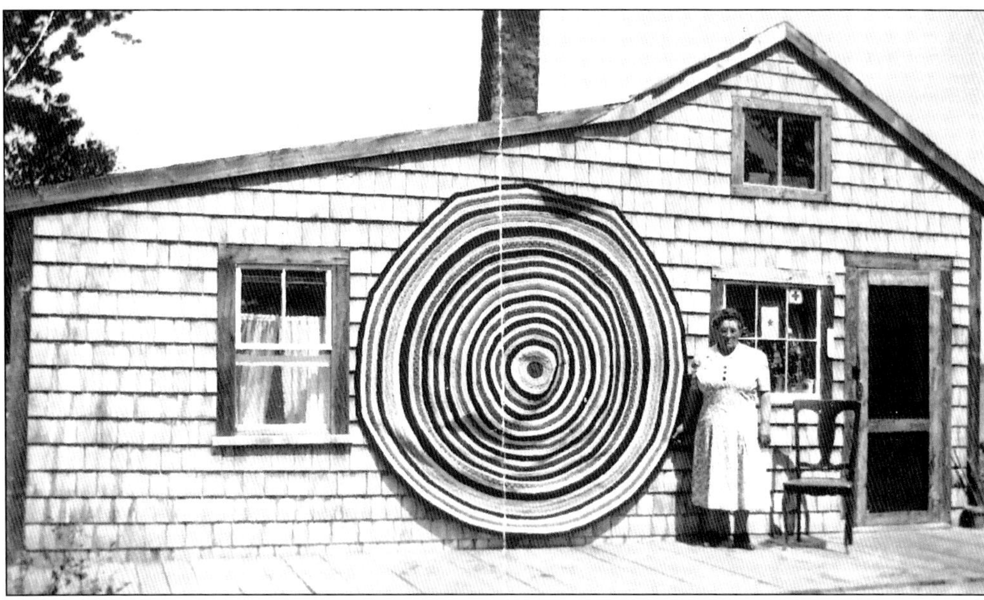

Cordelia Scott proudly displays her newly finished braided rug on the side of her home on Wallace Circle in West Point, about 1944. The star on the banner in the window represented her son Carlton, then in the service, and the cross above and to its right signified a donation to the Red Cross.

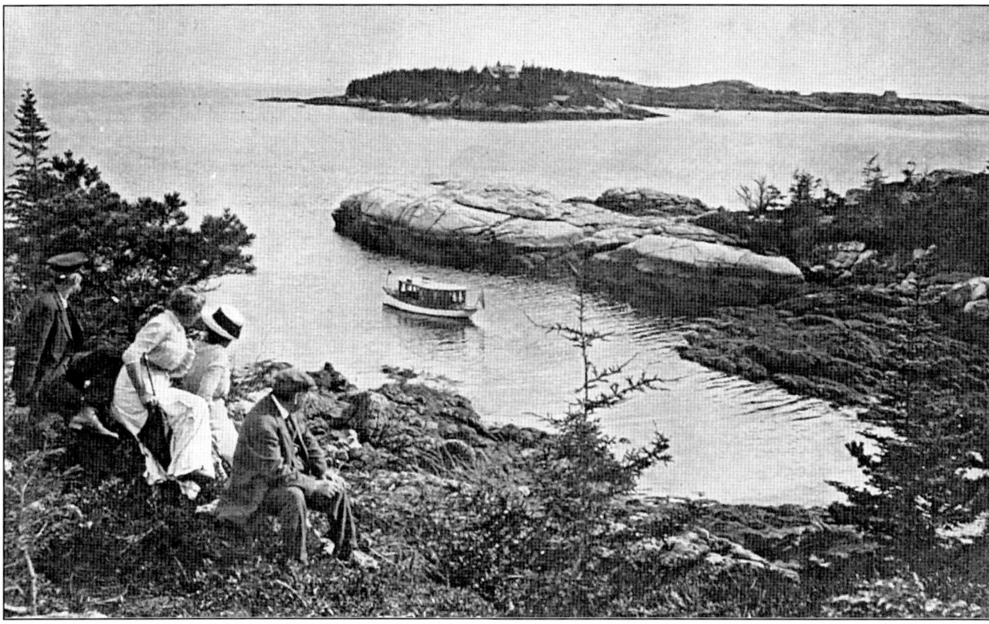

The Larrabees and the Bryants enjoy a view of Cat Point and Cat Cove at West Point (with the Wood Islands beyond).

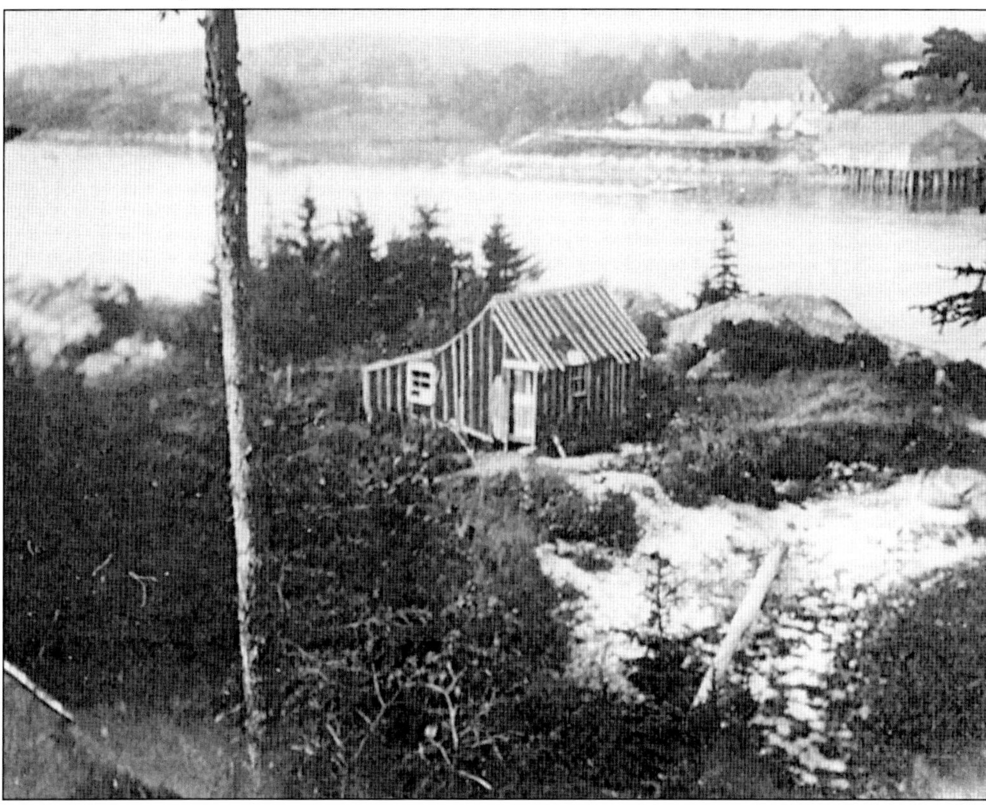

In this pre-1912 photograph, Ridley's Landing and Wharf, Sebasco, are visible in the background. The building in the foreground was on Malaga Island.

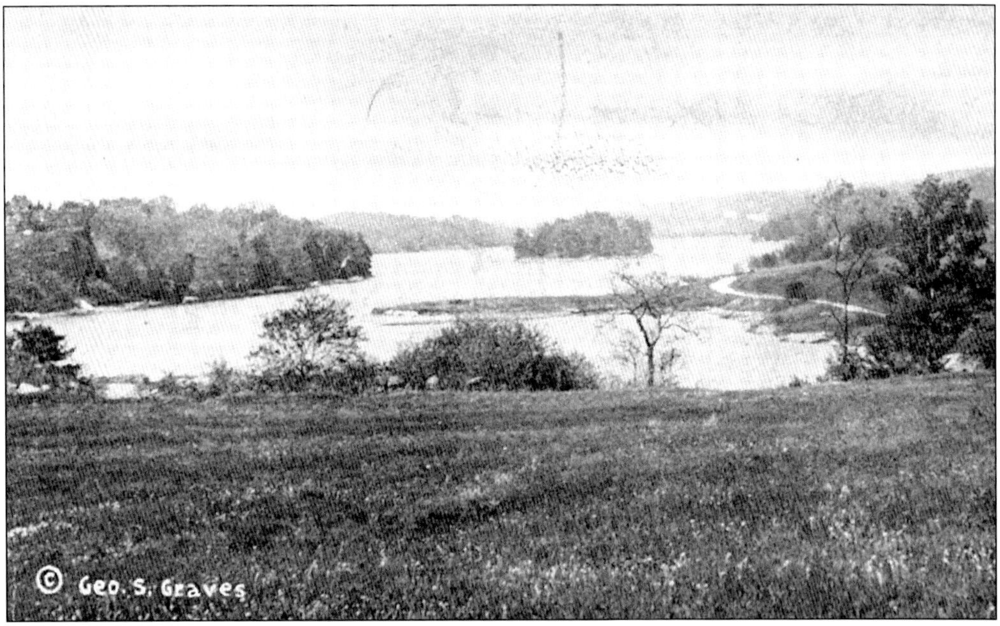

The Basin, with its narrow inlet from the New Meadows River, provides a quiet haven for boaters seeking shelter from rough seas. Trees have replaced the open spaces that bordered The Basin in the early 1900s.

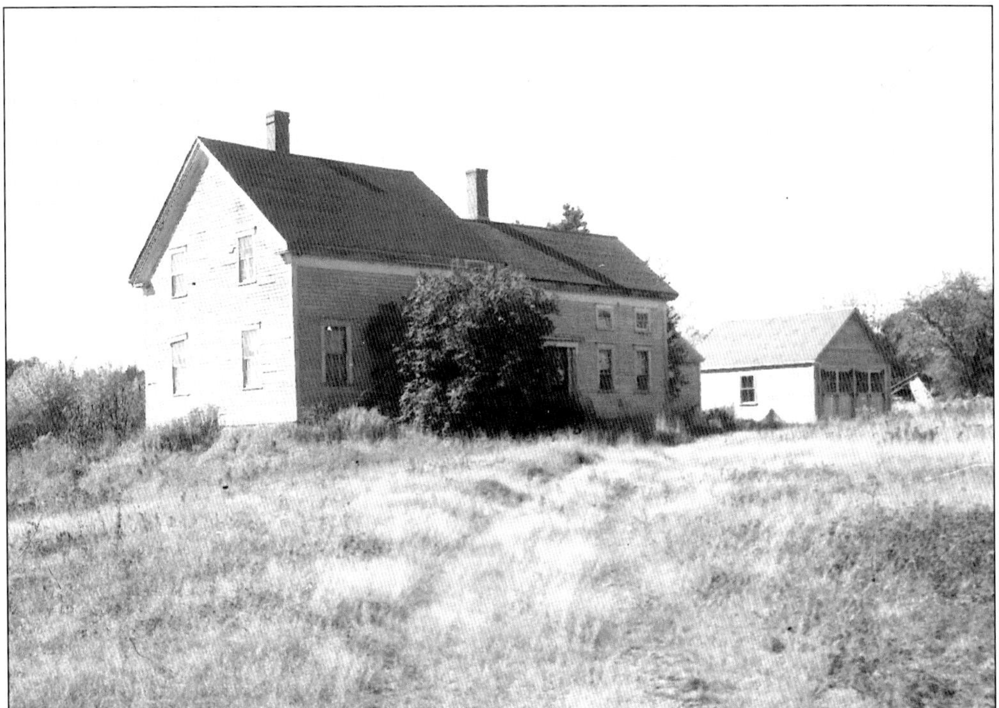

The Perry farm in Meadowbrook, built around 1800 but shown here *c.* 1963, was originally known as the Old Winnegance Farm and later the T.C. Hughes farm. In 1969 the property was purchased by John and Leslie Darling and converted into Meadowbrook Campground.

Two

SCHOOLS AND CHURCHES

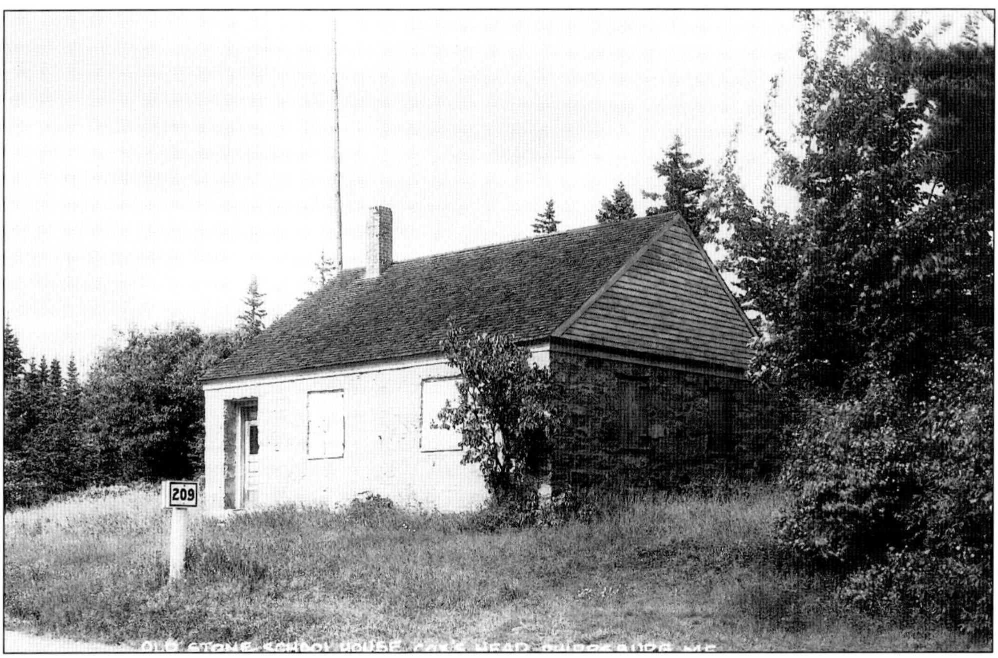

Each community had its own school. The majority of them were one-room schools containing all grades, kindergarten through grade eight. Until secondary transportation began in 1952, those students wishing to go on to school would find their own transportation to Bath or attend one of the boarding academies in the state. The Stone Schoolhouse near Cox's Head, built in 1836, served the students of the Percy District until it closed in 1926. At that time the students were transferred to the Parker Head School. In front of the schoolhouse was a sign indicating that Route 209 once ran through Parker Head and on to Popham.

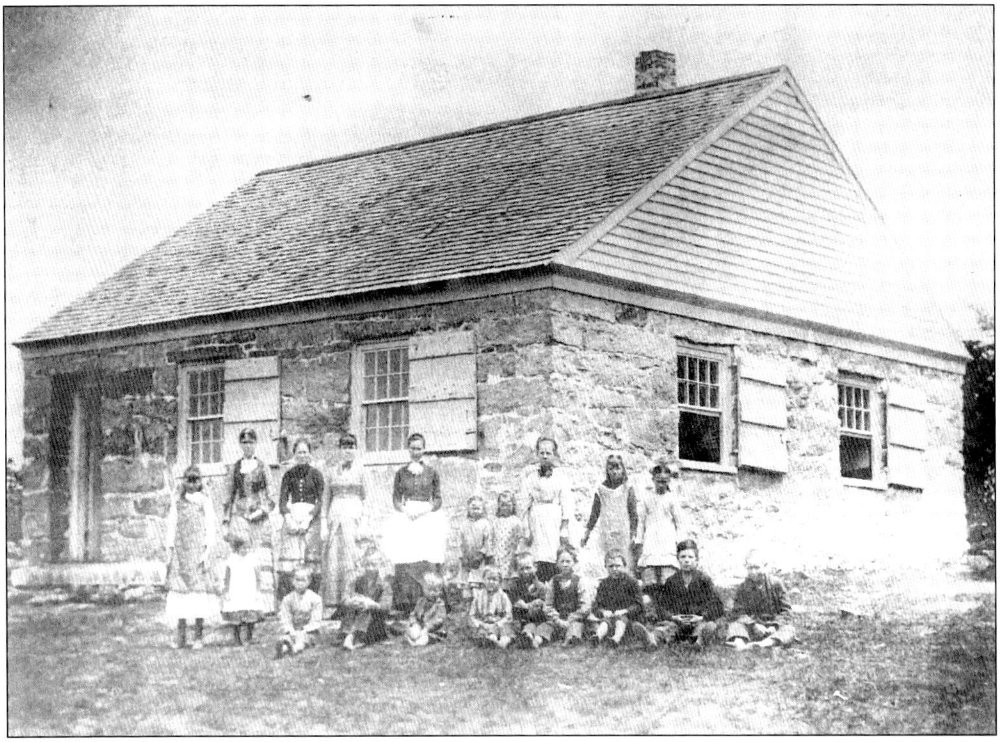

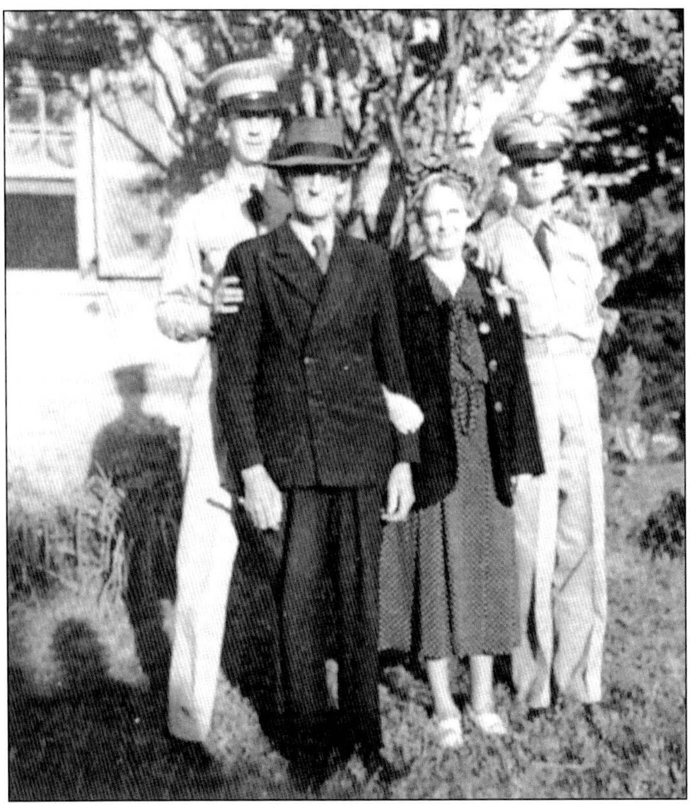

The students of the Percy District School pose in front of the Stone Schoolhouse in the 1880s or 1890s. Seated second from the right was the Perkins boy (the grandfather of Earle Perkins, who traveled to the South Pole with Admiral Byrd). He reportedly was extremely proud to be the only boy in school with shoes!

Edward and Eleanor Thomas and their two sons, Edward Jr. (left) and Fred (right), stand in front of the Stone Schoolhouse near Cox's Head in the early 1940s. The Thomases owned a farm nearby. Mrs. Thomas at one time taught at the Percy District School.

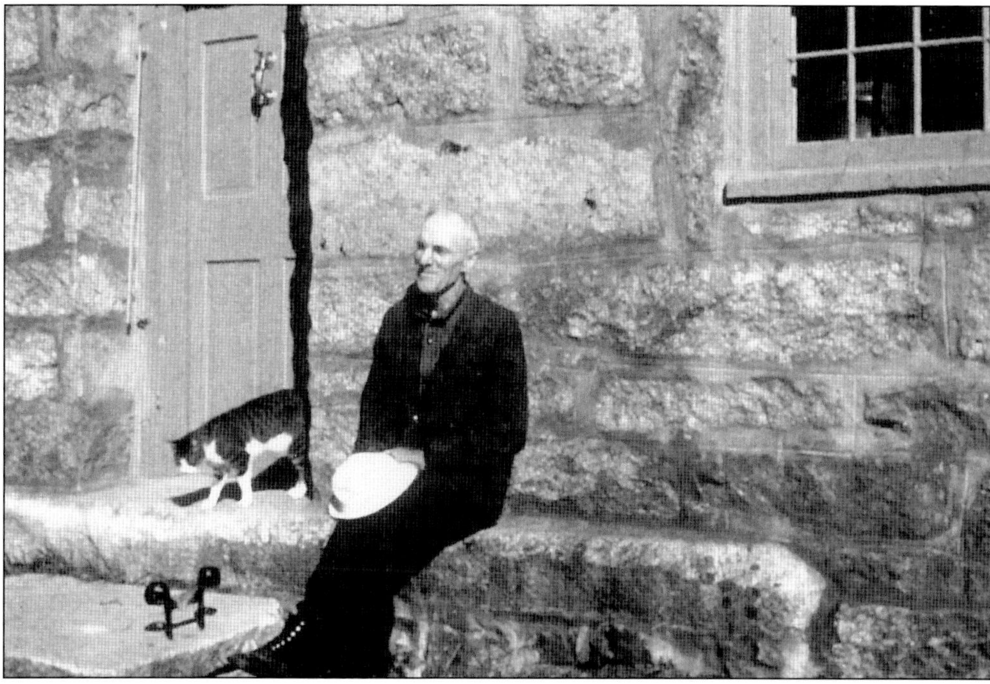

Nathaniel Percy poses *c.* 1950 in front of the McLanathan home, formerly the Percy District School. The Percy family originally owned the land where the school was constructed.

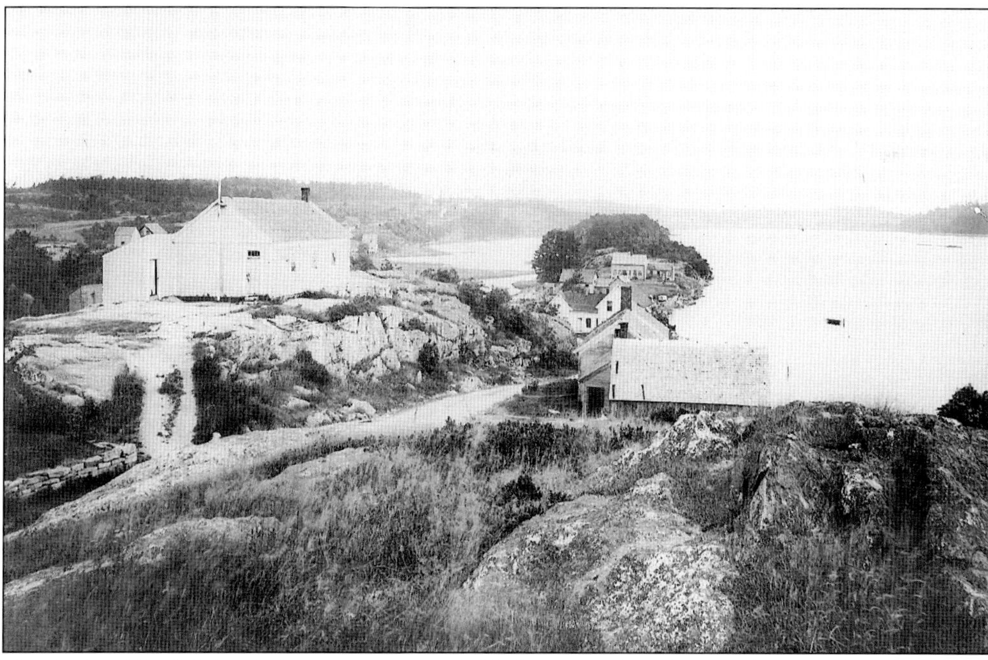

The Parker Head School, shown here *c.* mid-1800s, sat high on ledges; fortunately, no students were ever seriously injured by falling from them. The house pictured across the road was owned by John and Alice Rollins and burned in July 1947, while the former summer home of Dr. Bonny at the foot of the hill was burned by the town in about 1960. To the right is the Parker Head Mill Pond, which provided ice for harvesting from the 1870s through the late 1890s.

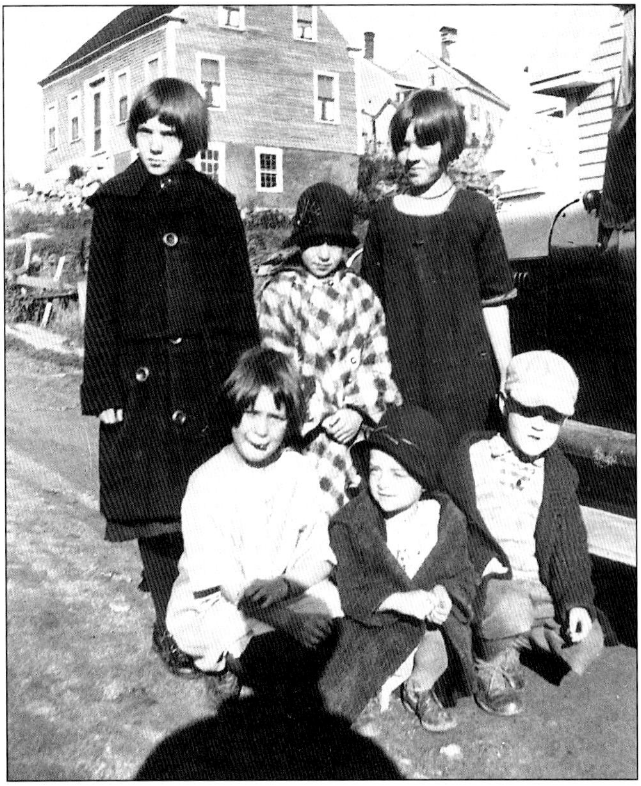

These youngsters from the Parker Head School are, from left to right, as follows: (front row) unknown, Mildred Harrington, and Leo Hamel; (back row) Flossie Wyman, Francis Kreidler, and Priscilla Wyman. They are standing in front of the Parker Head Post Office.

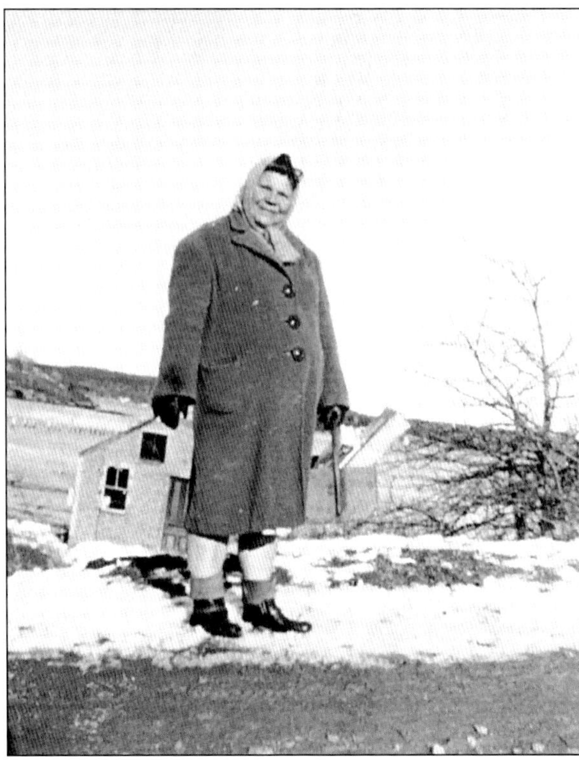

Teacher Alice Lowell walks home from the Parker Head School carrying her schoolwork in the ever-present clam hod. She taught at the Parker Head School from 1947 until it closed in 1958. At that time she moved to the new consolidated school, where she became known as "Mrs. Kindergarten." Behind her is the Parker Head Wharf.

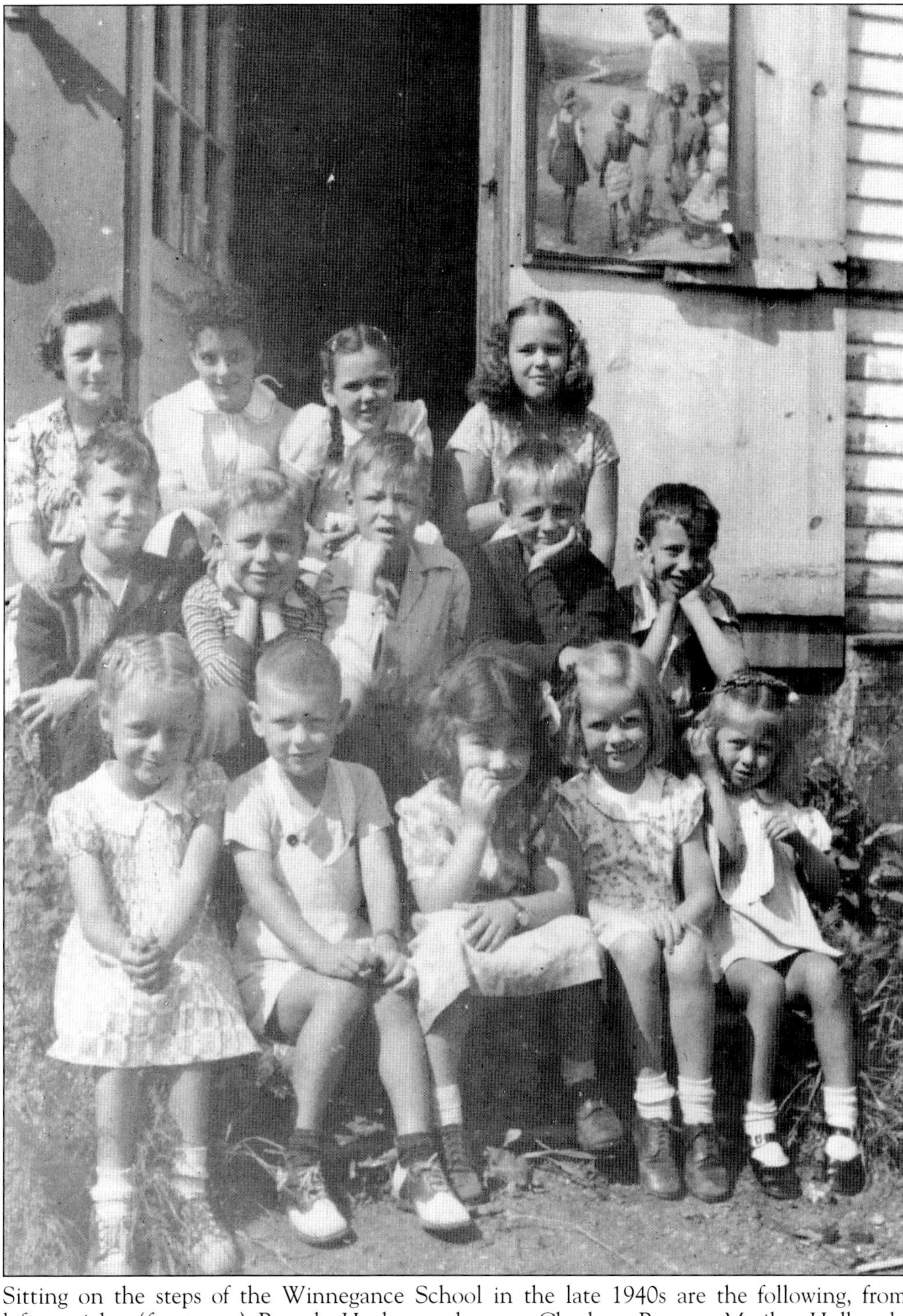

Sitting on the steps of the Winnegance School in the late 1940s are the following, from left to right: (front row) Beverly Hughes, unknown, Charlene Brown,, Marilyn Holbrook, and Madelyn Holbrook; (middle row) Milton MacDonald, unknown, David Dyer, Harold Mott, and Artie Totman; (back row) Theresa Williams, Edith Hawkes, Marilyn Bates, and Marilyn Spinney.

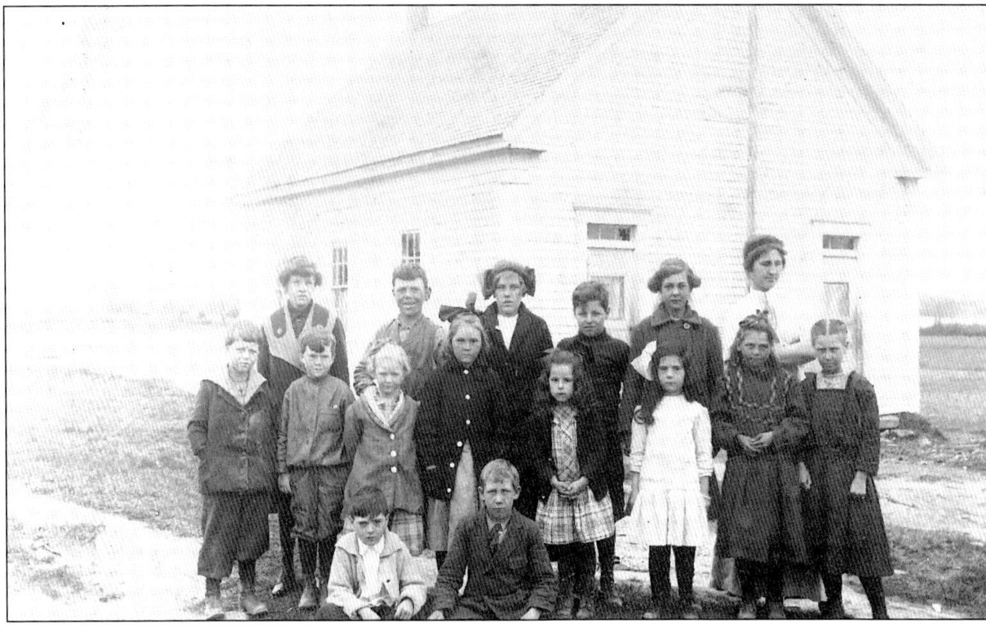

Posing c. 1915 in front of the Phippsburg Center School are, from left to right, as follows: (front row) Tommy Allegrin and John Davis; (middle row) Edward Heald, Arthur MacDonald, Ruth Heald, Clara Perry, Marilla Williams, Elsie Allegrin, Maud Heald, and Blanche Heald; (back row) Lillian Roderick, Jimmy Heald, Doris Davis, John Williams, Eleanor Harrington, and Esther Fox (teacher).

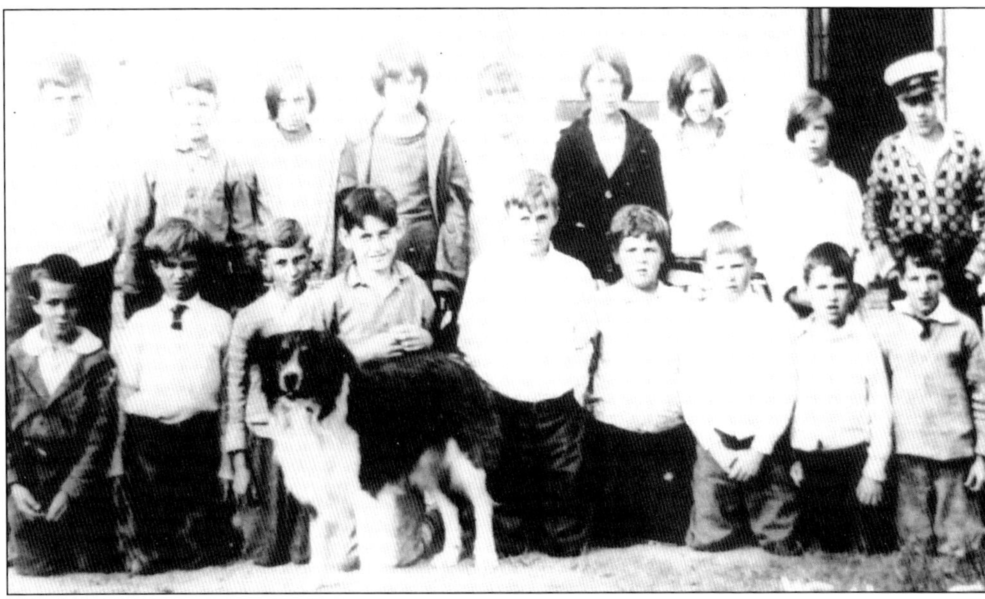

This group, pictured in front of the Phippsburg Center School, is this class of 1928. From left to right they are as follows: (front row) Lester Beals, Carlton Brown, Leland Smith, John Hamilton McCourt, Irving Harrington, Maurice Pushard, Wesley Harrington, Arthur Harrington, and Ernest Brown; (back row) Mark Harrington, Durwood Wyman, Grace Brown, Catherine McCourt, Charles Doughty, Nettie Beals, Julia Smith, Elsie Brown, and Raymond Brown. Durwood Wyman's dog Duke is also in the picture.

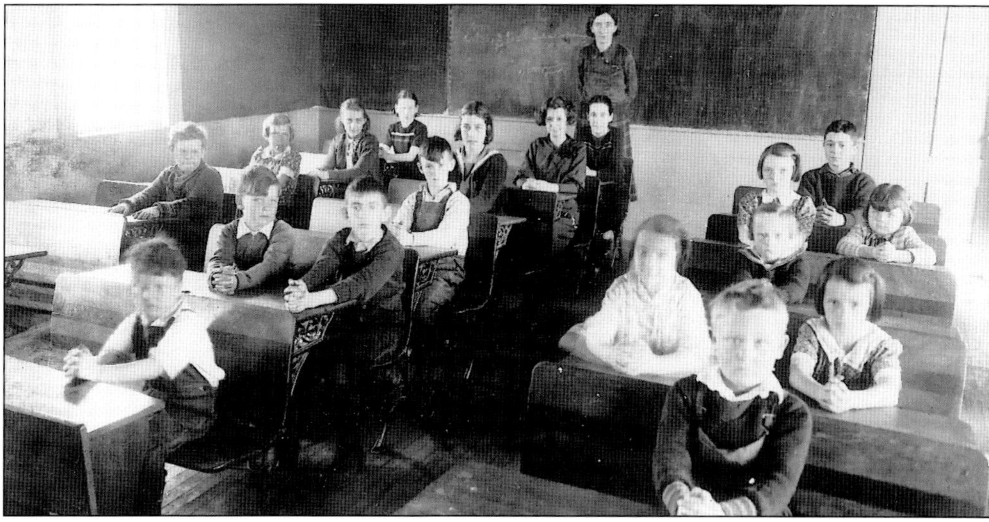

Susie Barbour, a teacher, posed with her students for this group picture in 1938. Sitting at their desks in the Phippsburg Center School are the following, from front to back: (left row) Kedrick Palmer, Dorothy Davis, Martha Beals, and Ceres McCourt; (middle row) Richard Hart, William Doughty (left), Robert Beals (right), Charles Hart, Jane Buker, Bertha Doughty, and Carol McCourt; (right row) Lawrence Scott, Shirley Hart (left), Mabel Hart (right), Betty Bowker, Louise Hart (left), Jean Bowker (right), and Eugene Bowker.

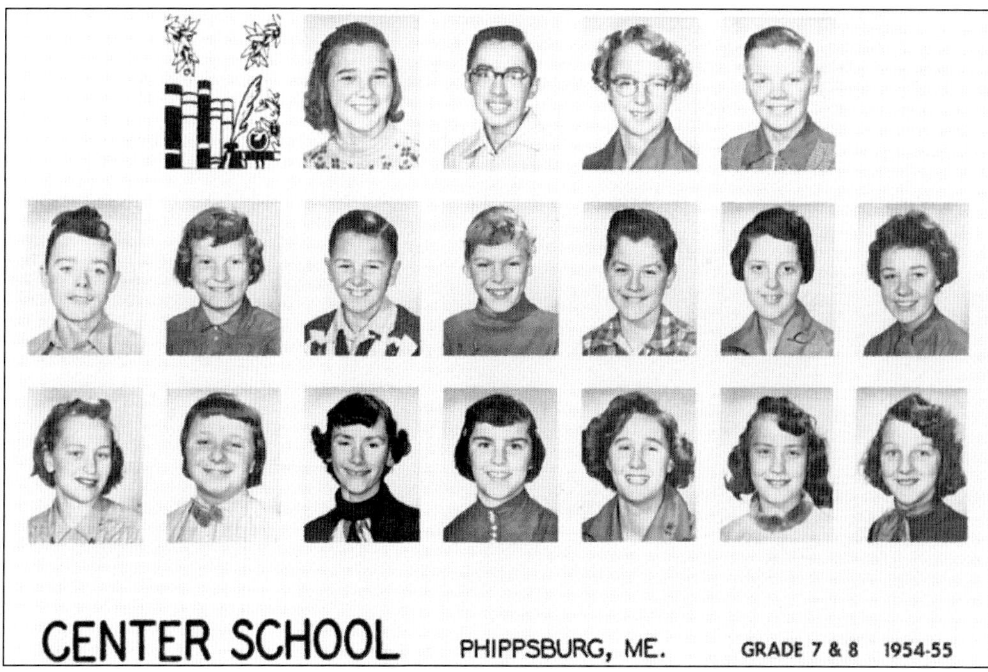

By the time these seventh and eighth graders attended the Center School in 1954–55, group pictures had been replaced with composite pictures. Shown here are, from left to right, as follows: (top row) Judy Moore, John McCourt, Marga Lee York, and Maurice Pye; (middle row) Warren Doughty, Patricia Holbrook, Johnny Libby, Roberta Pye, Robert Gray, Phyllis Eaton, and Diane Hamel; (bottom row) Betty Ann Wyman, Martha Robinson, Margaret Rogers, Marilla Totman, Nancy Senecal, Norma McDonald, and Donna Morse.

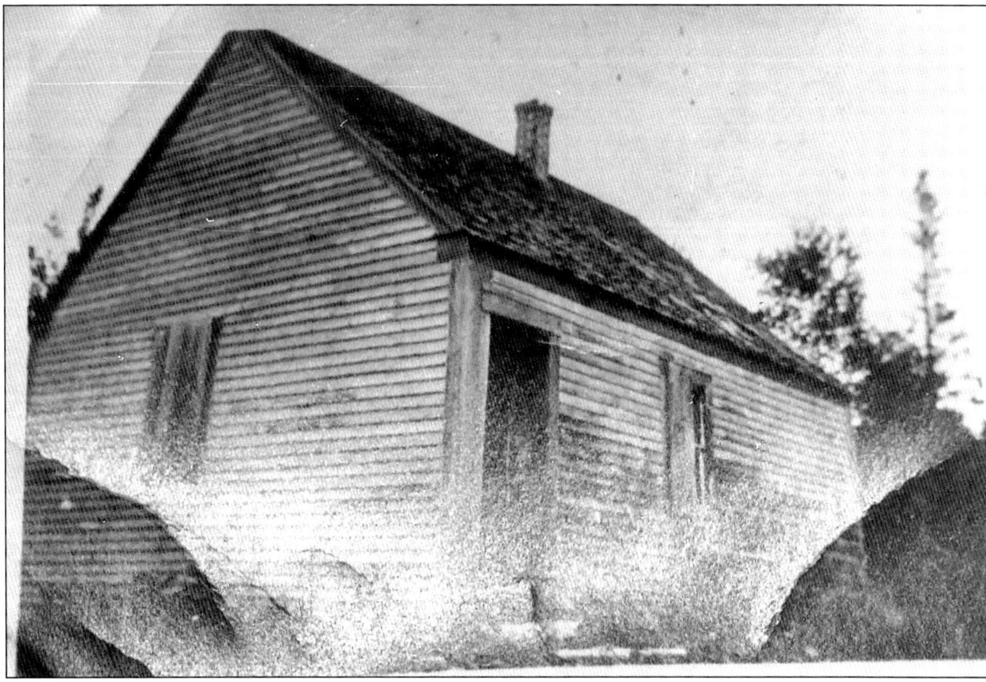

The Meadowbrook Schoolhouse was built in 1821. It was a typical one-room school for all grades, with a pot-bellied stove in the middle of the floor. It was torn down in 1917 due to the decline in population of the Meadowbrook area.

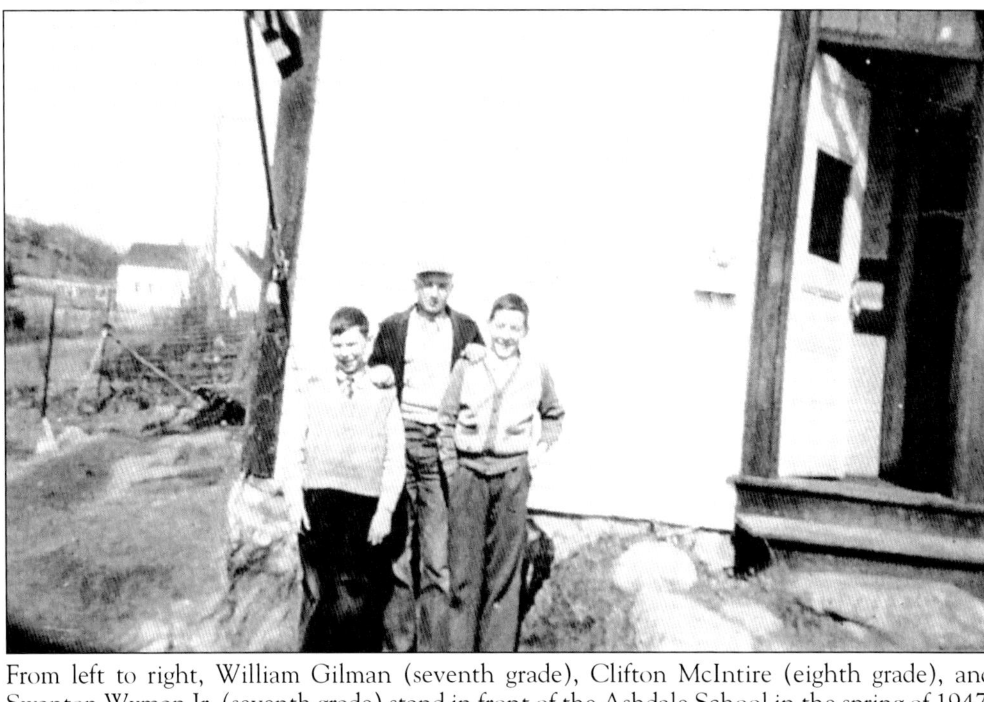

From left to right, William Gilman (seventh grade), Clifton McIntire (eighth grade), and Swanton Wyman Jr. (seventh grade) stand in front of the Ashdale School in the spring of 1947. The school opened in 1865 with Vilora J. Gilman as its first teacher. The last teacher to work here before the school closed in 1947 was Margaret Gilman, the wife of Vilora's grandson.

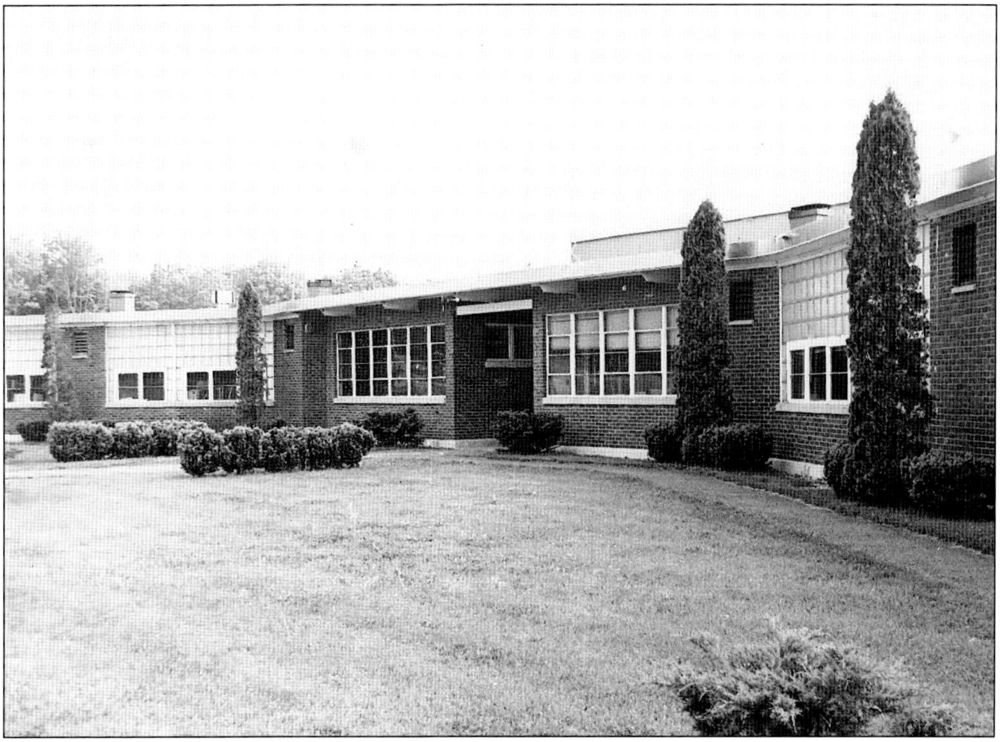

The district schools were replaced in 1958 by a consolidated school known as the Phippsburg Elementary School, which then served grades kindergarten through eight.

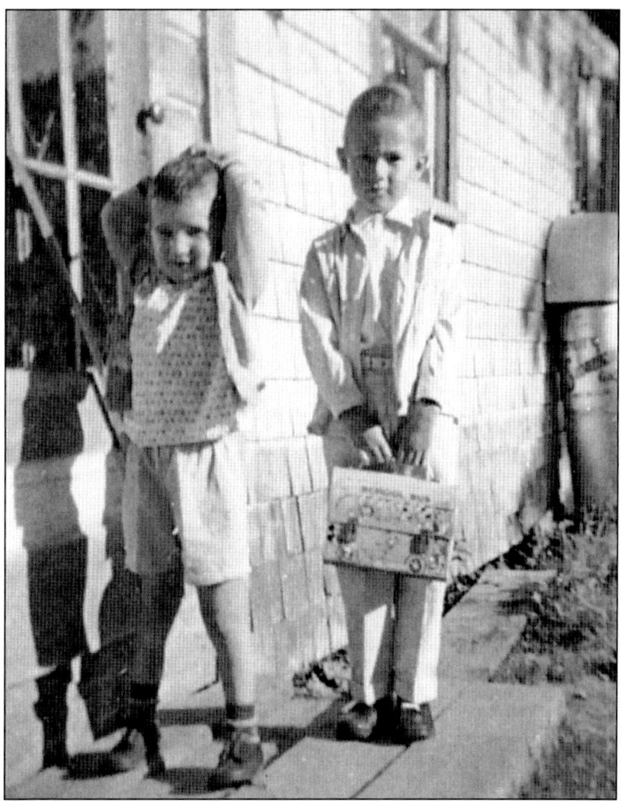

Roger Condon (right) is ready for his first day of school in September 1961. He was attending the new Phippsburg Elementary School. Staying at home is his younger brother Lyman.

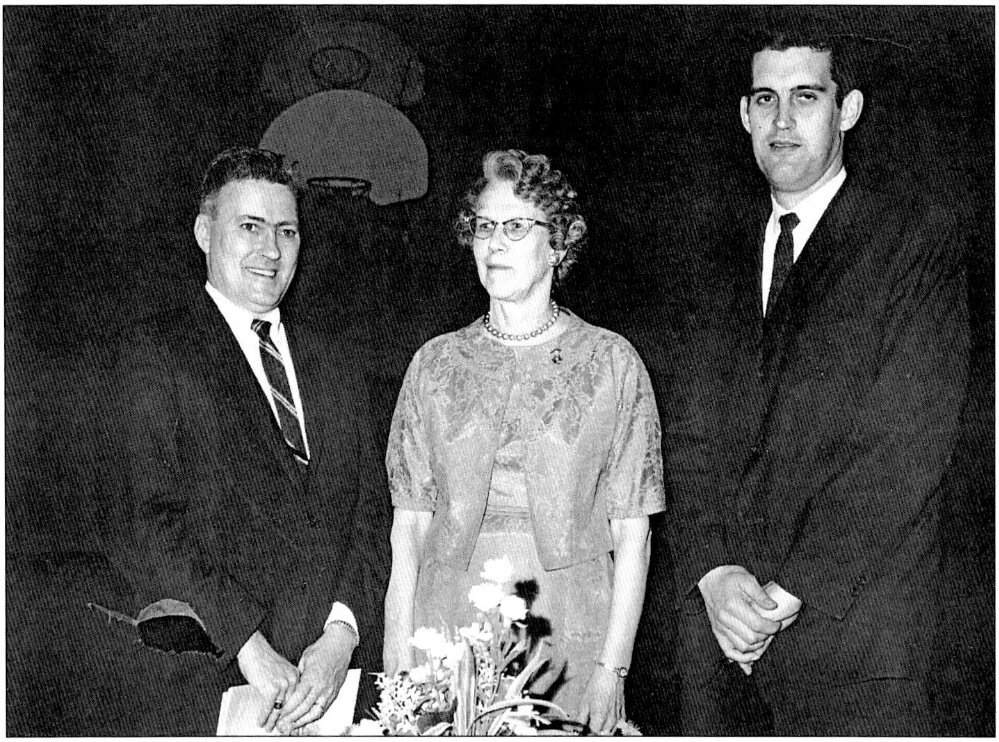

Margaret Gilman, president of the Phippsburg Teachers' Club (1966–67), retired from teaching second grade in 1967. With her are Superintendent Ronald E. Susee and Principal James H. Abbott Jr.

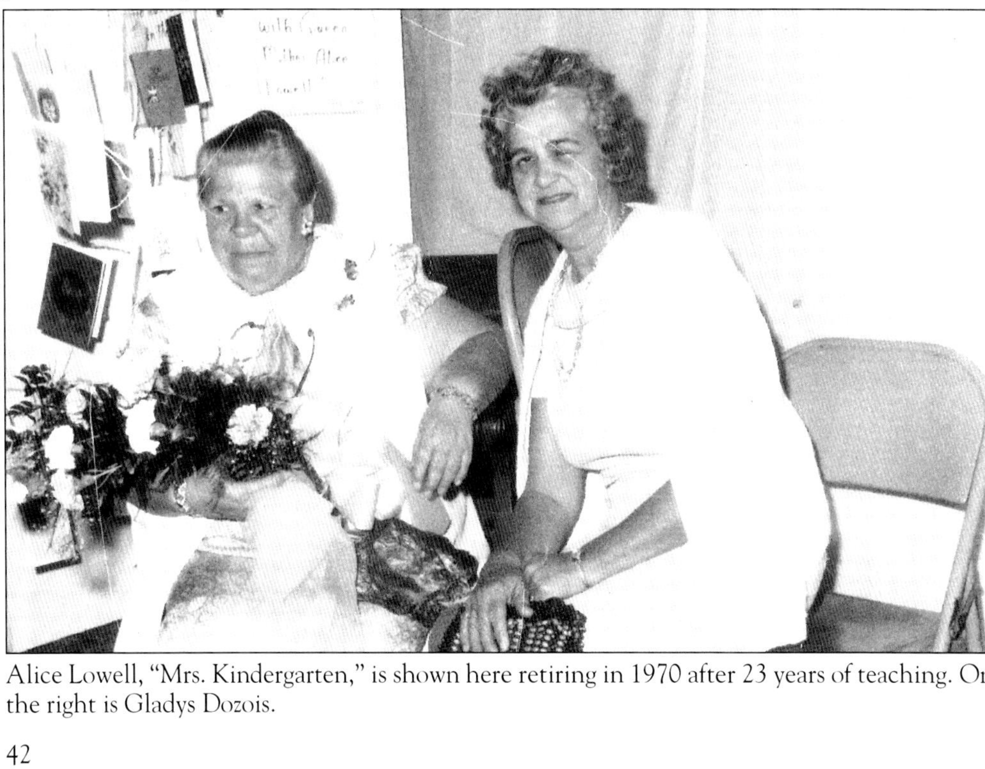

Alice Lowell, "Mrs. Kindergarten," is shown here retiring in 1970 after 23 years of teaching. On the right is Gladys Dozois.

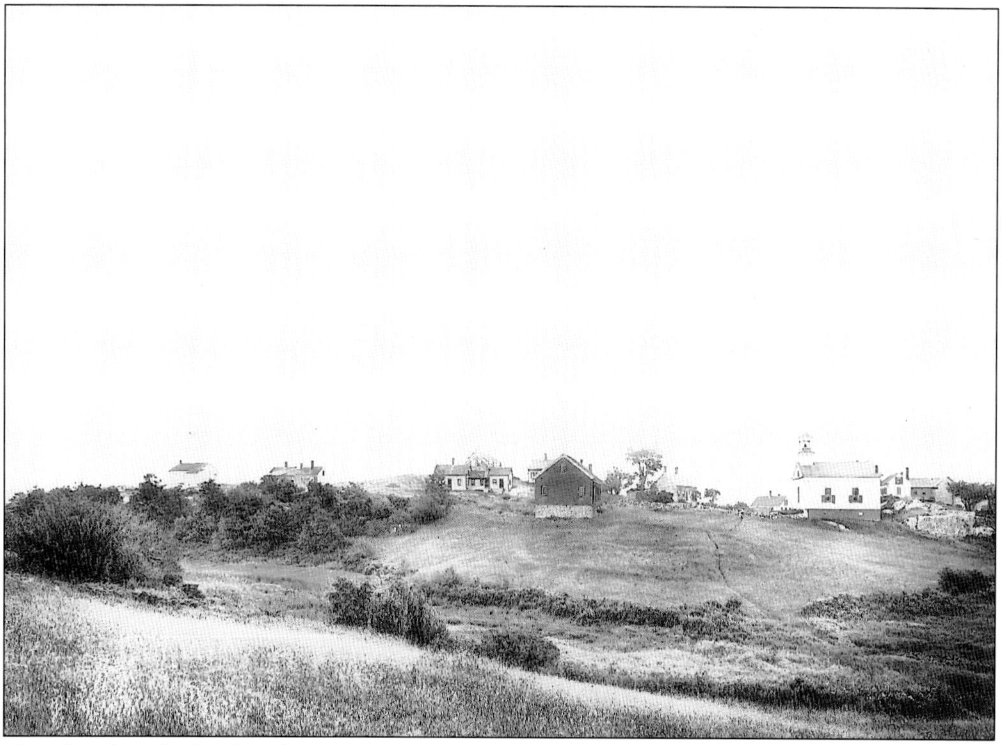

The church at Parker Head stood on a sharp corner in the center of the village. Seen across open terrain are the Parker Head Church (1846) at right and the Parker Head School (1847) at left. Between the two are several homes and Independence Hall (1897), also known as the Dance Hall. The hall later housed a store before it was razed in the mid-1900s.

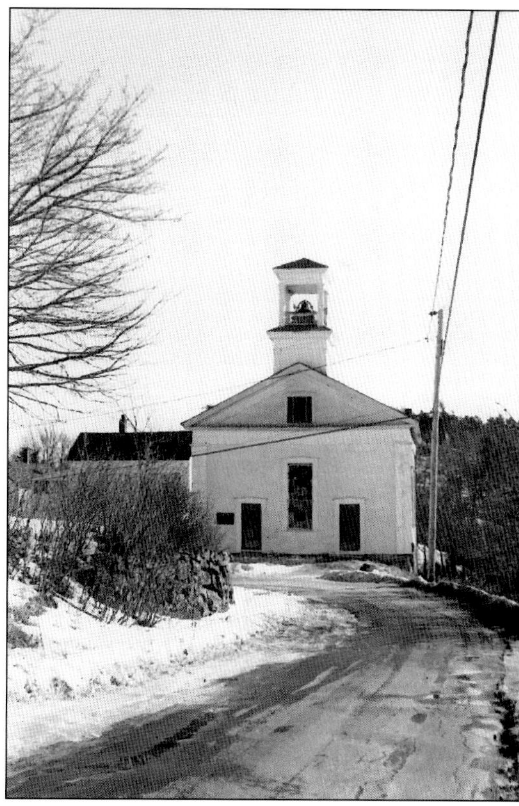

The Parker Head Church was built in 1846 as the Free Union Meeting House. In 1853 it became a Baptist church. Four pinnacles atop the steeple, evident on early photographs of the church, had disappeared by the time this picture was taken in 1966. In 1972, after many years of neglect, the church was torn down.

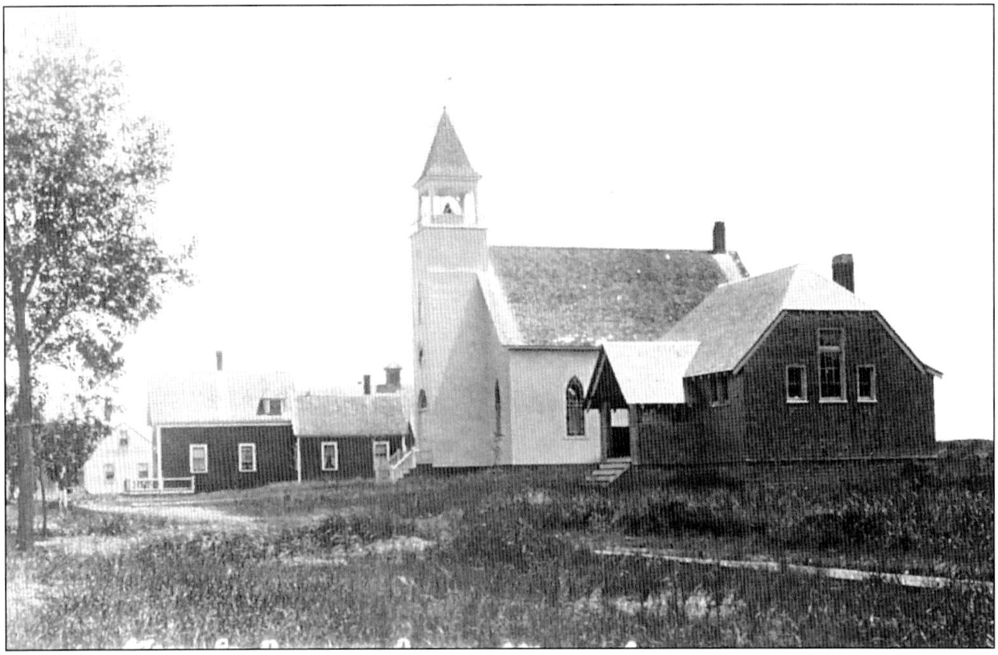

Popham Chapel (center) was built to serve the Popham Beach resort area in 1892–96. Vacationing ministers conducted Sunday morning and evening services. The library to the right was built in 1910 after numerous suppers, dances, and other fund-raising benefits were held.

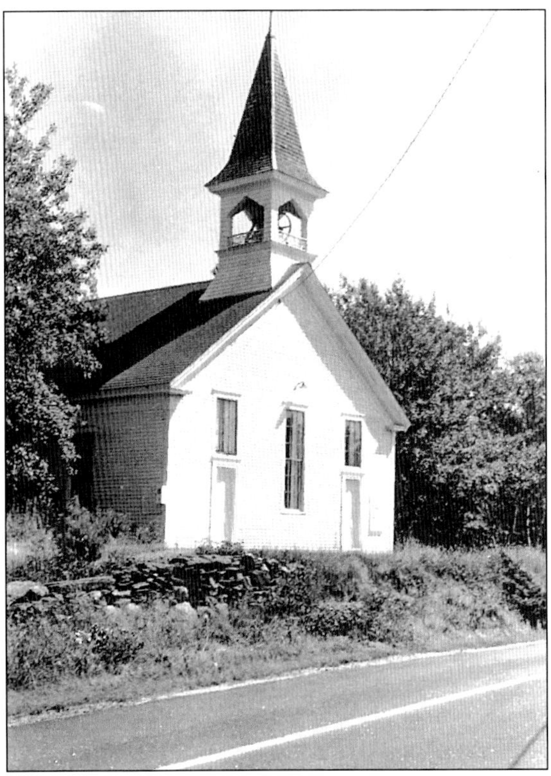

The Small Point Free Will Baptist Church, sitting high on a ledge overlooking the Small Point Road, is believed to have been constructed in 1828. It is located in the Ashdale section of town.

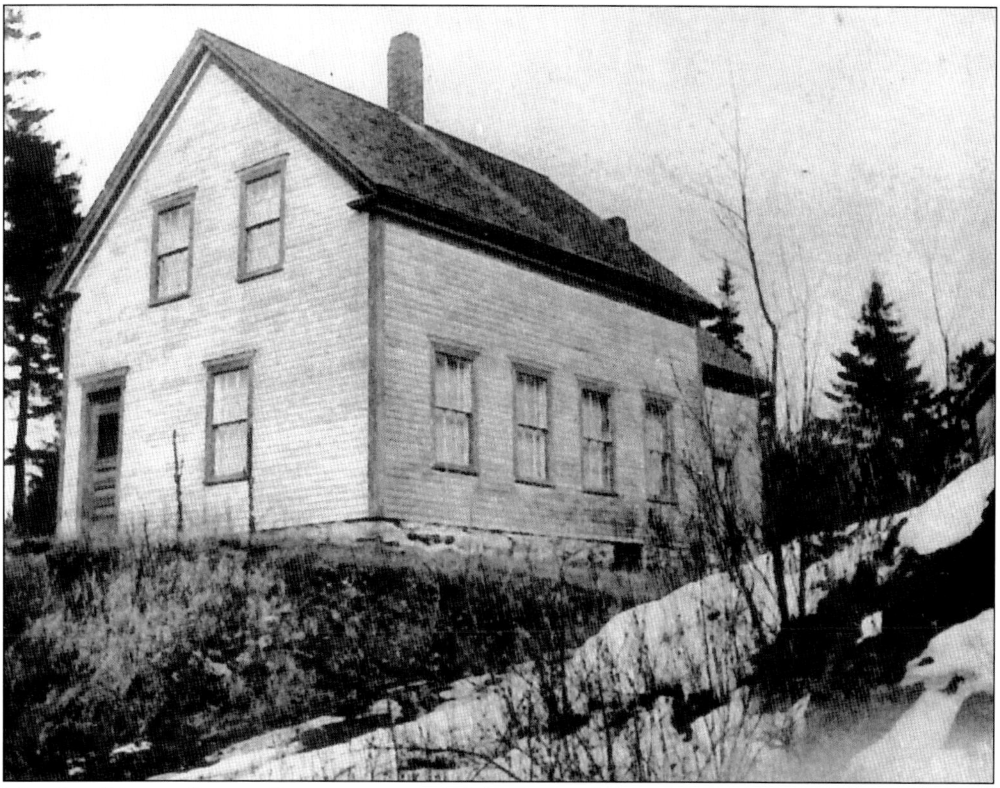

The Small Point Baptist Parsonage in Ashdale, shown here *c.* 1920s, also sits high on ledges well above the road.

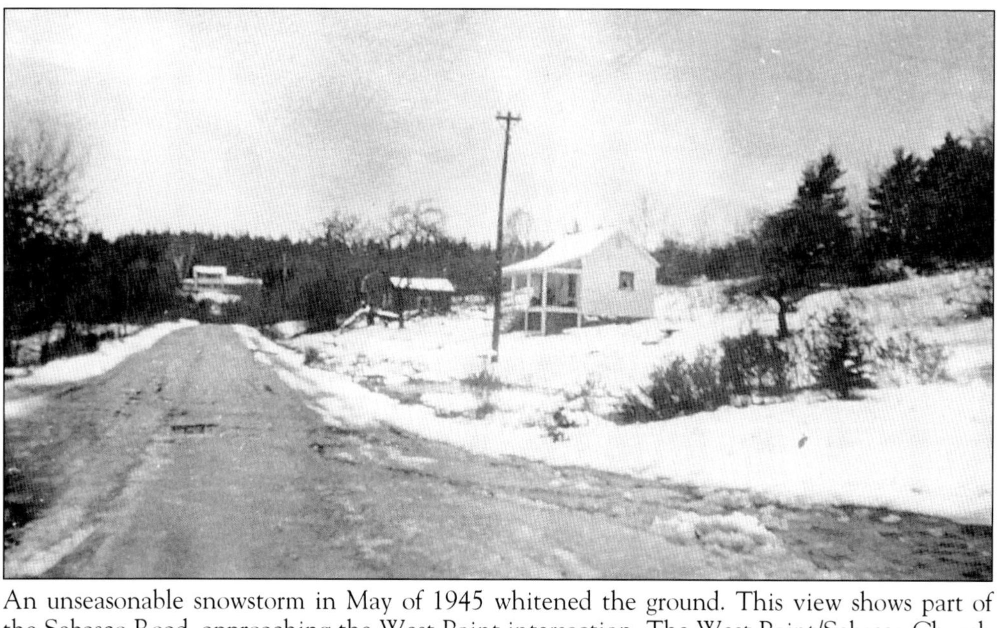

An unseasonable snowstorm in May of 1945 whitened the ground. This view shows part of the Sebasco Road, approaching the West Point intersection. The West Point/Sebasco Church parsonage is visible in the background.

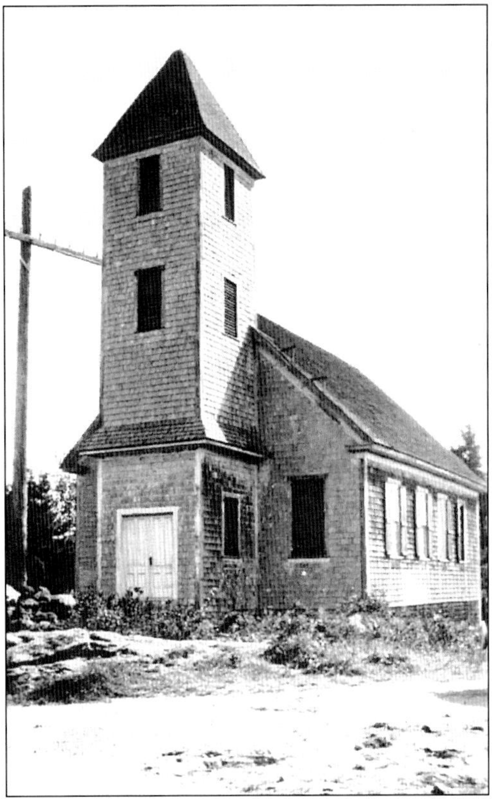

Dedicated community members spent 25 years raising funds before the Pine Grove Community Church in West Point was built in 1924. It is named for the grove where services were held before the church was constructed. This picture was taken in 1943.

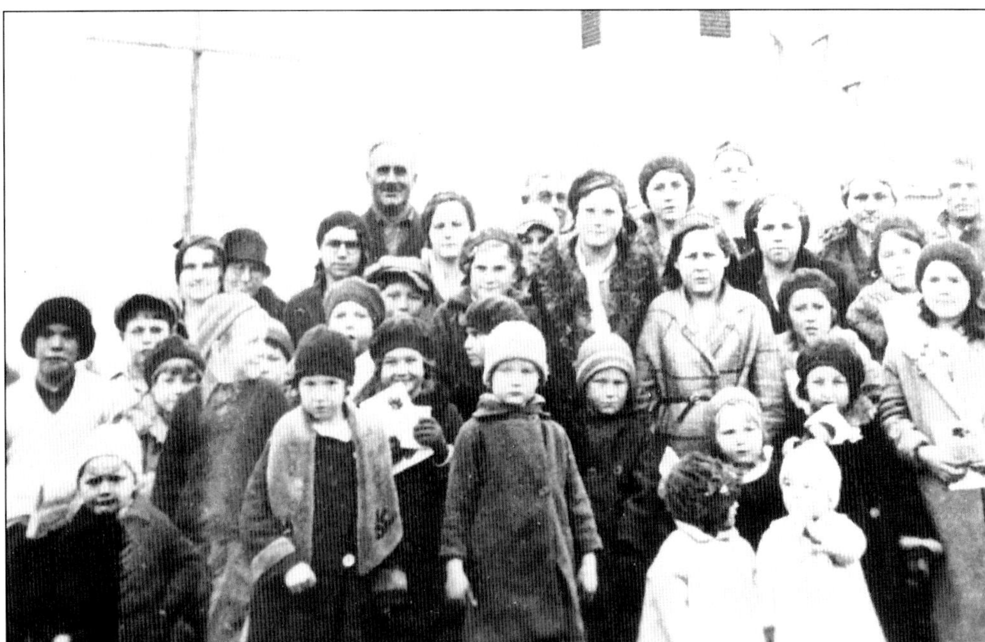

A West Point Sunday School class gathered in front of the Pine Grove Community Church in 1935. Several of those present bore familiar names, including Wallace, Scott, Parker, Hutchins, Gilliam, Atwood, Smith, and Alexander.

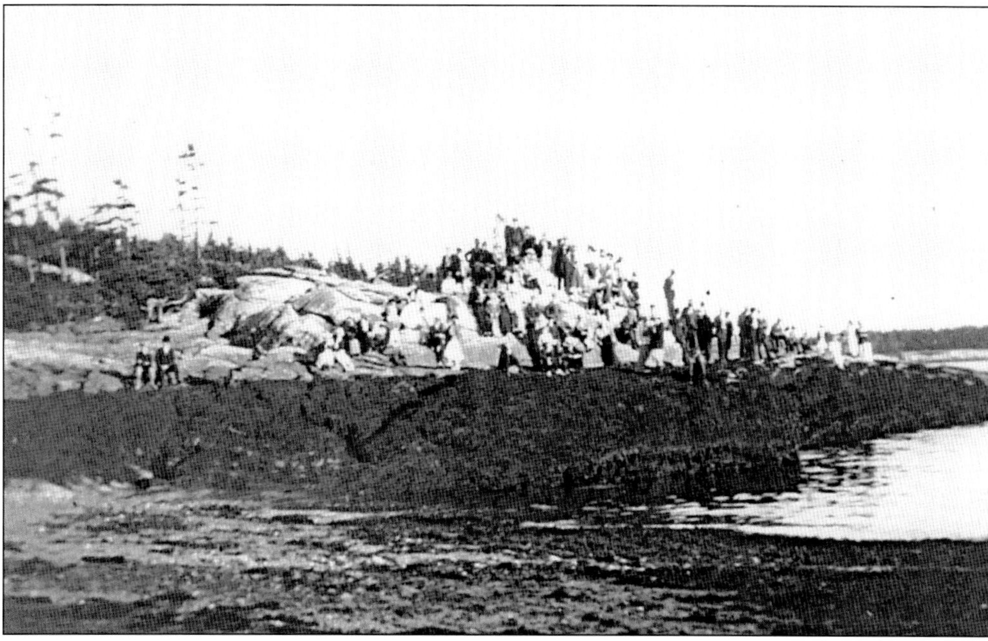

The congregation from the Pine Grove Community Church in West Point gathered at Cat Cove for a baptism. Often several people would come to be baptised at the same time. Reportedly, after one revival meeting, over 75 converts were baptized in the cold waters of the cove.

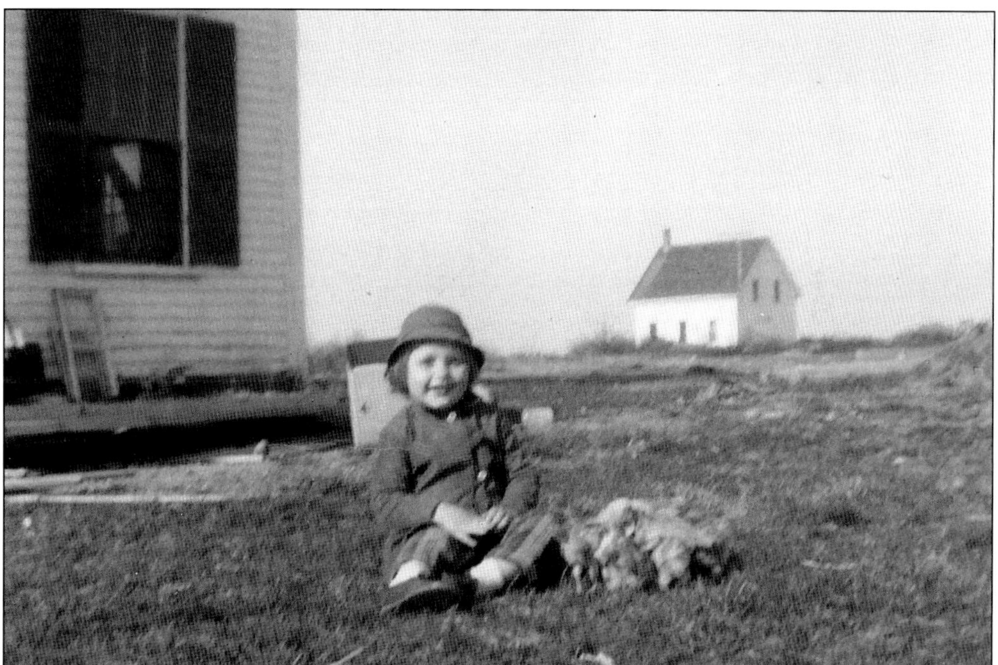

At one time the Sebasco Church stood on the hill south of Sebasco Village near the Butler homestead. It could be seen across the road from the Morrison farm, where Diane Hunt is shown playing in 1960.

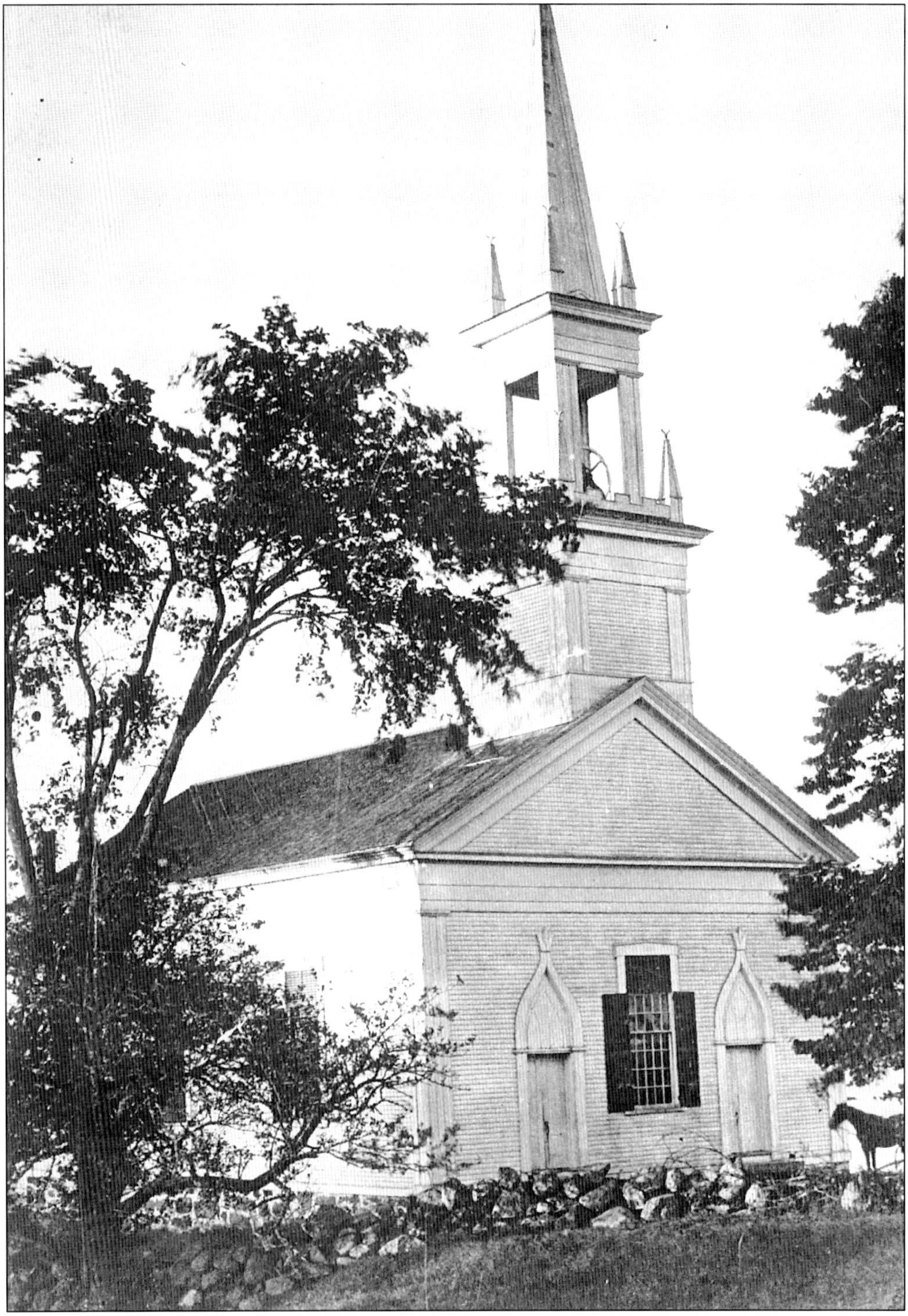

The Phippsburg Congregational Church was built in 1802 and was remodeled in 1847. This picture was taken prior to 1909, when the plain glass windows seen here were replaced with stained-glass memorial windows.

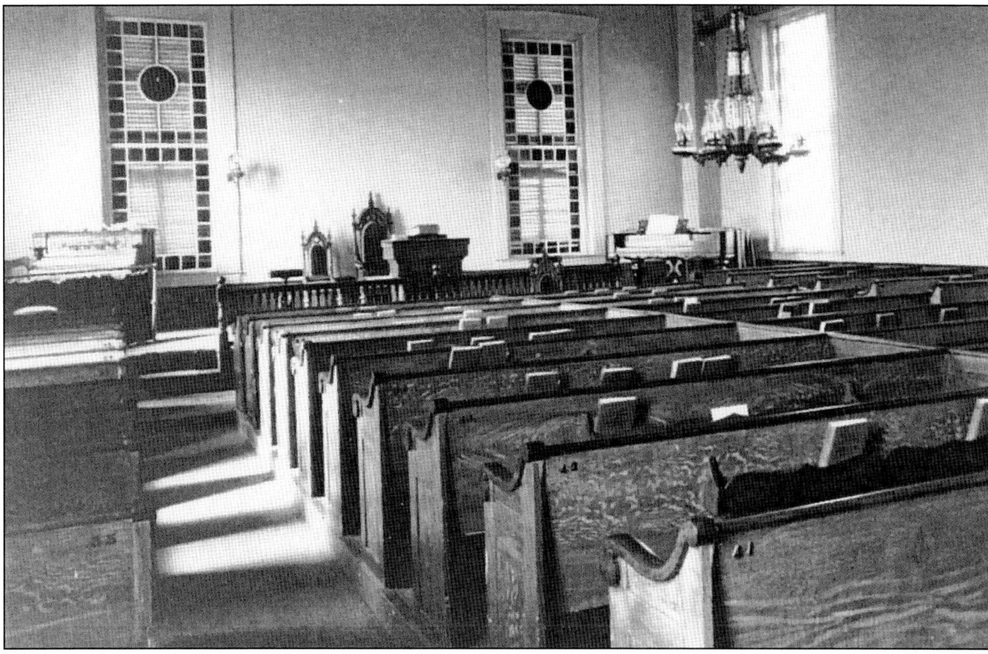

In 1909 memorial stained-glass windows replaced the original plain glass windows in the Center Church. The old windows were said to have been given to the donors of the new windows and may be found in houses in the area. At that time the pews were stained and hand grained.

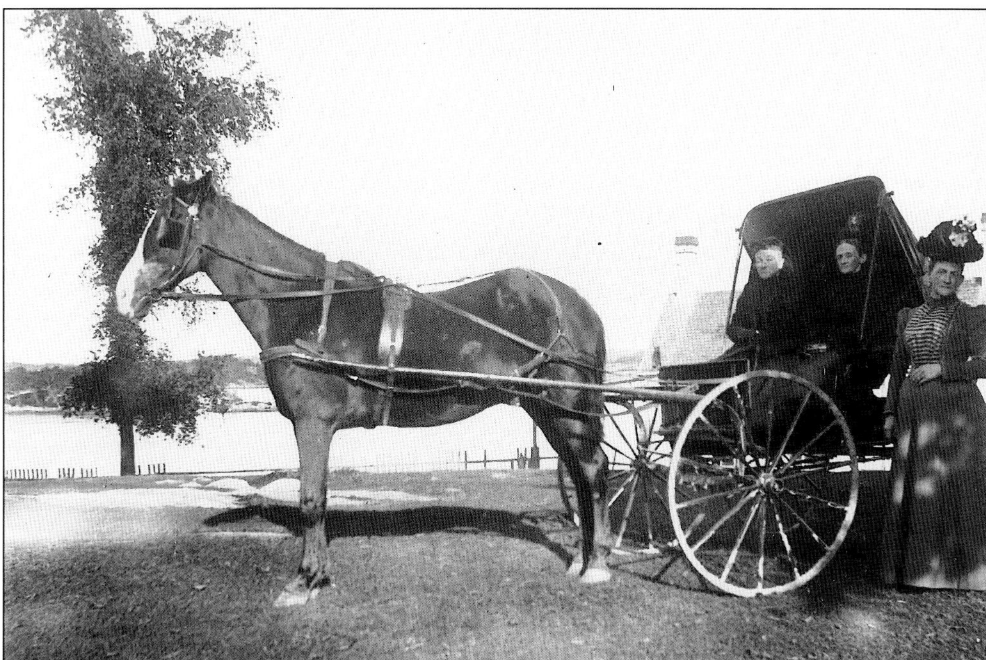

Three well-dressed unidentified ladies arrive at the Center Church around 1900. A fence separates the church property from the Minott home in the background.

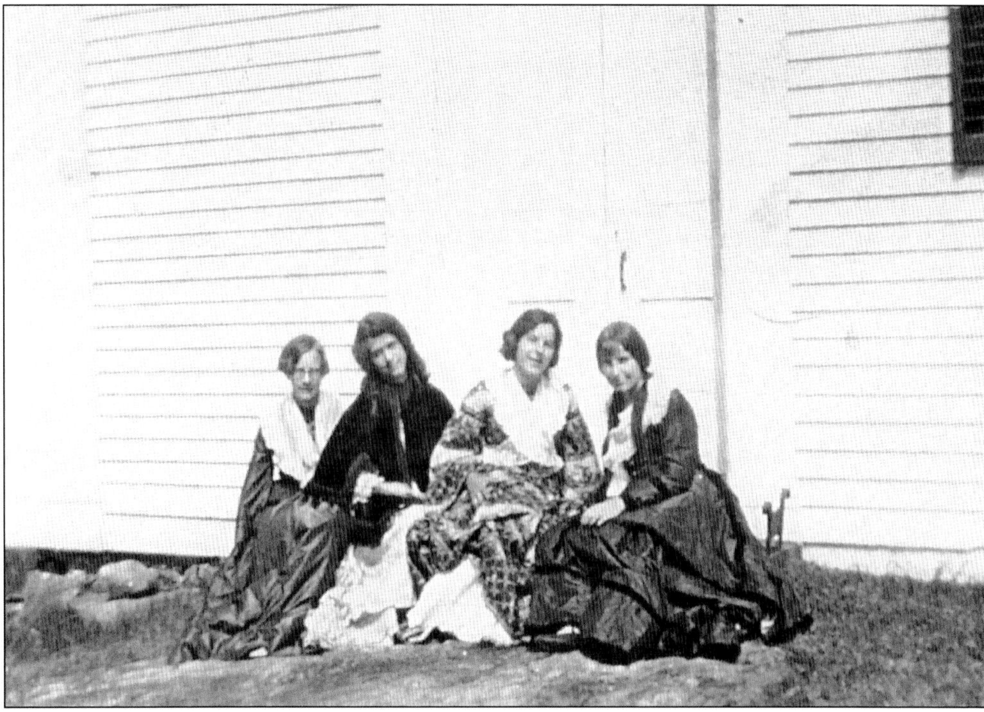

Pauline Wyman, Margaret Minott, Marilla Williams, and Anita Williams pose *c.* 1920s in front of the Phippsburg Center Church in old costumes.

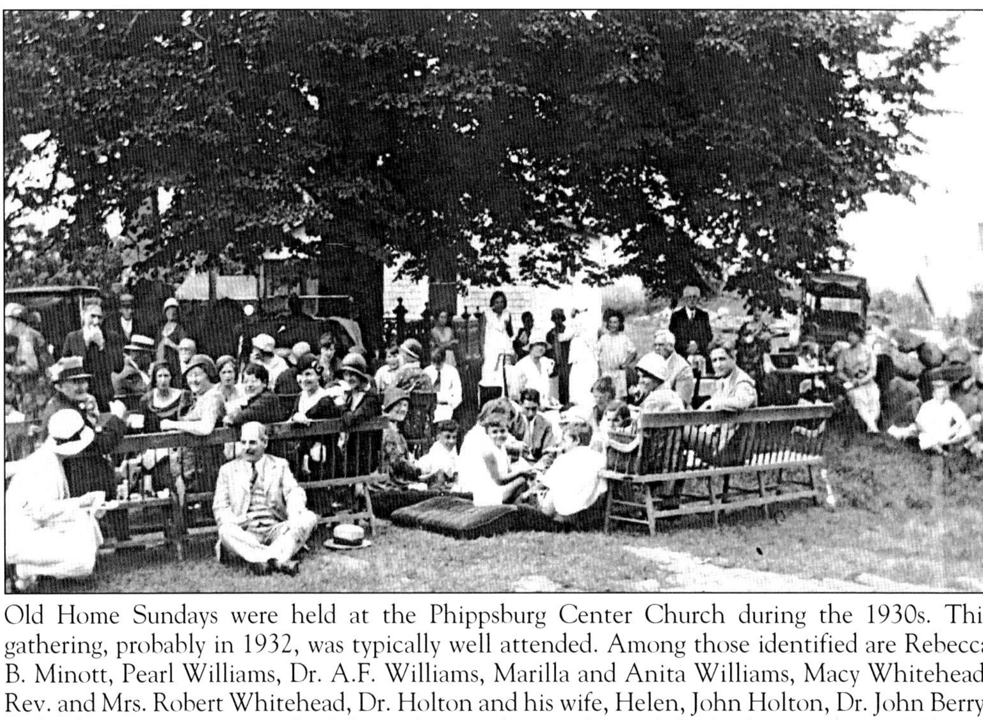

Old Home Sundays were held at the Phippsburg Center Church during the 1930s. This gathering, probably in 1932, was typically well attended. Among those identified are Rebecca B. Minott, Pearl Williams, Dr. A.F. Williams, Marilla and Anita Williams, Macy Whitehead, Rev. and Mrs. Robert Whitehead, Dr. Holton and his wife, Helen, John Holton, Dr. John Berry, and Ada Minott. Kamp Keebec's bungalow can be seen beyond the linden tree (see p. 99).

In 1952 the 150th anniversary of the building of the Phippsburg Congregational Church was celebrated with a special worship service and picnic. Dressed in their finery and posing for the camera are, from left to right, Mildred Rogers, Florence Rollins, Roberta Snipe, and Alice Lowell.

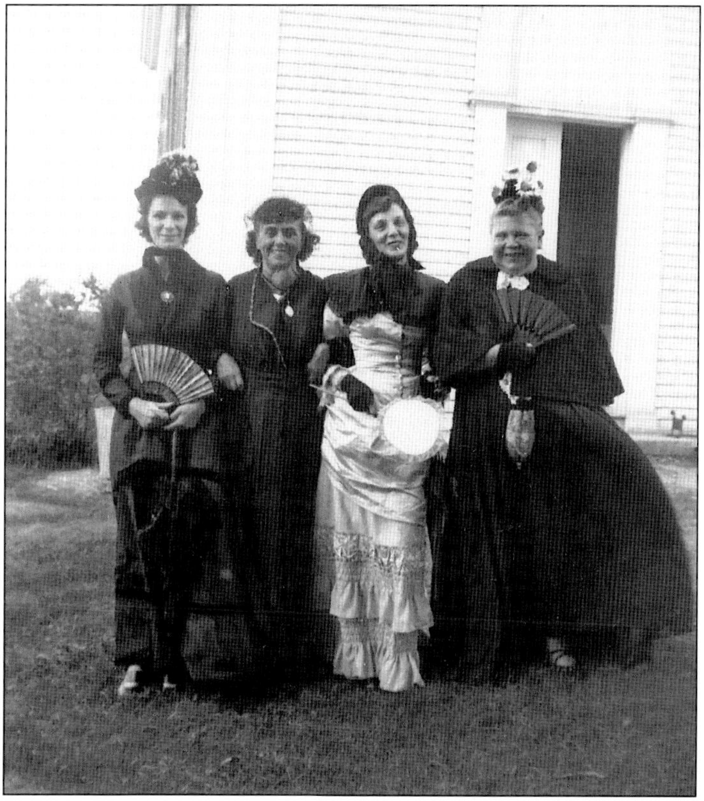

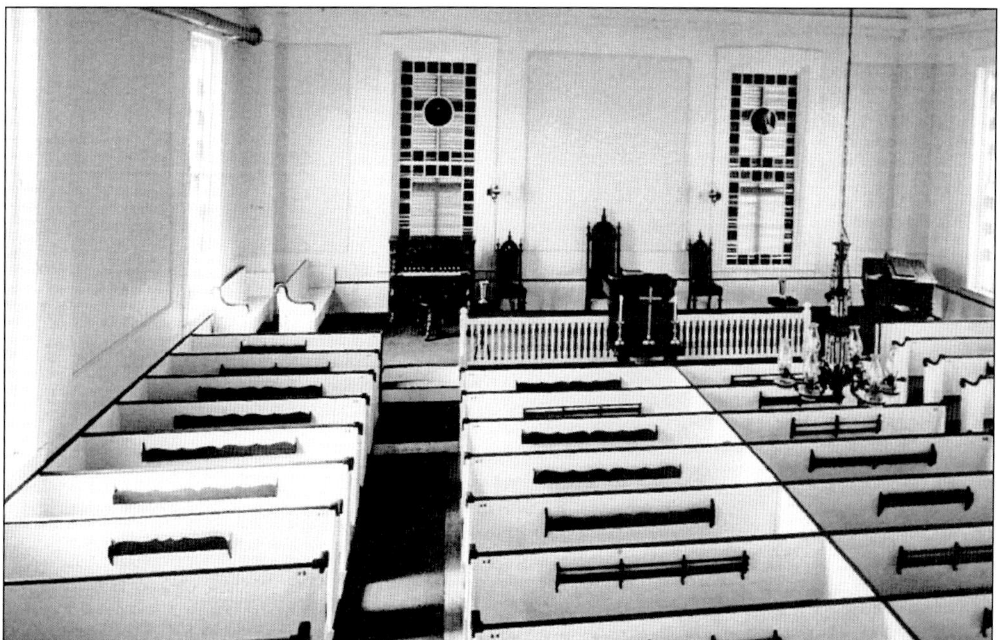

By 1952, when the anniversary celebration was held, the pews in the church had been painted white with dark trim. At this time the building was heated with one wood stove that sat at the back of the sanctuary with the stovepipe running the entire length of the room to the chimney.

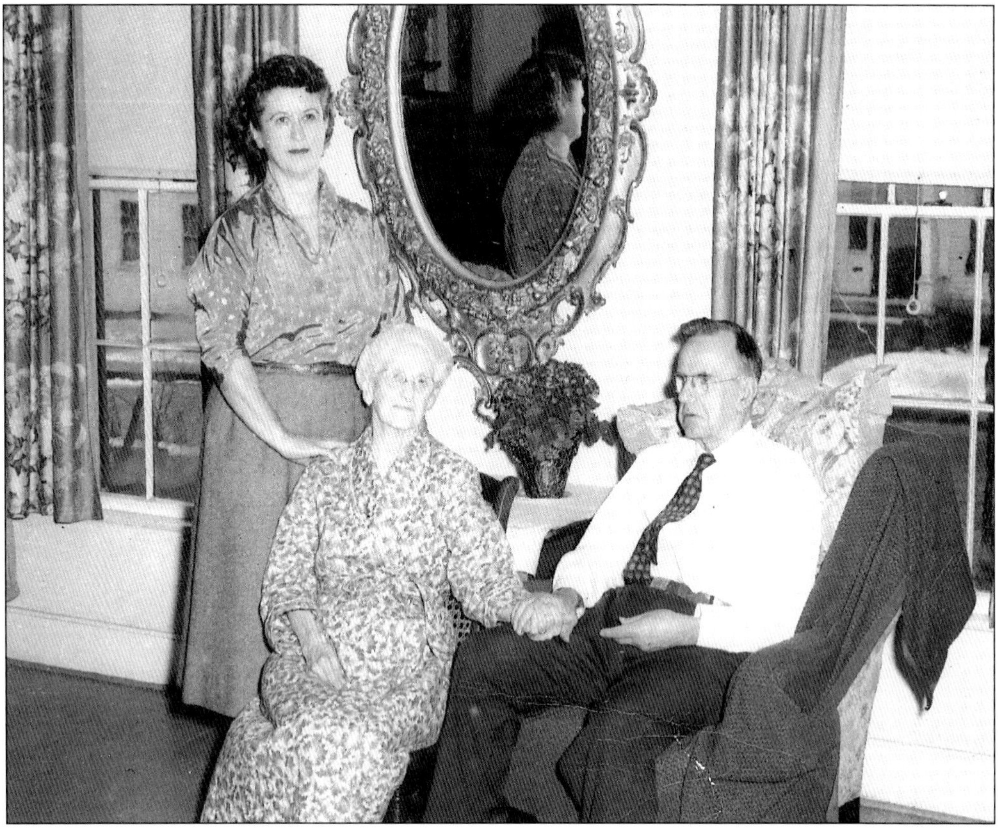

Rev. Charles Stevens served the Phippsburg Congregational Church while a student at Bowdoin College in the early 1900s, and his ordination into the ministry was held in this church in 1908. He posed with his wife, Lizzie (formerly Elizabeth Minott), and their niece, Margaret Minott Bennett.

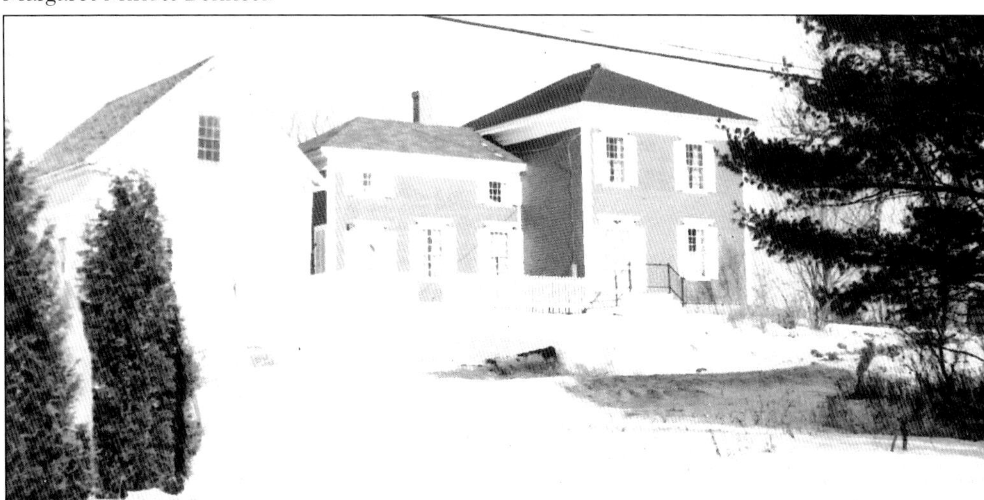

The home at the corner of the main road and the Parker Head Road was once owned by the Congregational Church and was used as a parsonage when needed. It was sold in 1967 to raise money for repairing the church steeple.

Three

COMMERCIAL AND GOVERNMENT BUILDINGS

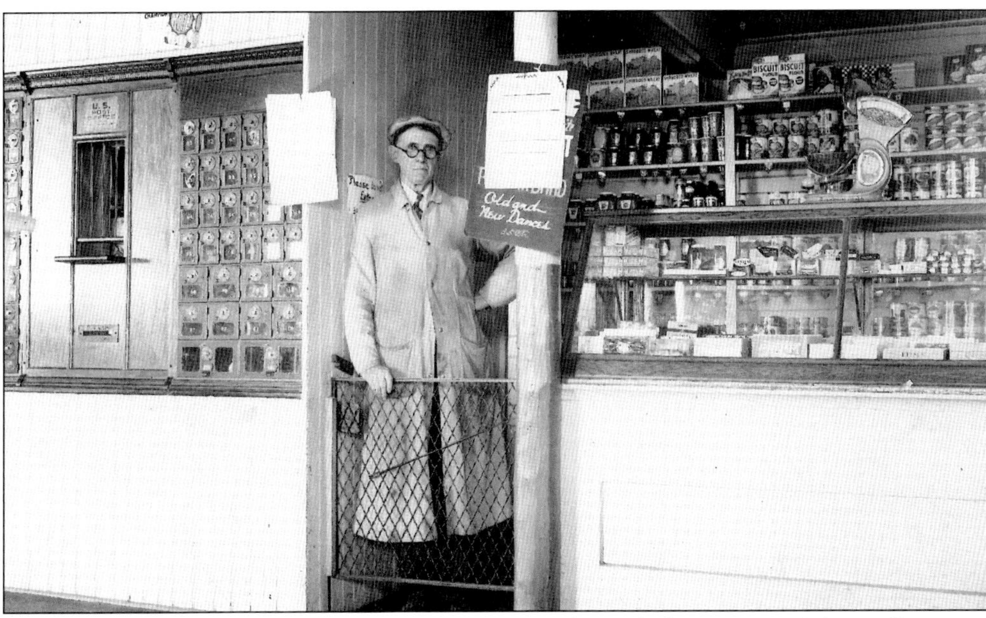

James C. Gilman, postmaster and store owner, stands inside his store at Sebasco Estates in the early 1930s. He had been postmaster for 33 years when he retired in 1946. Combining stores and post offices was a typical practice; the post office sometimes moved from one store to another, depending on the political party of the administration.

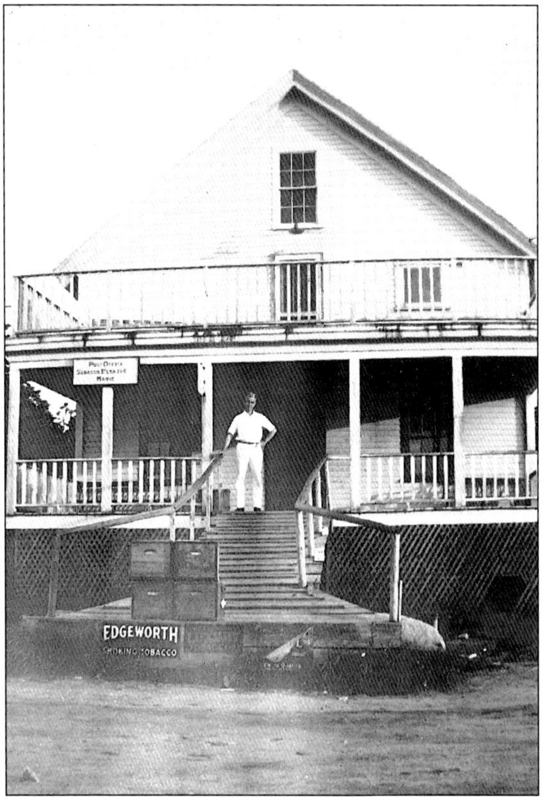

Gilman's General Store and Post Office at Sebasco Estates later became a dormitory at Sebasco Lodge. Walter Bartlett, a chef at the lodge, is shown here on the porch of Gilman's Store in the early 1940s.

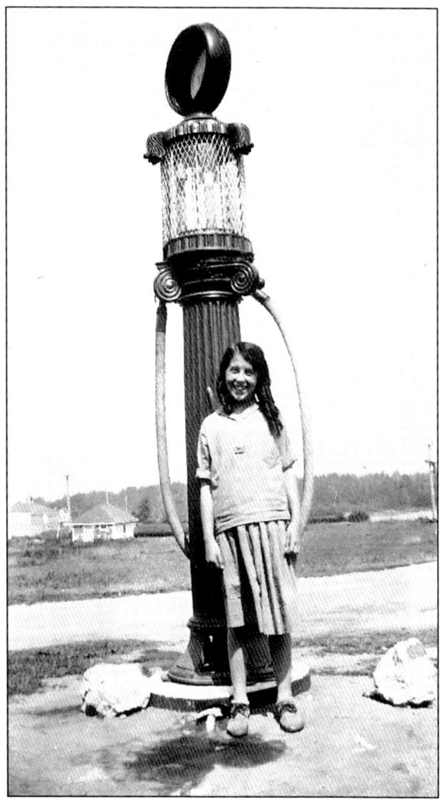

This gas pump stood in front of Gilman's Store by the lodge. Belle Lowell poses in front of the pump in about 1930.

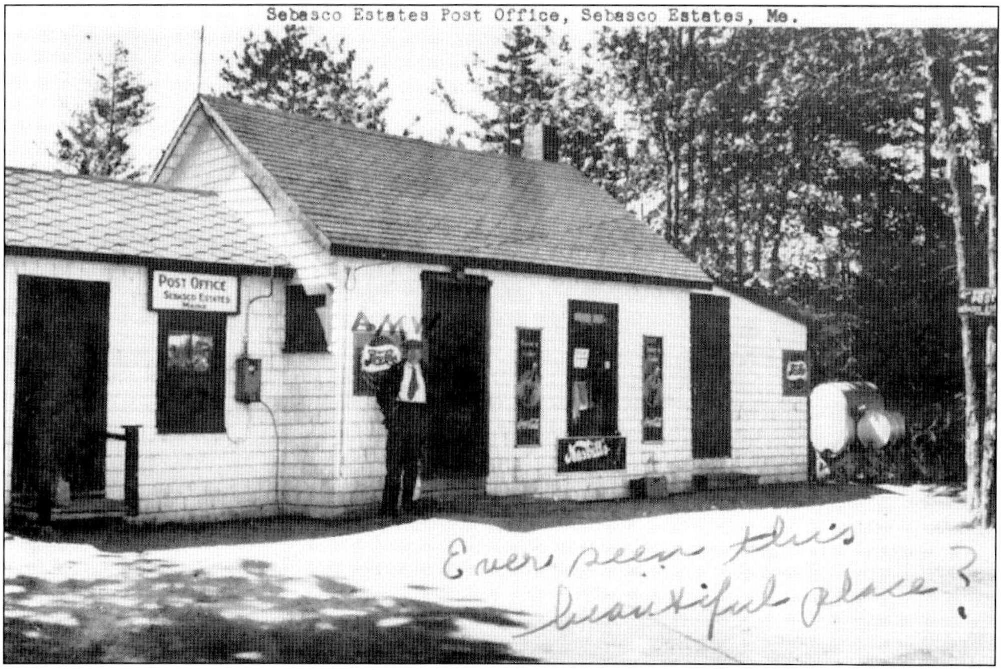

From about 1946 to 1960, the Sebasco Estates Post Office was located in Coffin's Store in Sebasco Village, with Arthur Wallace as its postmaster.

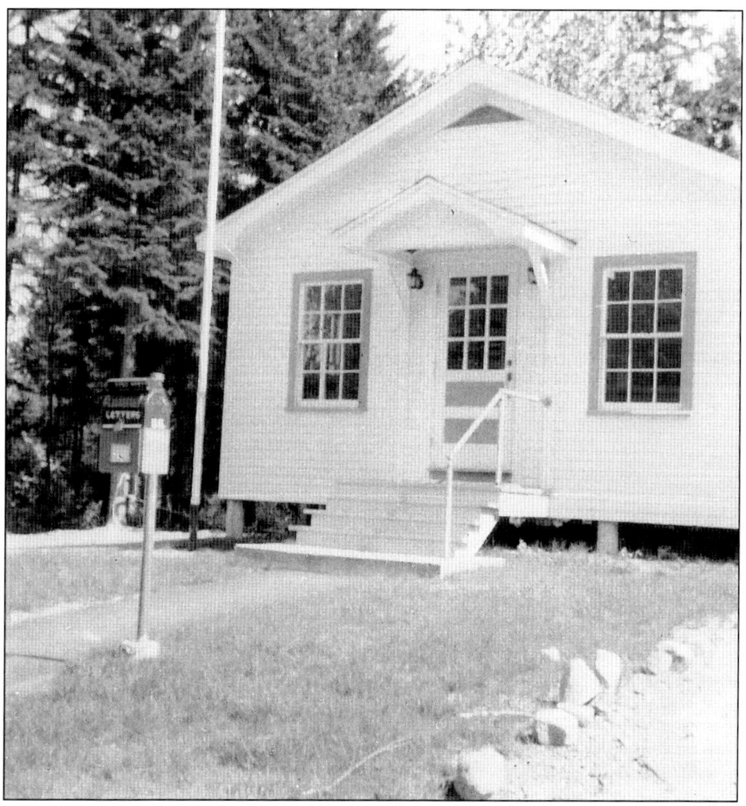

The Sebasco Estates Post Office moved from its location in Coffin's Store to its own building in 1960. Arlene Hamel was then postmaster.

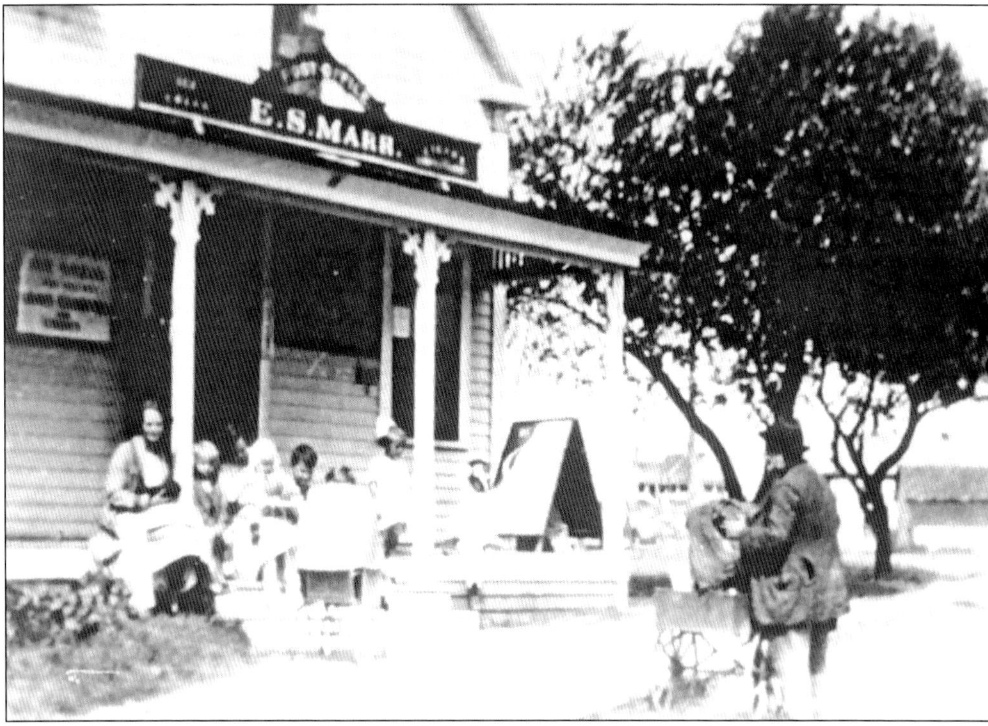

An organ grinder entertains local children in front of Marr's Store, one of Popham's general stores at the turn of the century. Marr's Store at times housed the post office.

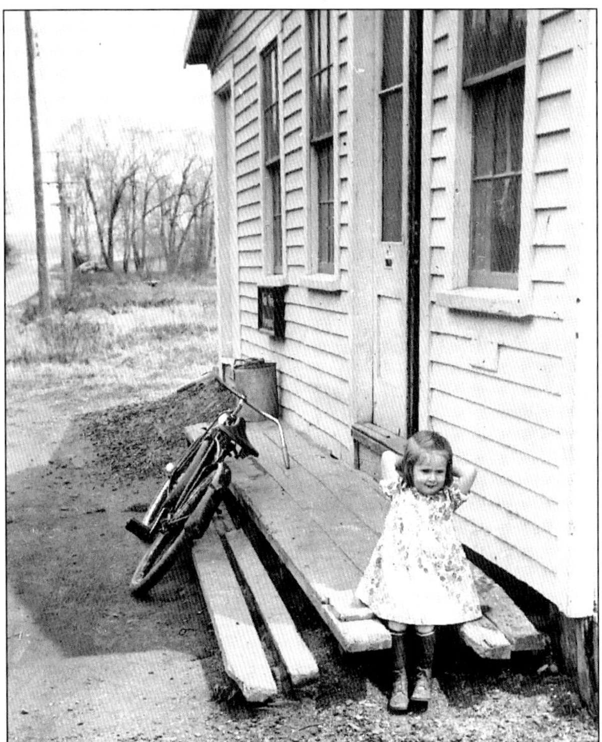
In April 1943, Laura Libby played in front of the store and post office at the Center where her mother, Arlene, was assistant postmaster.

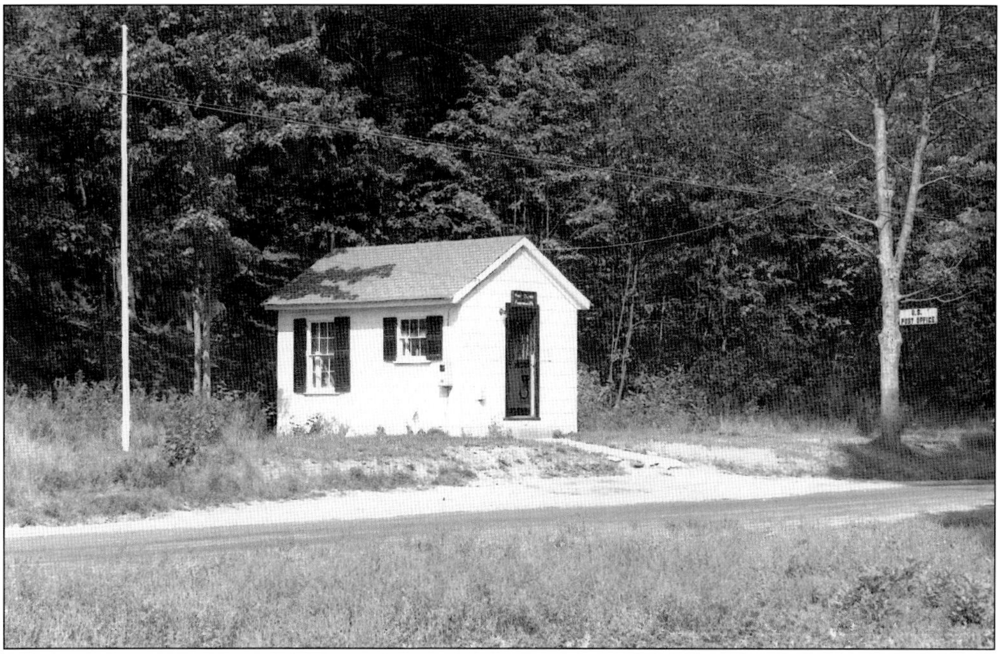

In 1946 the Phippsburg Center Post Office moved to its own tiny building. A later addition nearly doubled its size, but even before that the postmaster, Priscilla Rainey, found room for a small lending library within the post office.

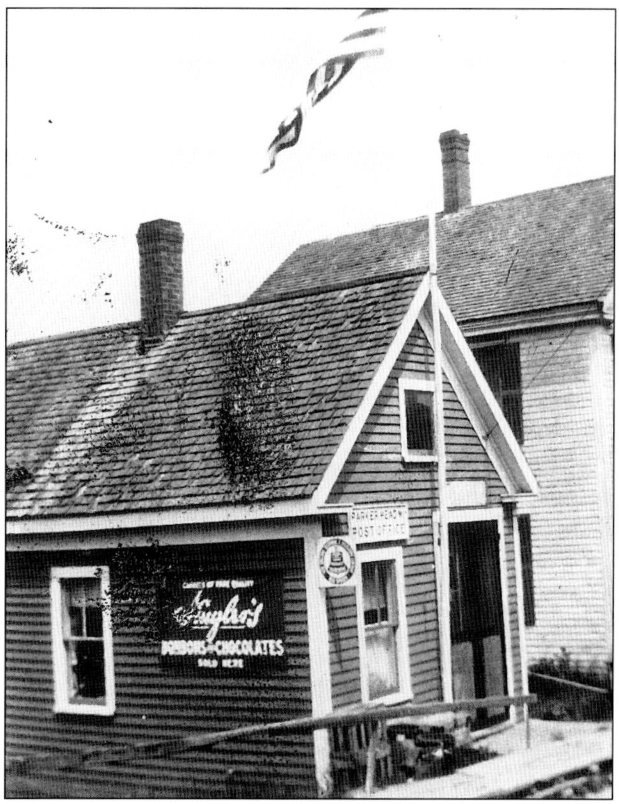

The Parker Head Post Office offered, in addition to mail services, a public telephone and confections.

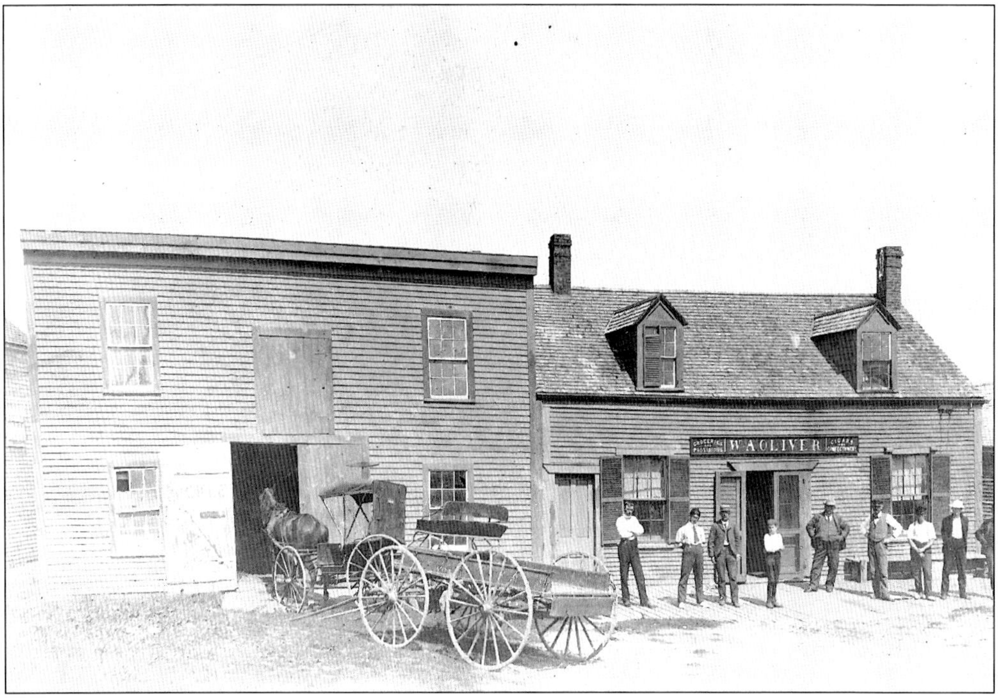

Groceries, provisions, cigars, and confections were among the items available at W.A. Oliver's Store in Parker Head. He owned the store at the village end of Mill Pond Dam between 1901 and 1906.

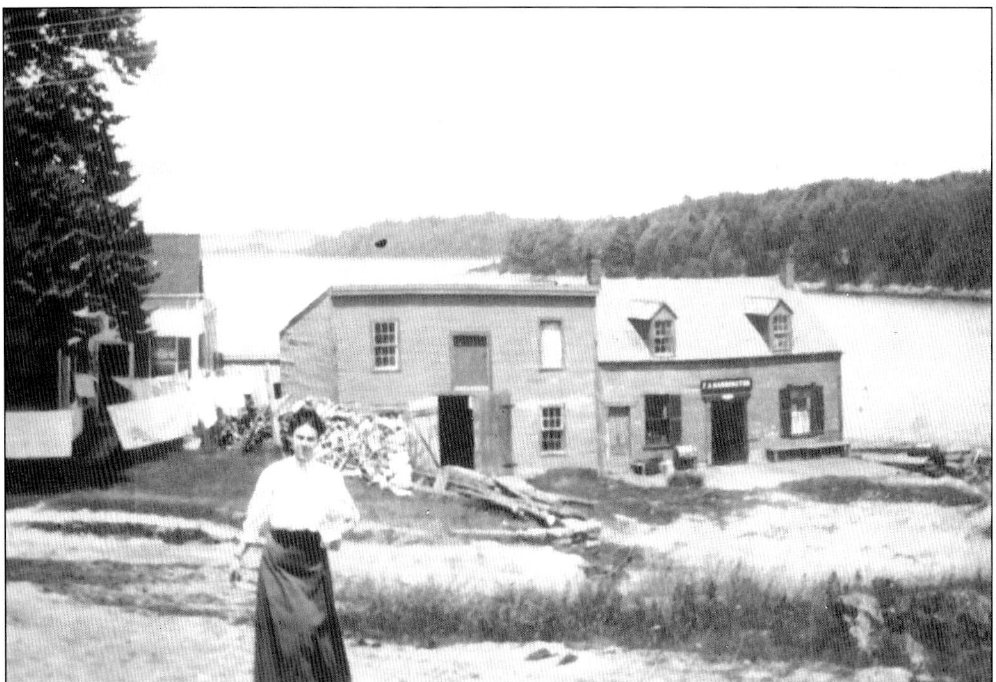

By 1906, W.A. Oliver's Store had become Harrington's Store. A photographer caught Frances Oliver Marks on the road near the store and the Ed Wyman homestead (with laundry).

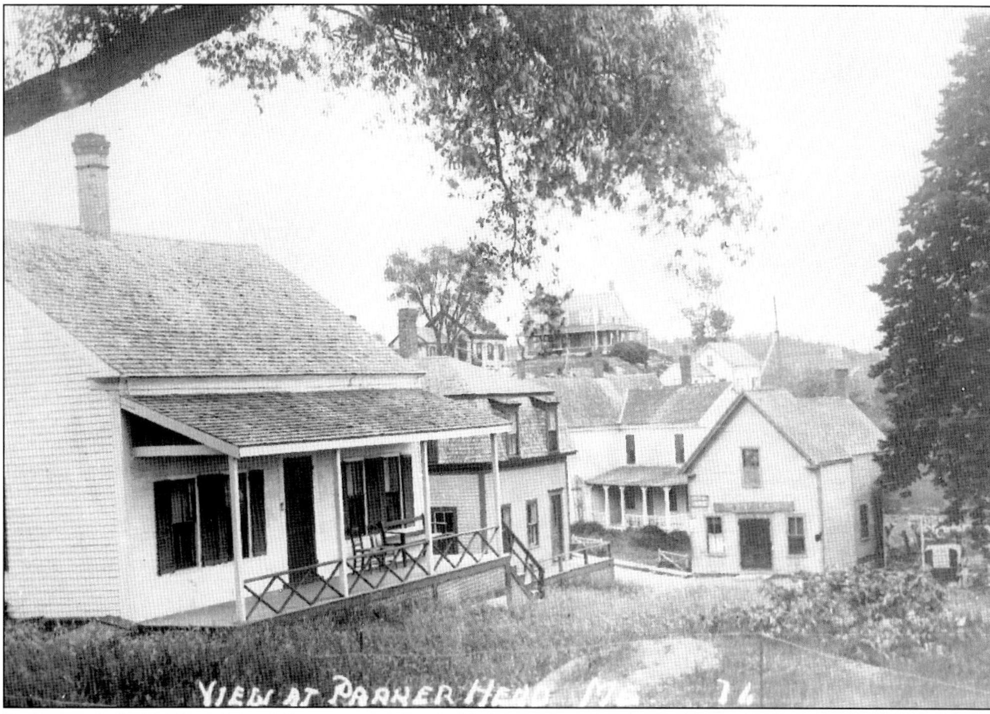

Before 1917 Parker Head businesses included George Duley's Store and Lizzie Harrington's boardinghouse, both shown near the center of this picture (see p. 17). The Grinlowe house in the foreground burned in the 1930s.

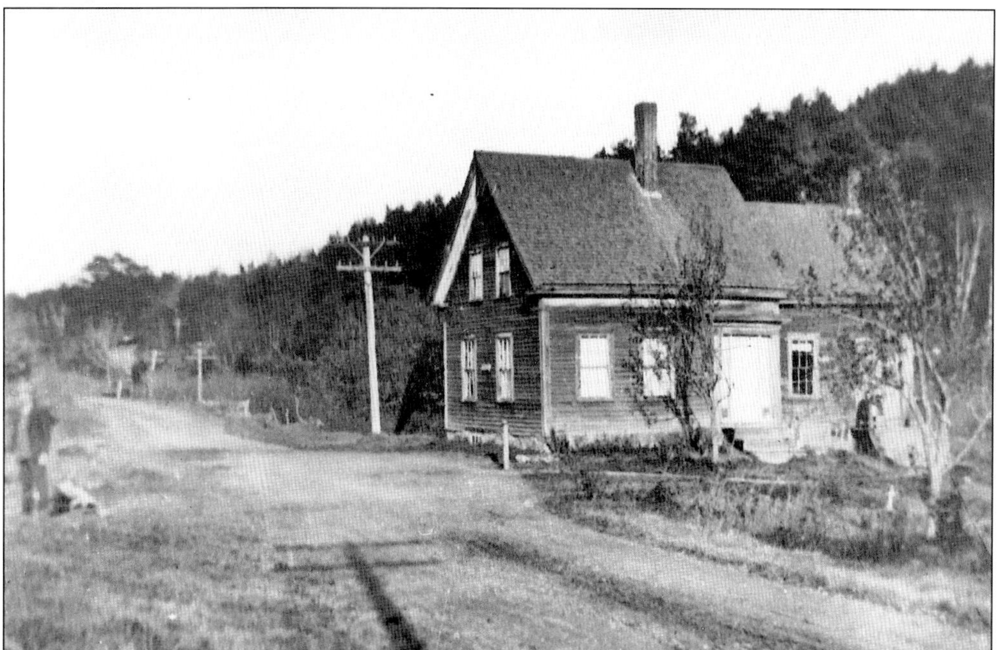

The Ashdale Post Office was located in the Benjamin Lowell house in about 1904. Sometime later, the road was straightened and rebuilt, moving it to the west.

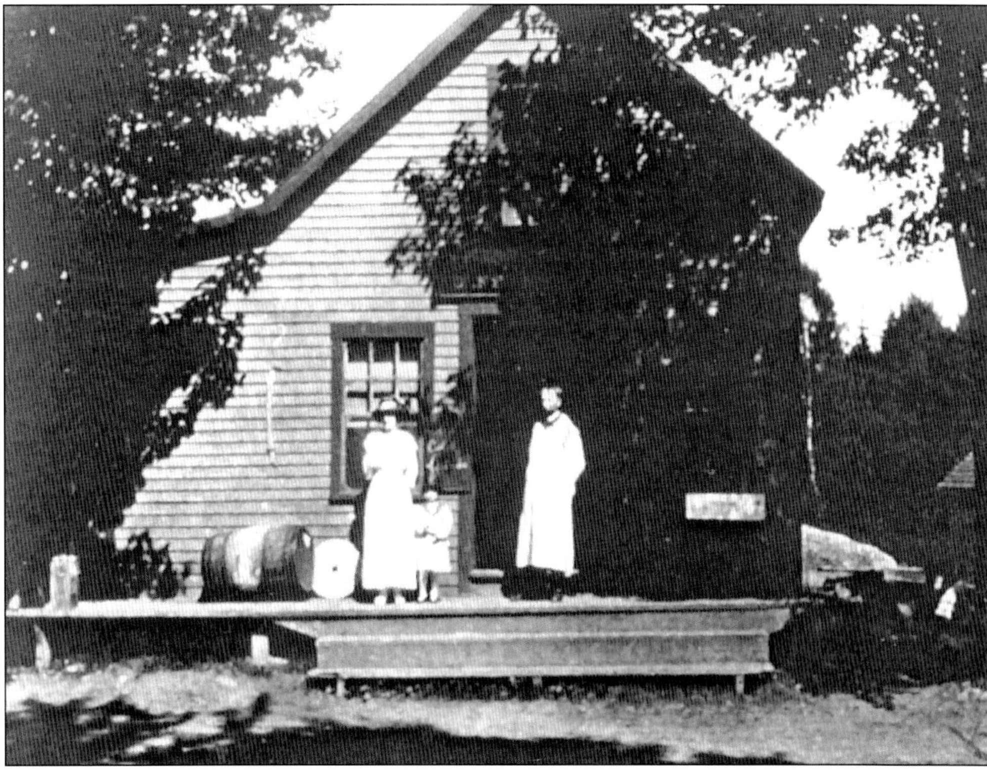

In 1914 Harry Hosmer stood in front of his store at Saw Mill Corner in Ashdale. Mr. Hosmer was also a plumber.

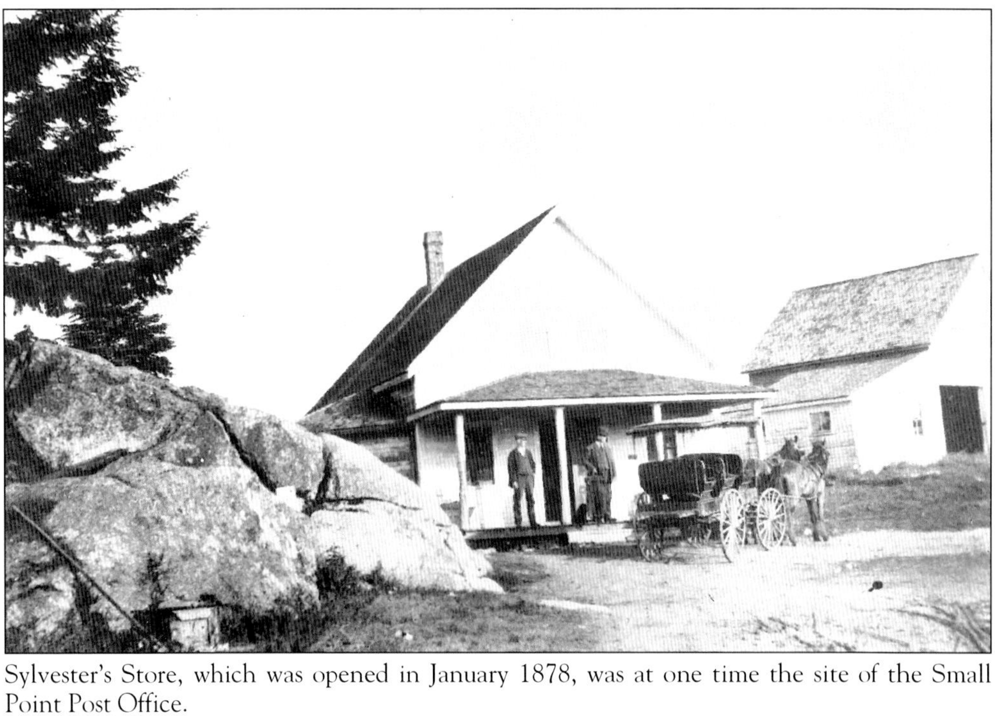

Sylvester's Store, which was opened in January 1878, was at one time the site of the Small Point Post Office.

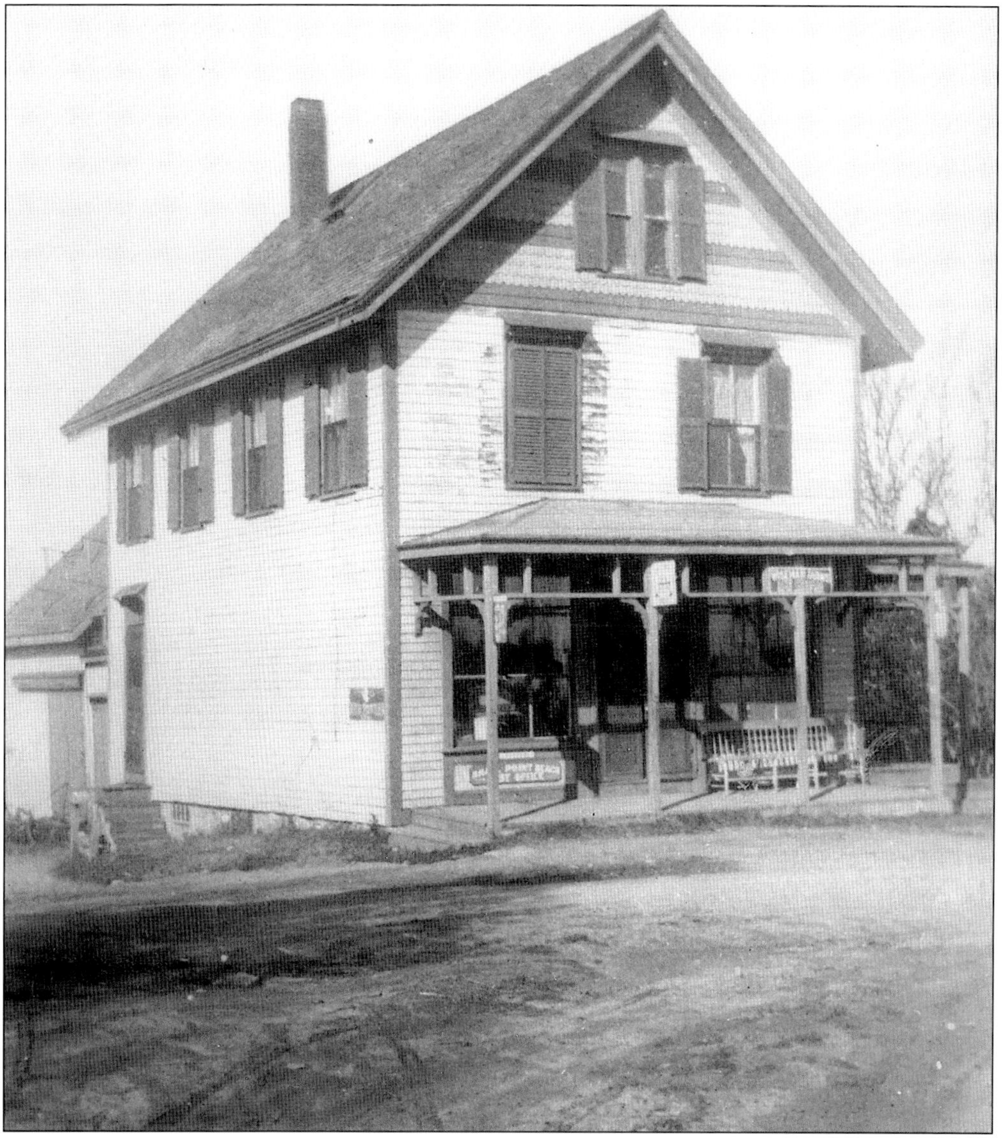

Later the Small Point Beach Post Office was housed in Wyman's Store across the road from the Small Point Club development. Originally built *c.* 1890 by Walter Chase, the store was purchased by Martin Wyman around 1910. He and his family ran the store until it closed in 1985; for most of those years they ran the post office as well.

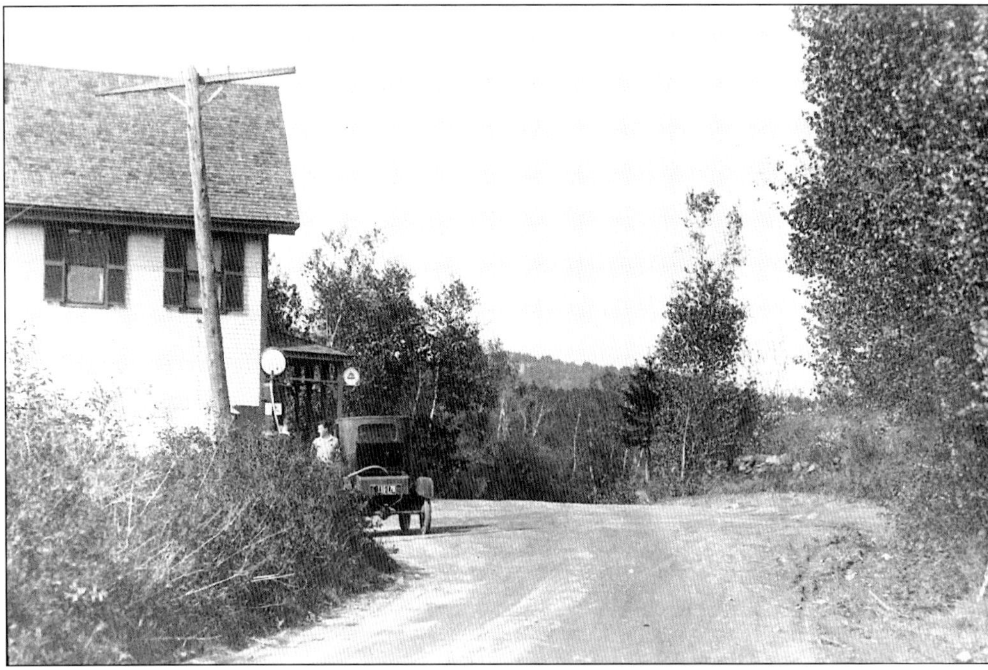

Wyman's Store at Small Point Beach also had a public telephone and sold gasoline.

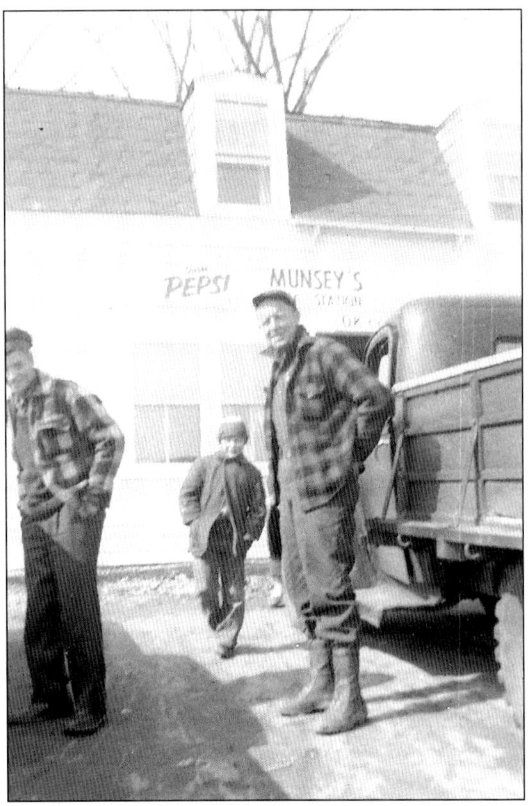

Munsey's Gulf Station and Store (known as O.K. Corral) was one of the businesses in Winnegance. Owner Lester Munsey, together with Charlie Williams and Keith Atwood, are shown here in front of the store in 1959.

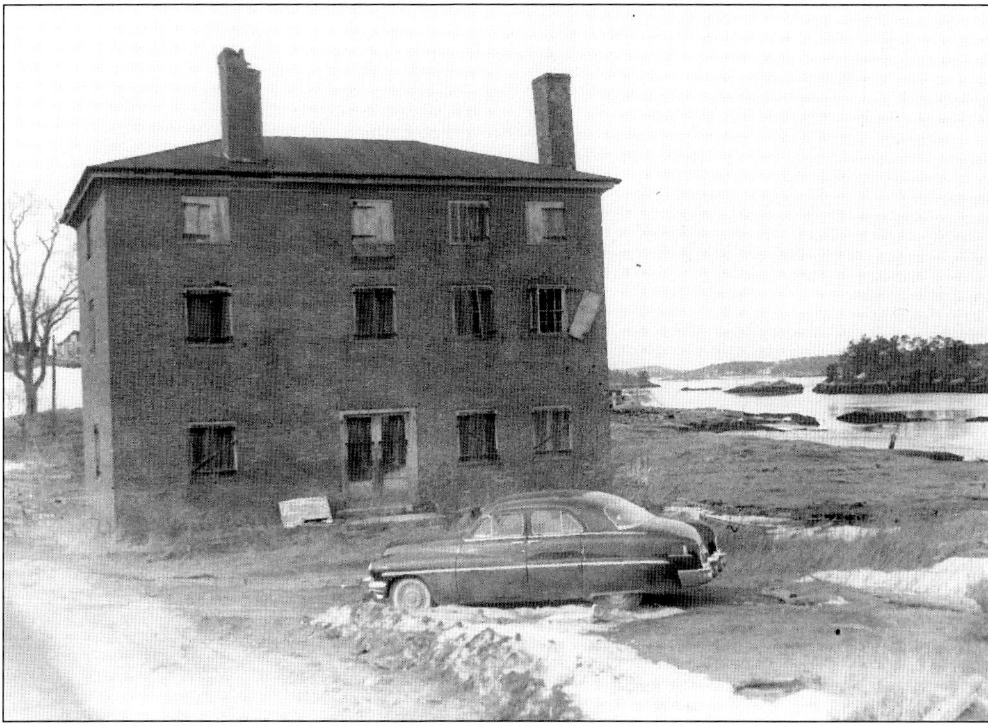

The brick store at the Minott Shipyard at Phippsburg Center housed the post office at various times. By 1956 the store was in disrepair; it was razed three years later.

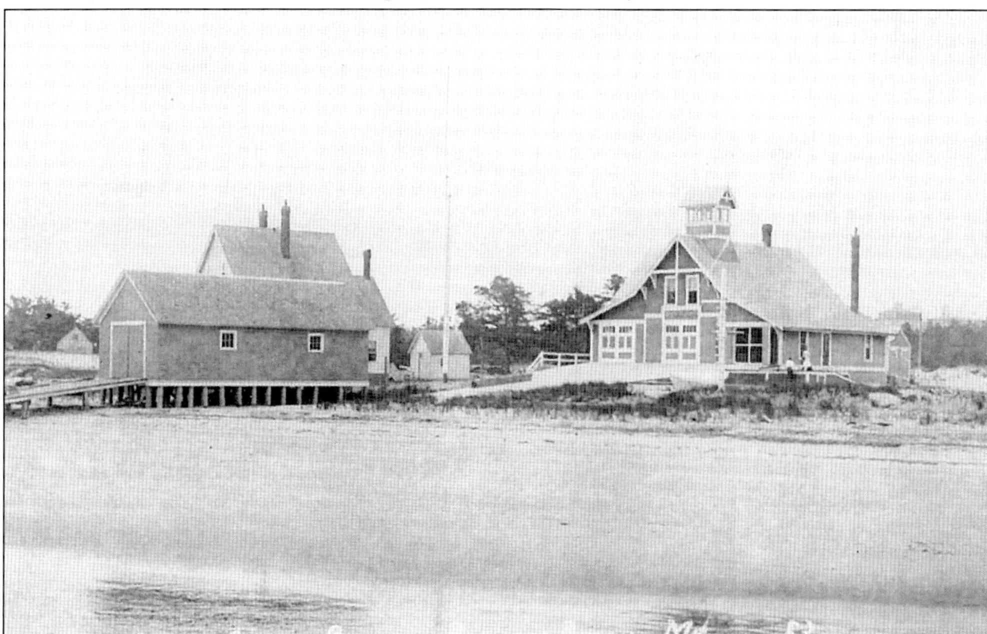

The U.S. Life Saving Station, originally called the Hunnewell Beach Life Saving Station, was in this location by 1893. In 1935 it became the Popham Beach Coast Guard Station and served the area until it closed in September 1971.

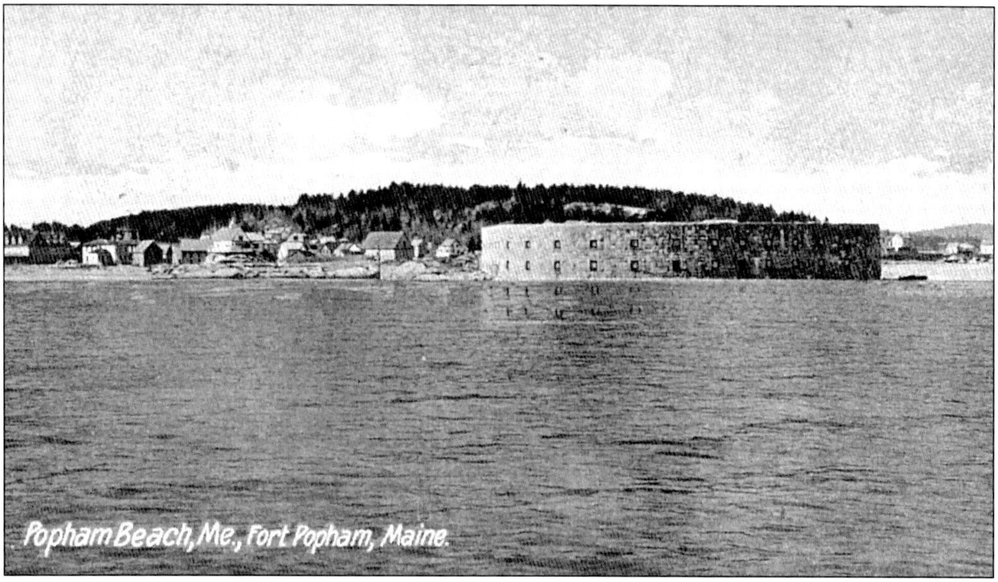

Fort Popham, constructed on a site that had earlier housed a wooden blockhouse, was built in 1865. Though it was never completed, it was manned during the Civil War, the Spanish-American War, and World War I.

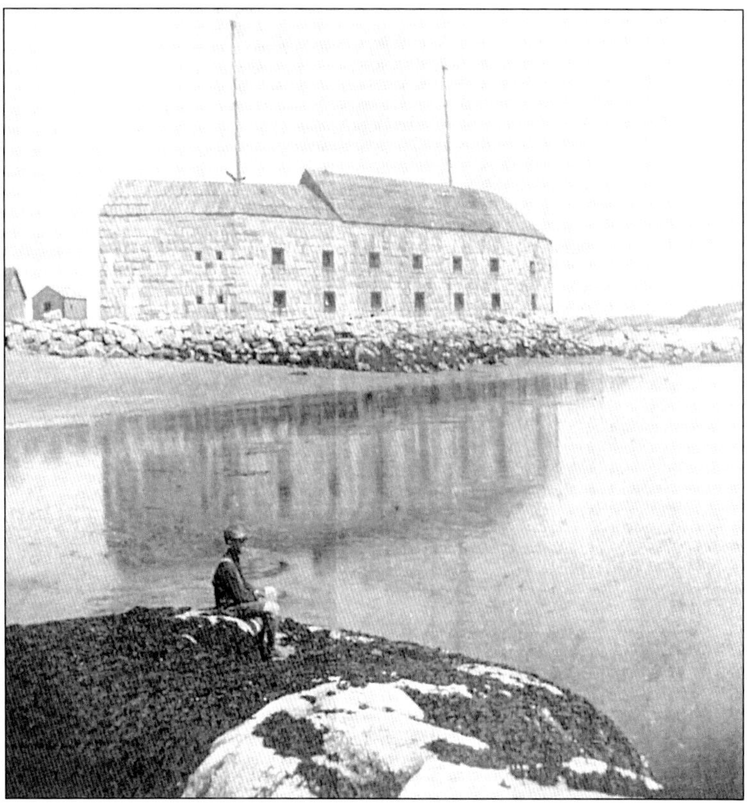

In this c. 1886 picture Fort Popham, still under construction, had a wooden roof.

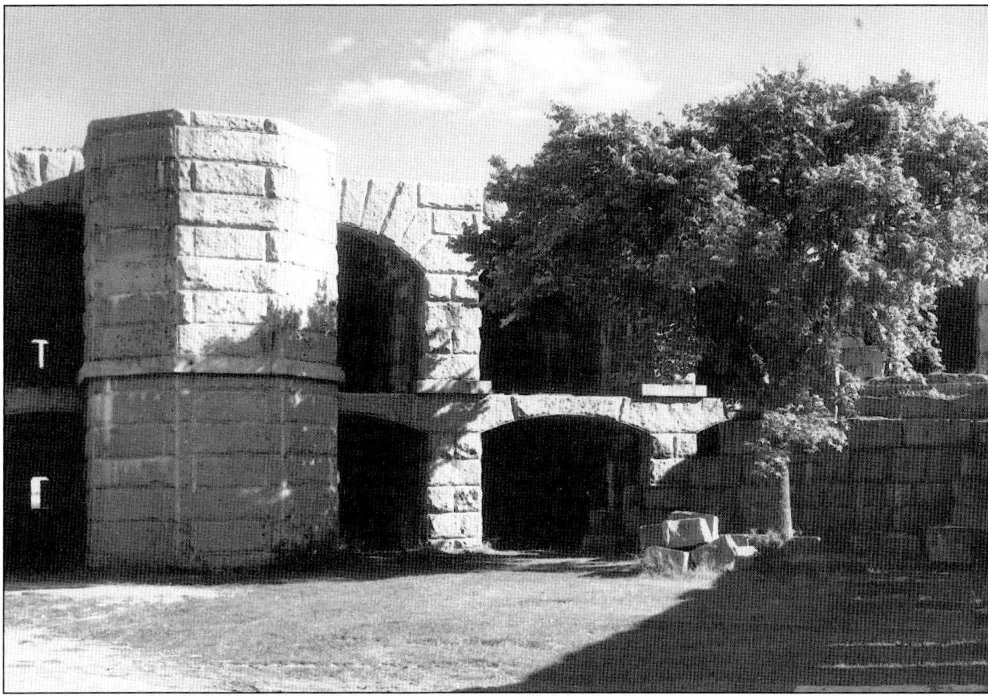

The tower-like construction on the left was one of two circular granite staircases inside Fort Popham. Blocks of the unfinished fort could still be seen under a tree in the 1950s.

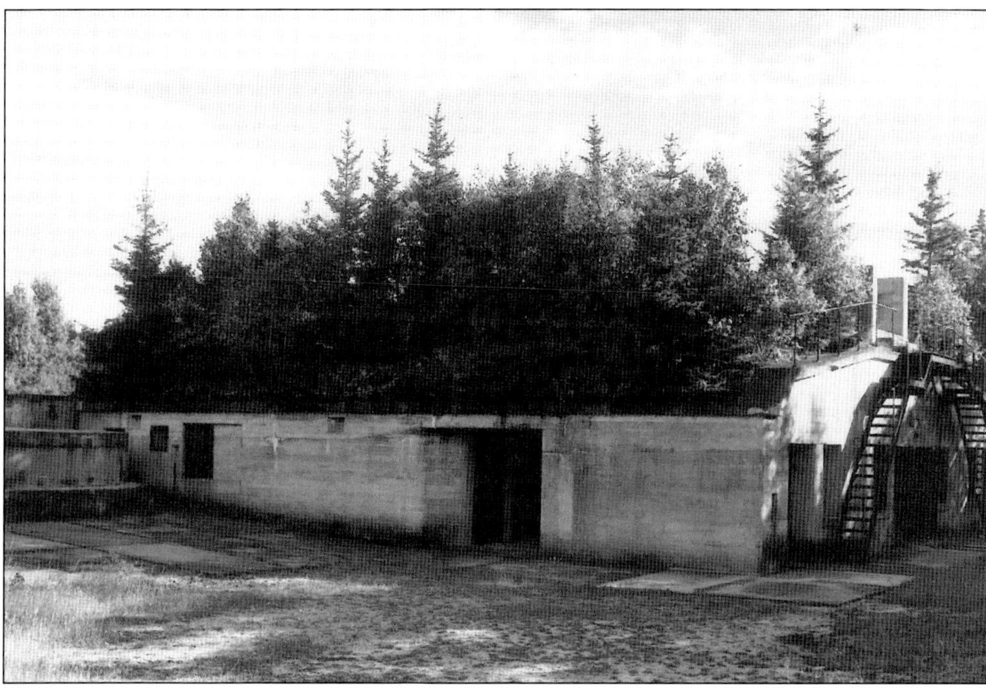

This c. 1950 picture of Fort Baldwin, manned in both World War I and World War II, was taken before vandals removed much of the metal construction.

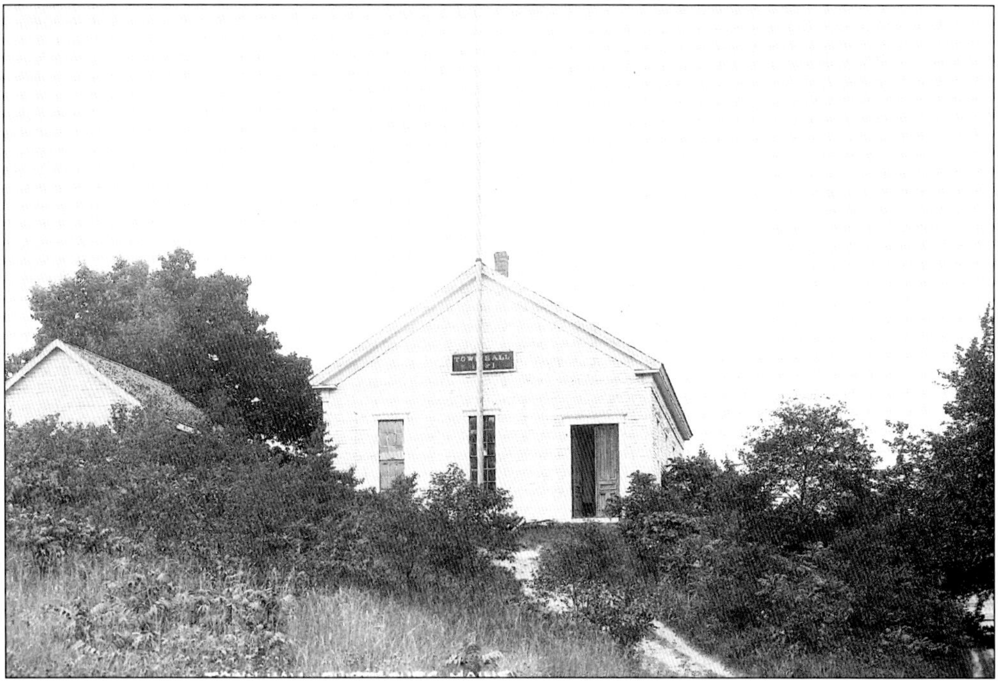

The town hall, built in 1881, remained in use until 1958, at which time the town offices were moved into the new elementary school. The hall was sold in 1969 but was later reacquired, moved to its present site across from the elementary school, and returned to its original role in 1988.

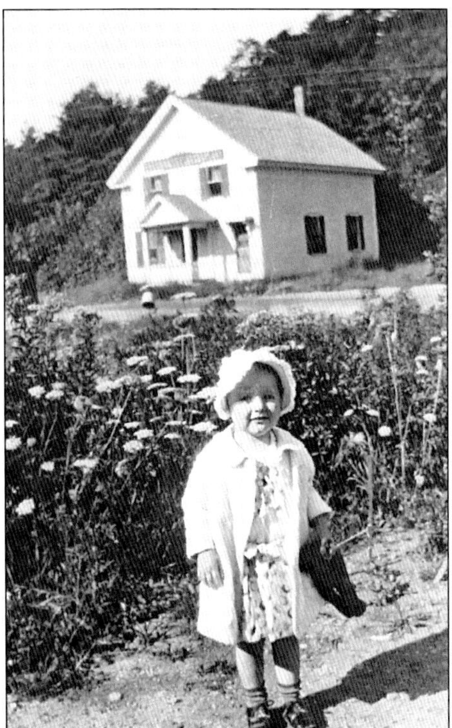

Ardenne Perkins, clutching her teddy bear, stands *c.* 1932 amidst the flowers at Phippsburg Center across from the Albert F. Totman Public Library, which was just south of the Center Store. Originally called Percy Hall, it was built about 1856 for use as a community hall. The building belonged to the Center Church from 1886 until 1923, when it was purchased by the town for a library. It was moved to its new location next to the Phippsburg Historical Museum on the Parker Head Road in 1984.

Four

Occupations

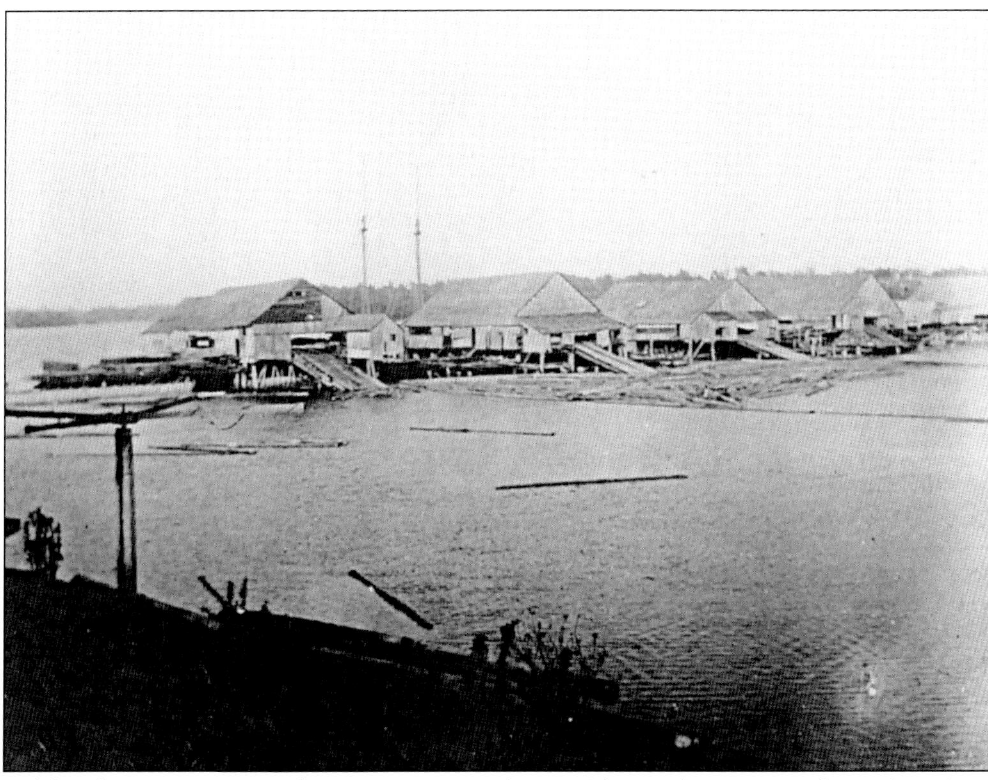

Tidal mills were constructed in various areas of town. The northernmost mills in Phippsburg were at Winnegance. The logs in the water would soon be sawed into lumber and possibly loaded onto the schooner (note the masts visible behind the mills) for shipment to distant ports.

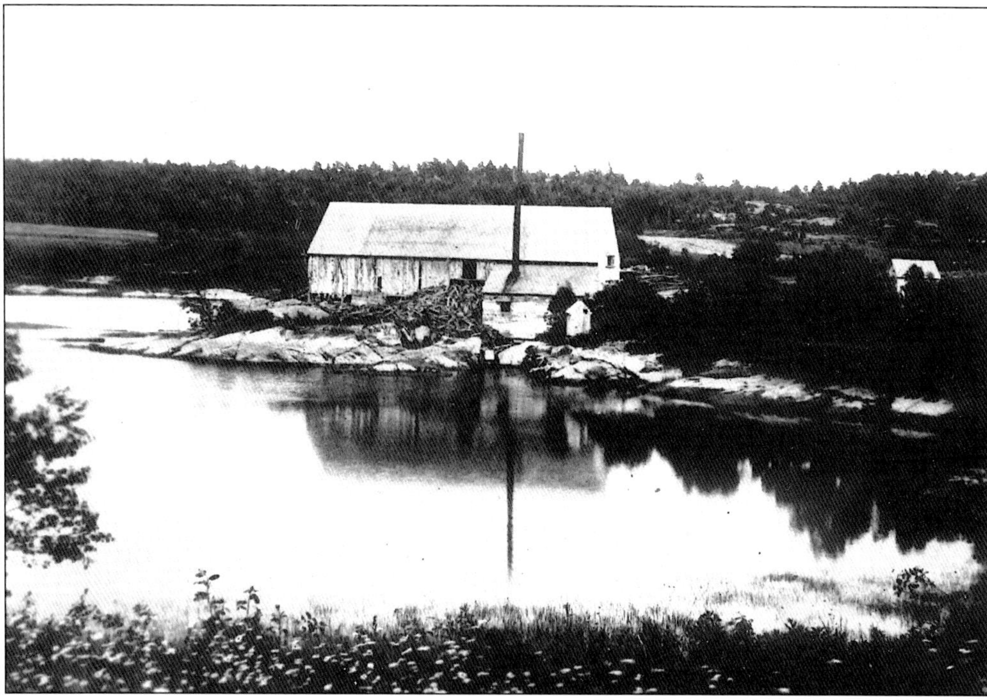

The Perry Sawmill, another example of the use of tides to power mills, was located at the south side of The Basin in the Sebasco area of town. In 1914 the remains of the old sawmill were removed by Freeman Merritt, who developed Sebasco Estates.

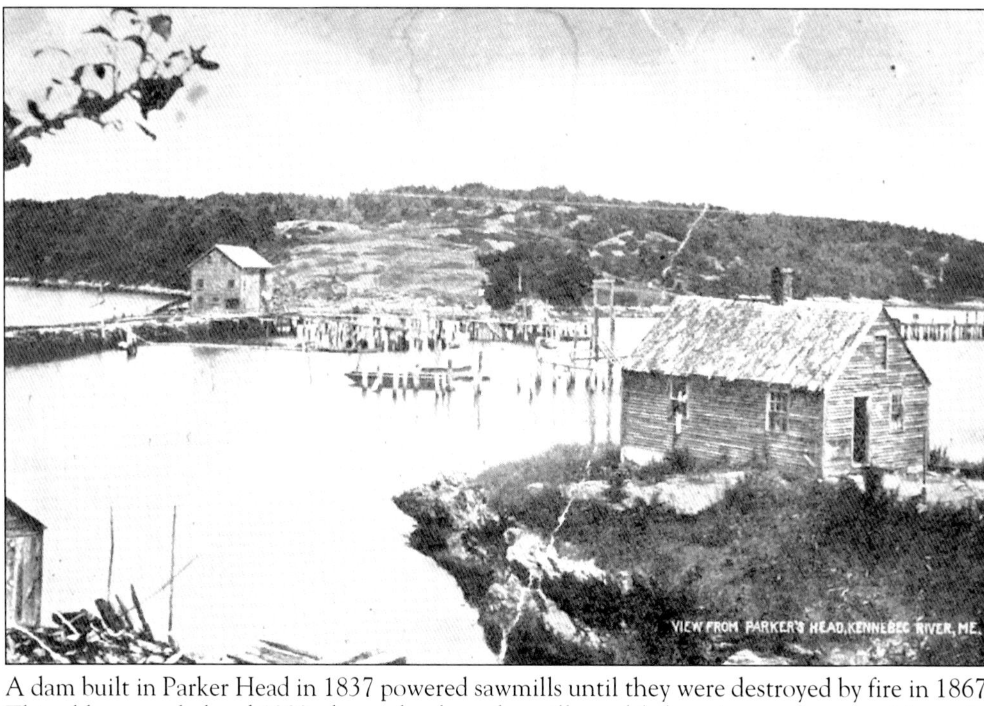

A dam built in Parker Head in 1837 powered sawmills until they were destroyed by fire in 1867. This old postcard, dated 1909, shows the dam, the mill pond (where ice was harvested from the 1870s through the late 1890s), and an old building on Pork Point.

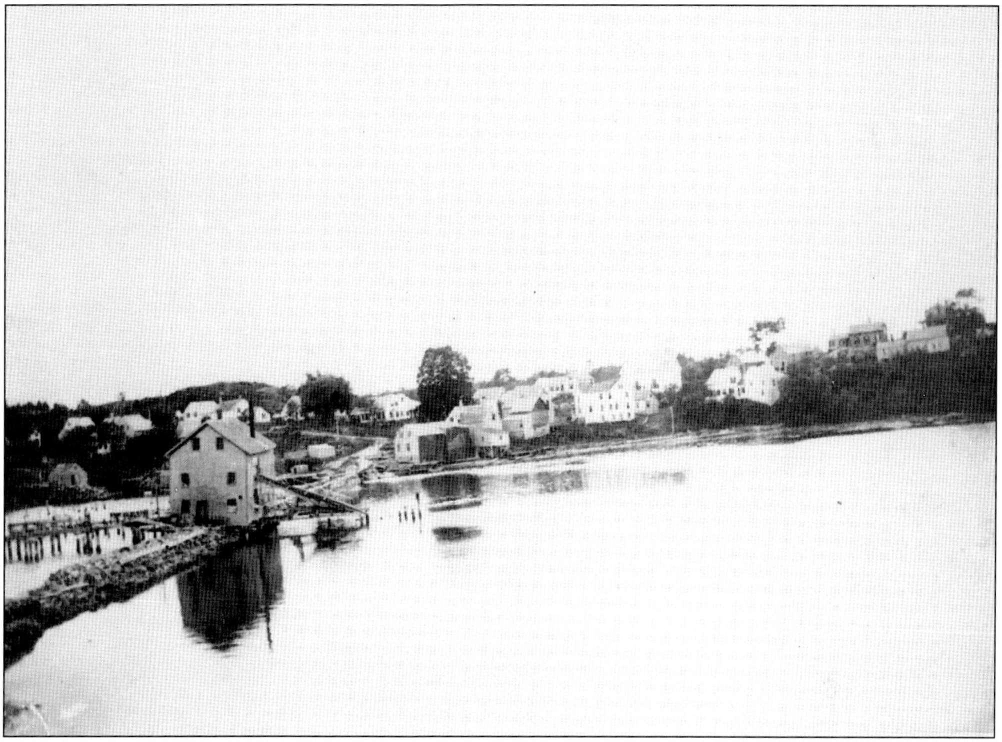

Wharves are visible on the left in this image of the icehouse at the Parker Head Mill Pond. In the background, at the end of the dam, was Parker Head Village.

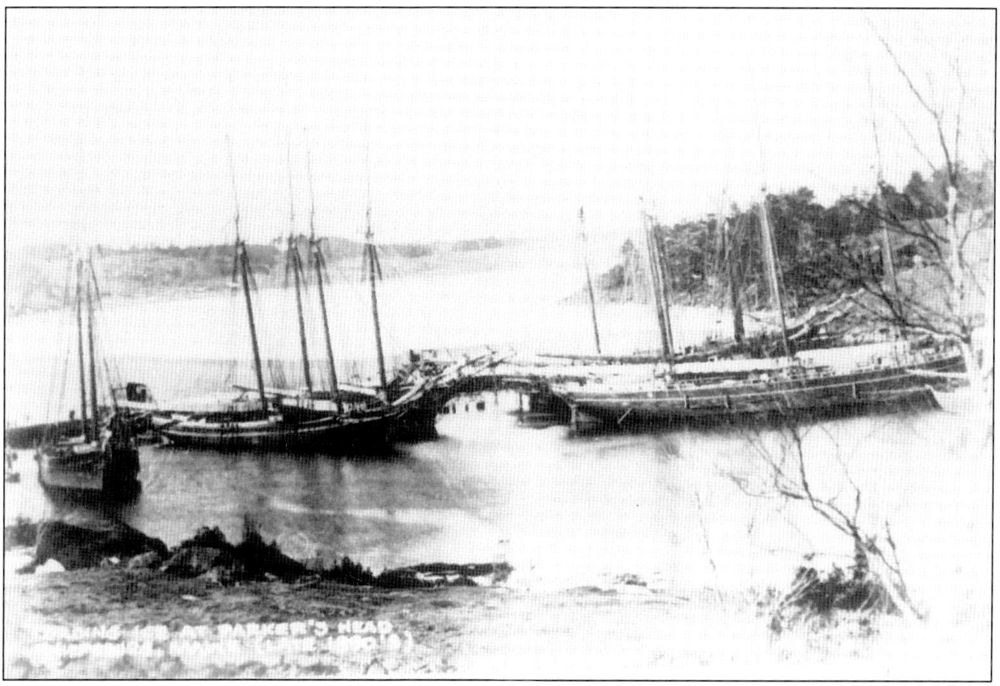

At least five schooners are shown here being packed with ice at the Parker Head Dam in the late 1890s.

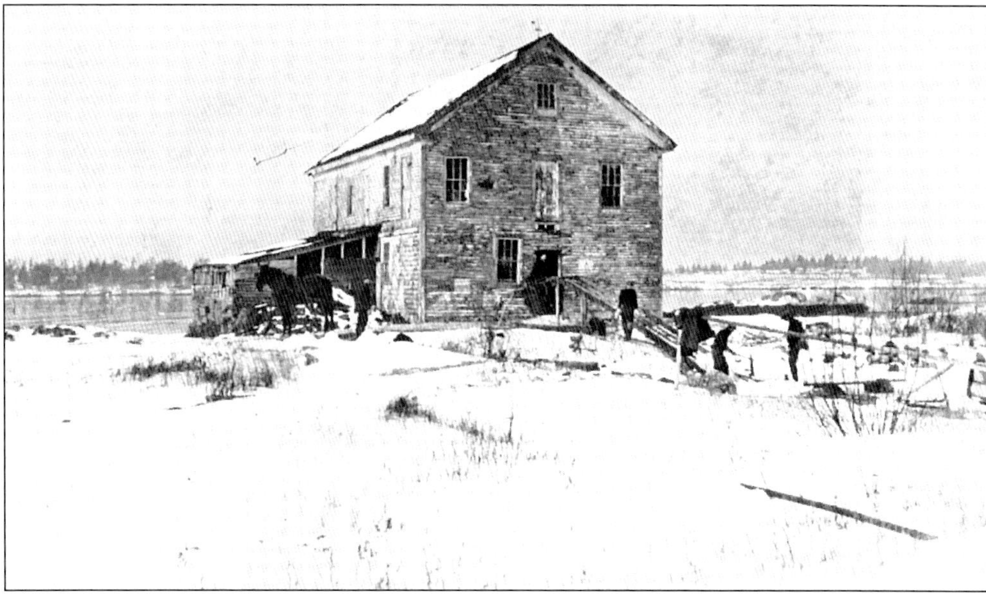

The ice business was an important industry in nearly every part of town from about 1880 through the turn of the century. Cornelius Creek in Sebasco was dammed up to create Cornelius Pond. Ice harvested from the pond was packed between layers of sawdust in the icehouse (shown here c. 1900) and shipped from Horse Island Harbor to southern and European ports.

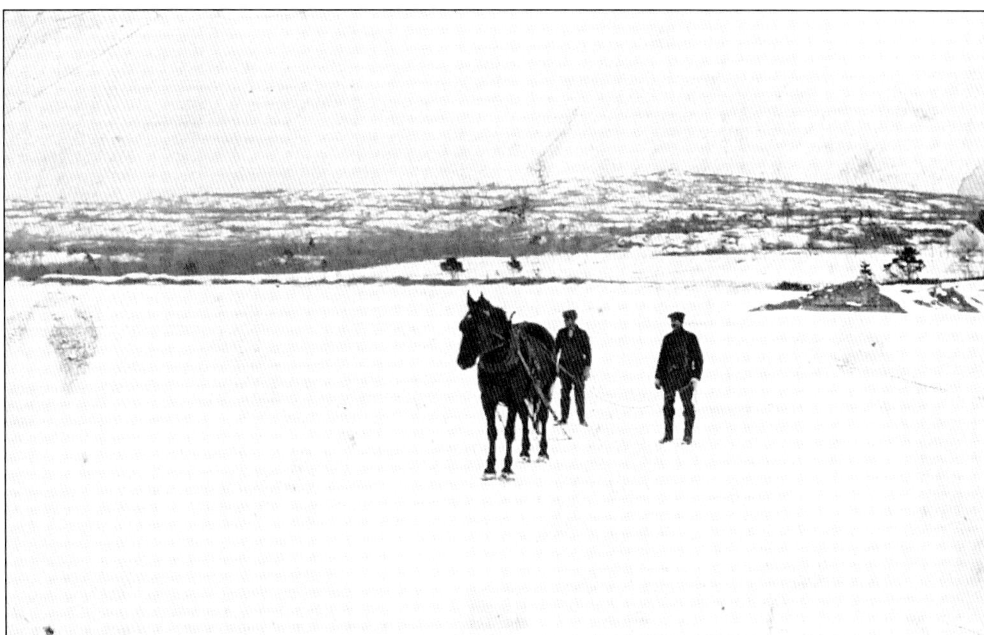

Horses were used to score the ice for cutting. Behind the horse and workers in this c. 1900 image taken at Sebasco was Merritt Mountain, known earlier as Mount Hunger.

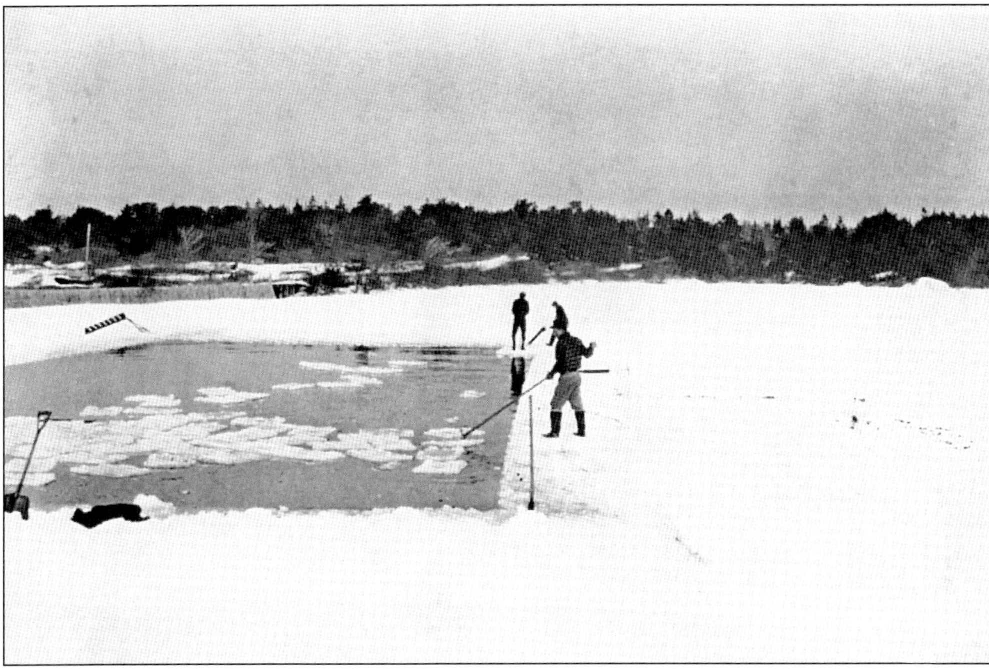

The ice was then cut into blocks, removed from the water, and stored in the icehouse until it was shipped during the coming months.

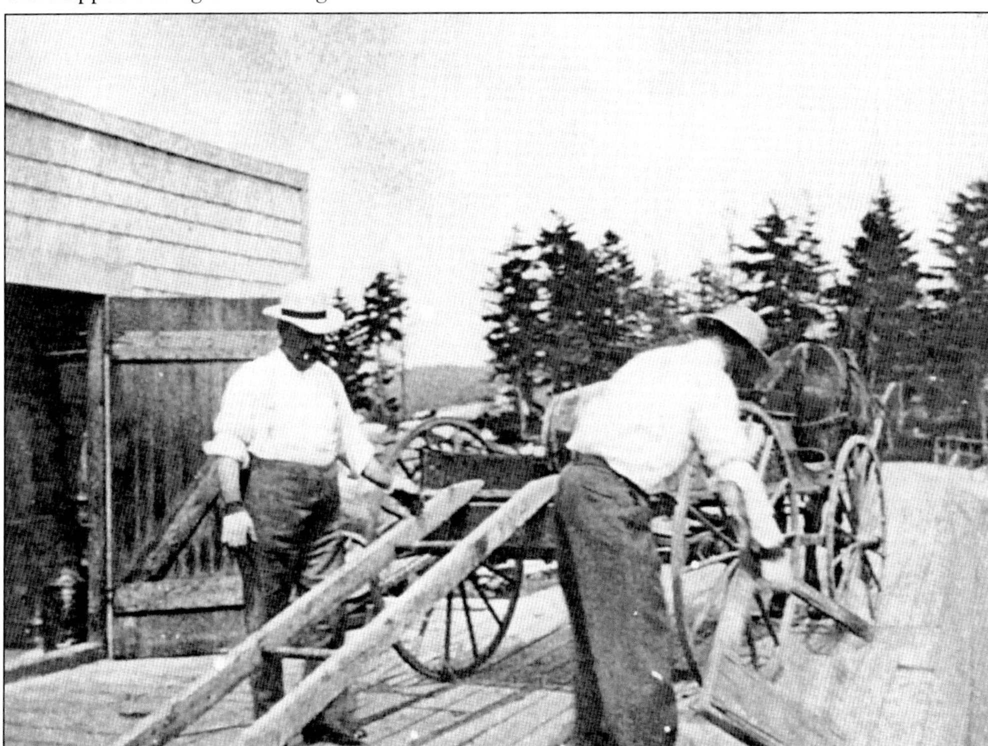

Billy Beals has just loaded a barrel of molasses onto a wagon near Cornelius Pond, *c.* 1910. The ladder-like ramp simplified the process.

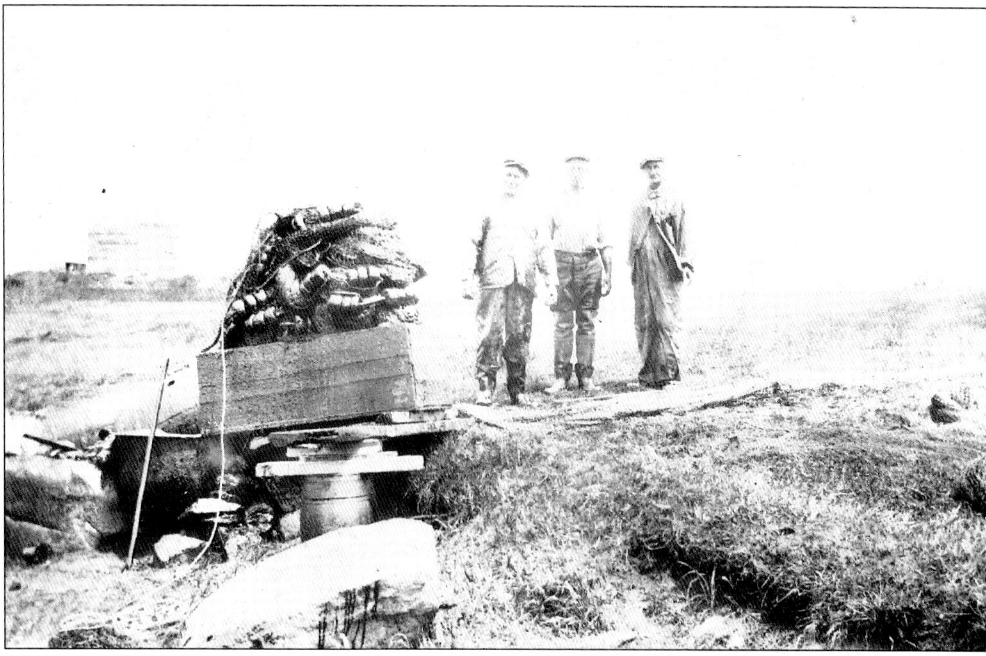

Alvin Pye (left), Ernest Pye (center), and Niles Webber pose *c.* 1920 near Alliquippa in Small Point. Beside them is a crate of fish nets with floats.

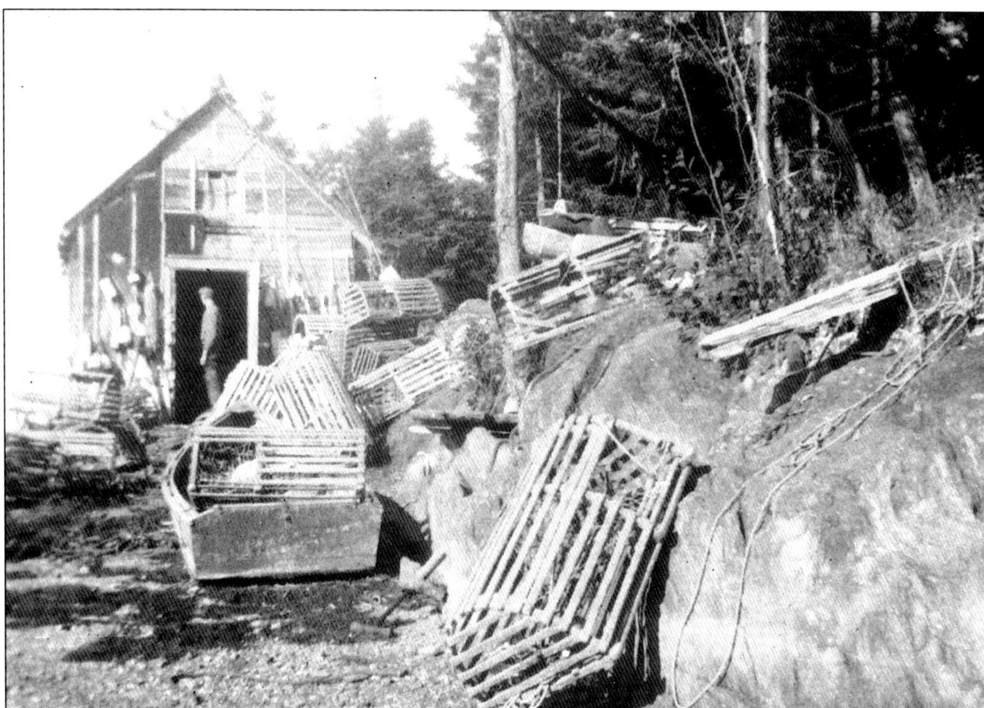

Cliff Pye stands in the doorway of Maurice Pye's fishhouse at The Branch in Small Point. Note the buoys leaning against the fishhouse and the wooden lobster traps scattered about the area in this mid-1900s photograph.

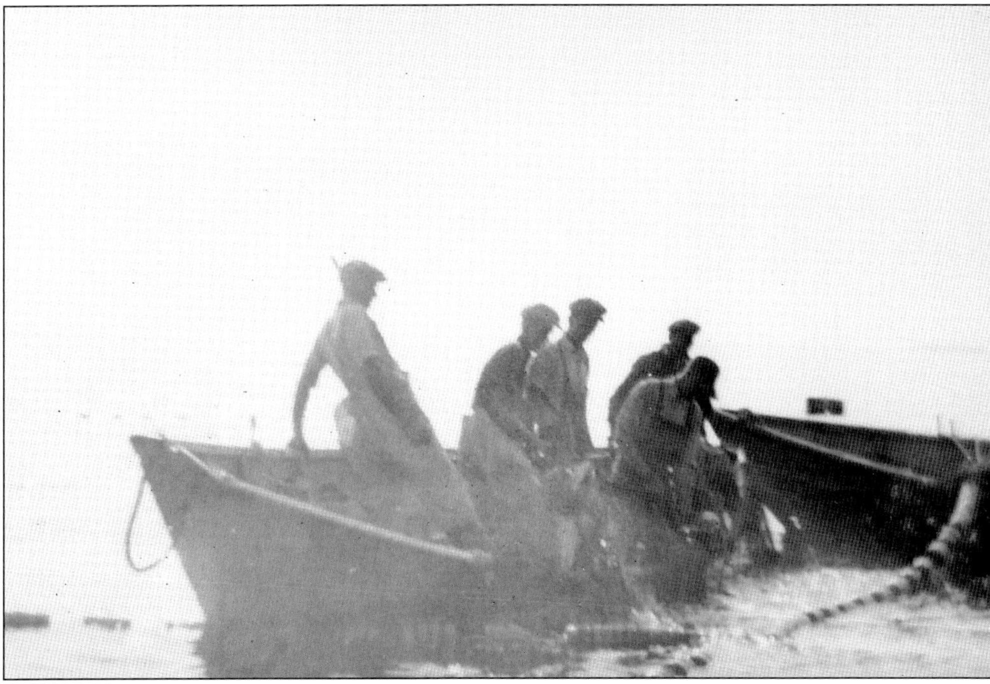

These Small Point fishermen were photographed pound fishing off Wood Island about 1933. Four of the men in the dories have been identified as Maurice Pye, Charles F. Pye, Clyde Pye, and Clifford Pye.

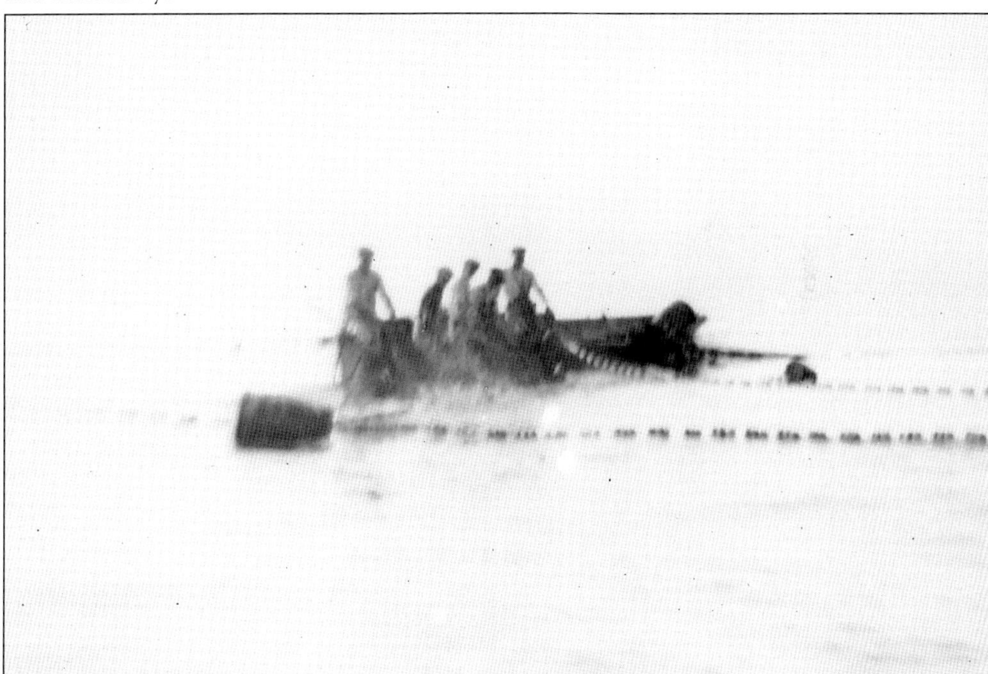

The pound net, suspended from barrels and cork floats, formed a pocket with a mouth to allow fish to enter as they swam by Wood Island. Fishermen working in dories hauled in the net and bailed the fish from the pound.

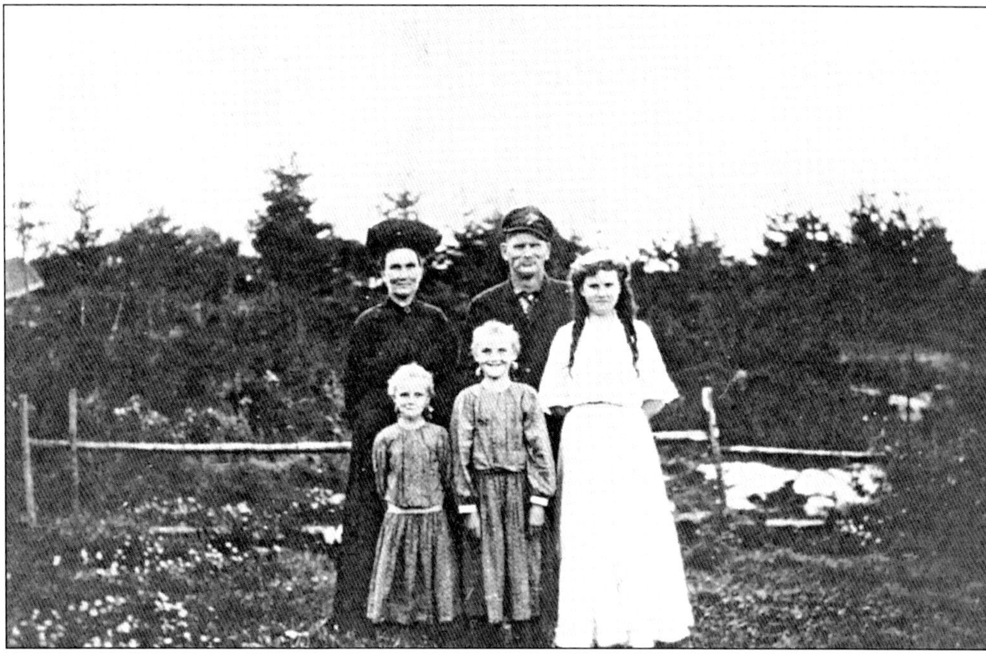

Fisherman Orlando Wallace poses *c.* 1906 with his wife, Almira, and their three daughters: Armerial (left), Ruby (center), and Clara (right). Orlando and Almira also had four older sons, all fishermen.

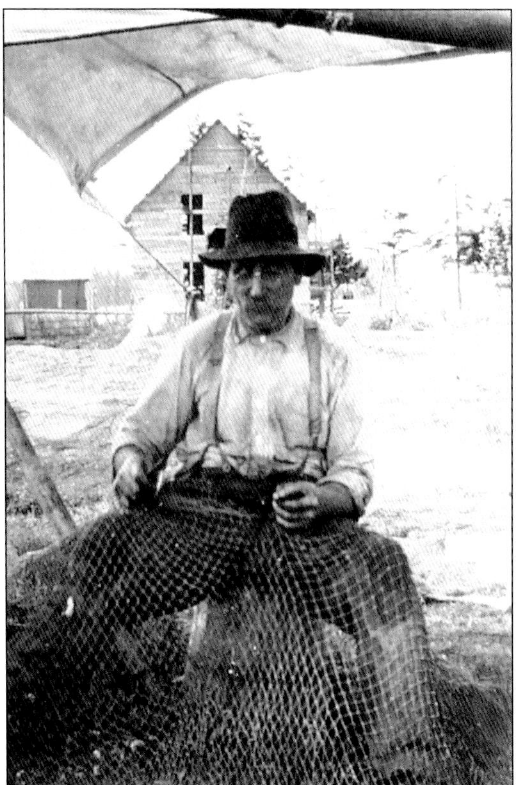

Albion Franklin "Frank" Wallace mends a fish net, *c.* 1920s. In the background is the home of Harry and Lillian Green at the Carrying Place in West Point.

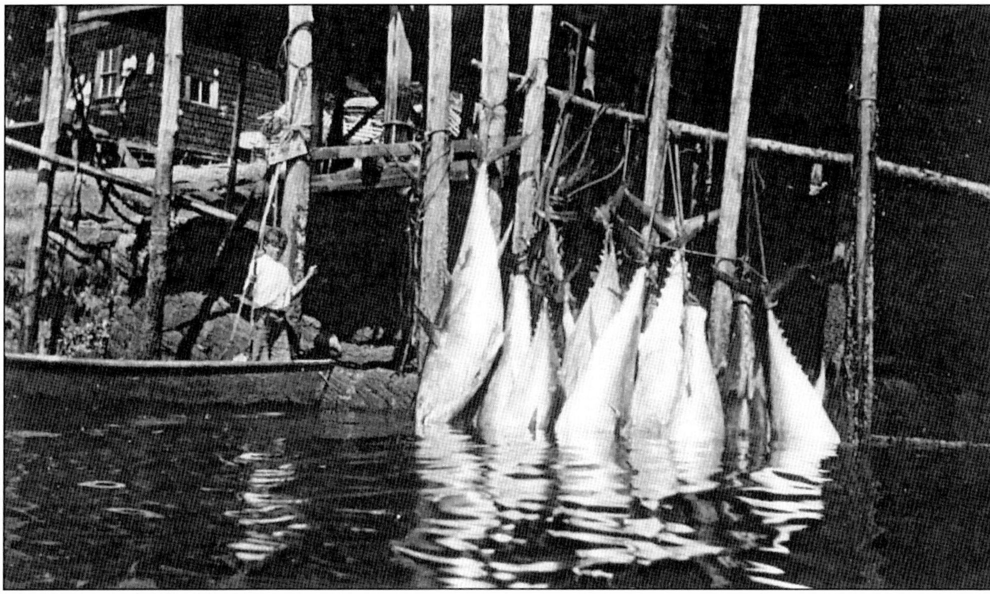
A successful catch of tuna hangs from a West Point wharf in 1935. The boy in the boat is Lawrence Wallace.

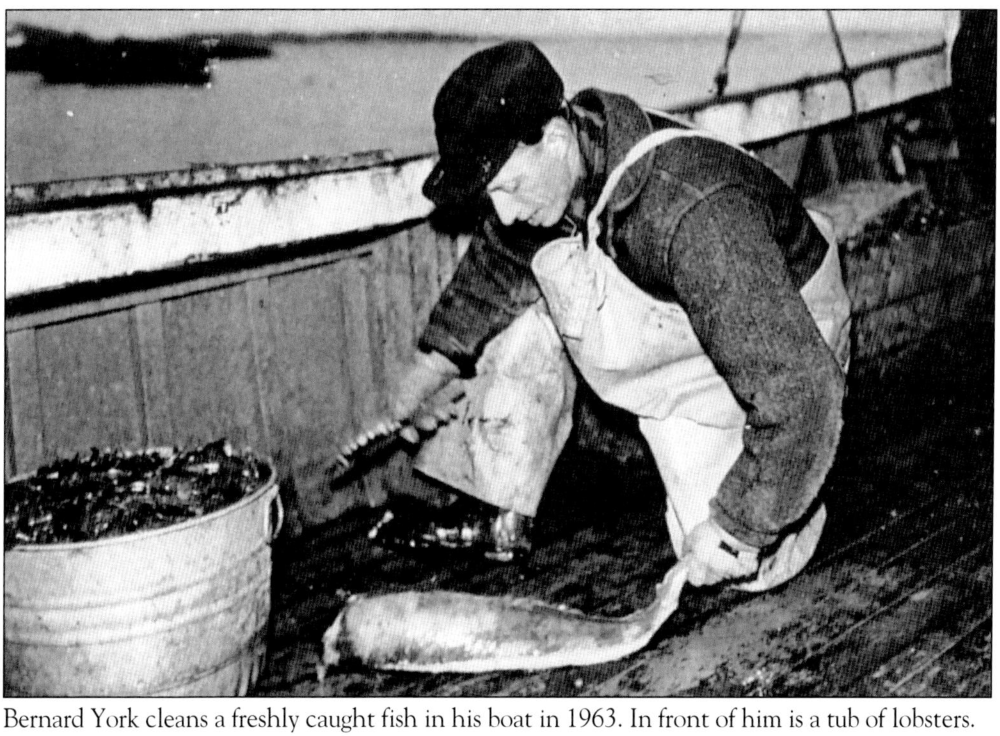
Bernard York cleans a freshly caught fish in his boat in 1963. In front of him is a tub of lobsters.

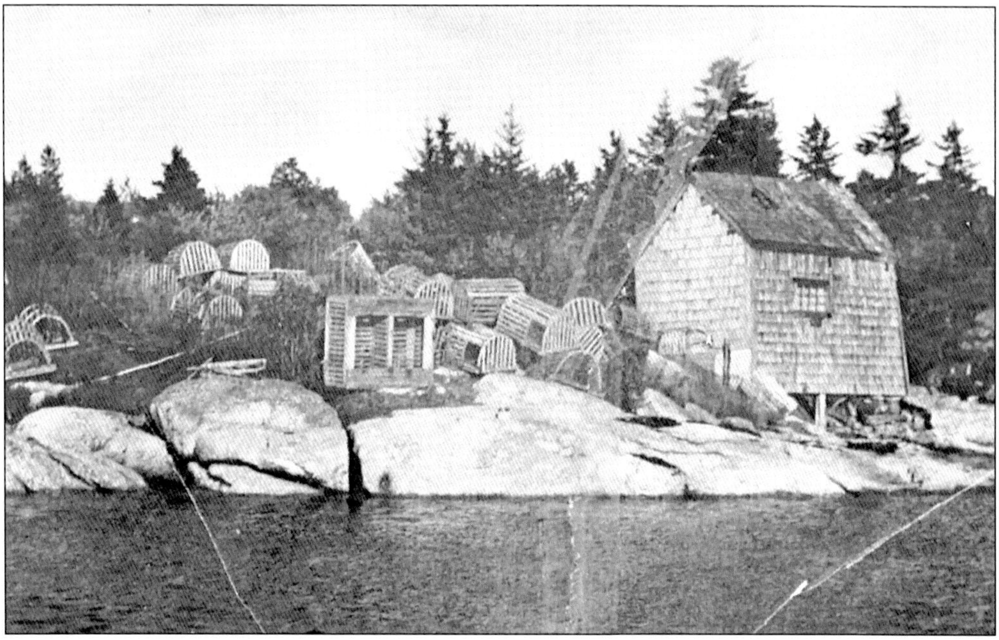

The lobster industry grew in importance after World War II. A fishhouse and wooden lobster traps cover this small island near Ridley's Landing in Sebasco in about 1950.

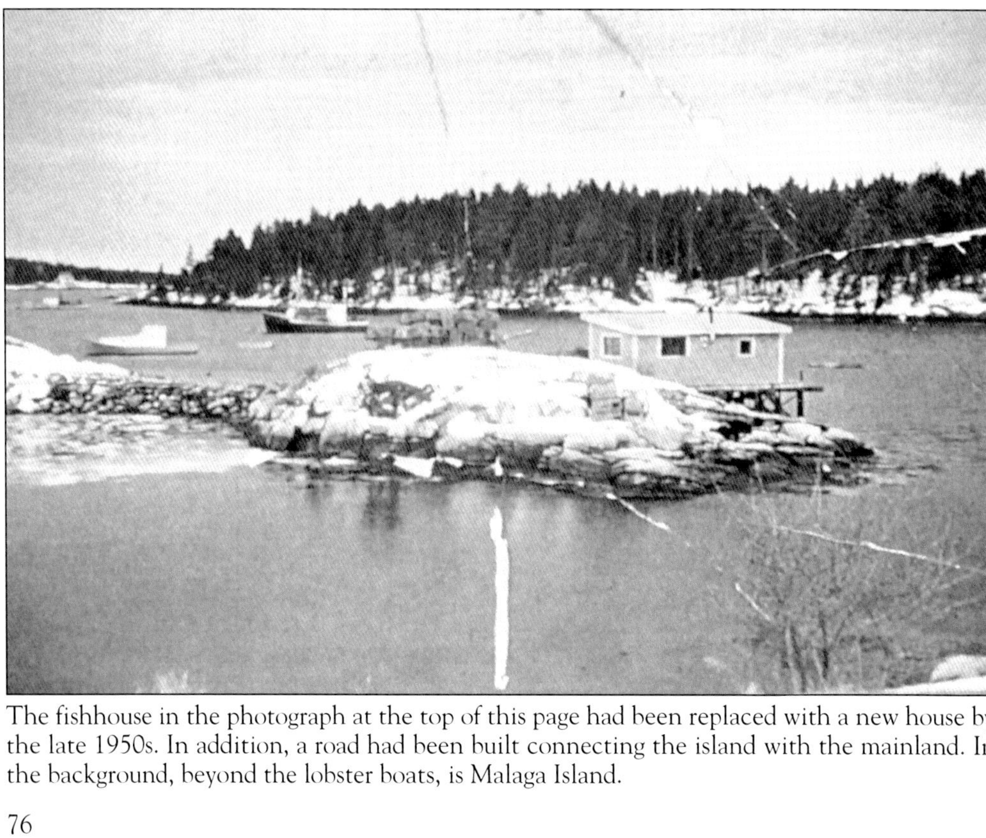

The fishhouse in the photograph at the top of this page had been replaced with a new house by the late 1950s. In addition, a road had been built connecting the island with the mainland. In the background, beyond the lobster boats, is Malaga Island.

In 1953 Alvin Charles "Ally" Wallace was photographed building wooden lobster traps in his fishhouse in West Point. By the mid-1970s many fishermen were using wire traps instead of the traditional wooden ones.

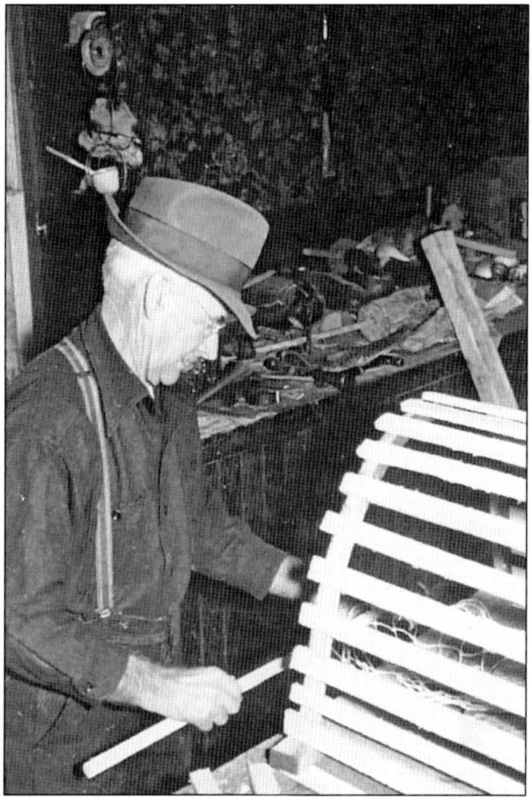

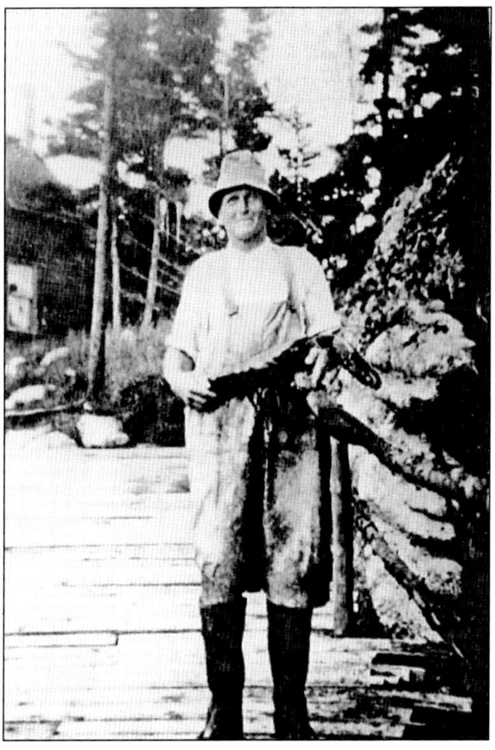

Oscar Gilliam of West Point proudly holds a huge lobster, *c*. 1920. Today this lobster would be illegal, too large to keep.

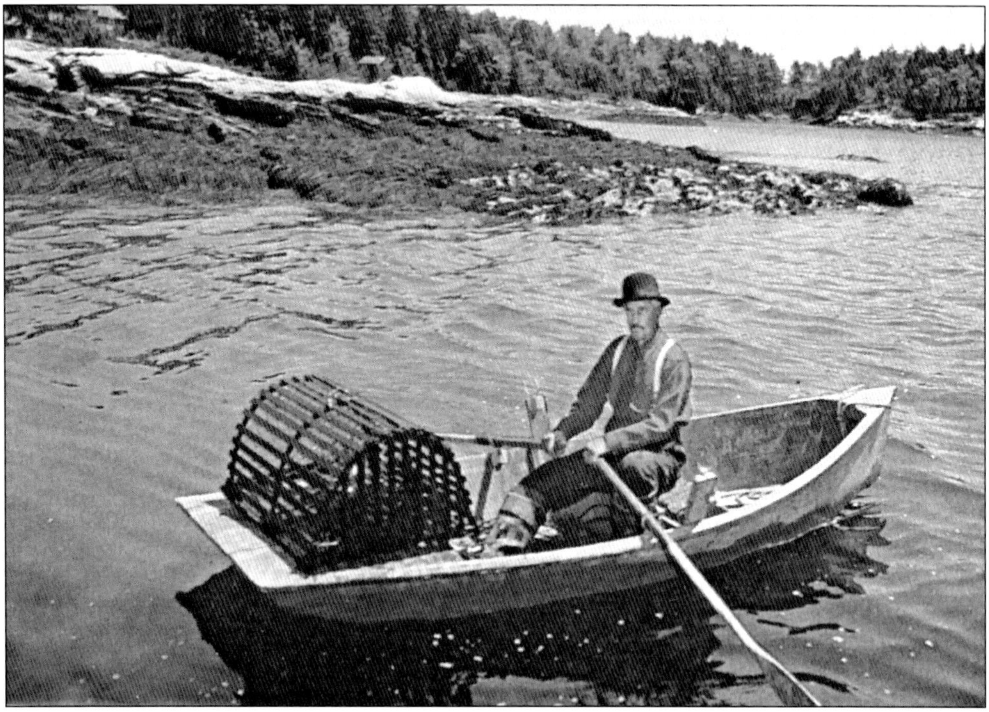

Alonzo "Lon" Lowell was often seen in his derby hat pulling his traps around Round Cove in Sebasco. Rock Gardens Inn and Cottages referred to him as "our lobsterman" in their advertising.

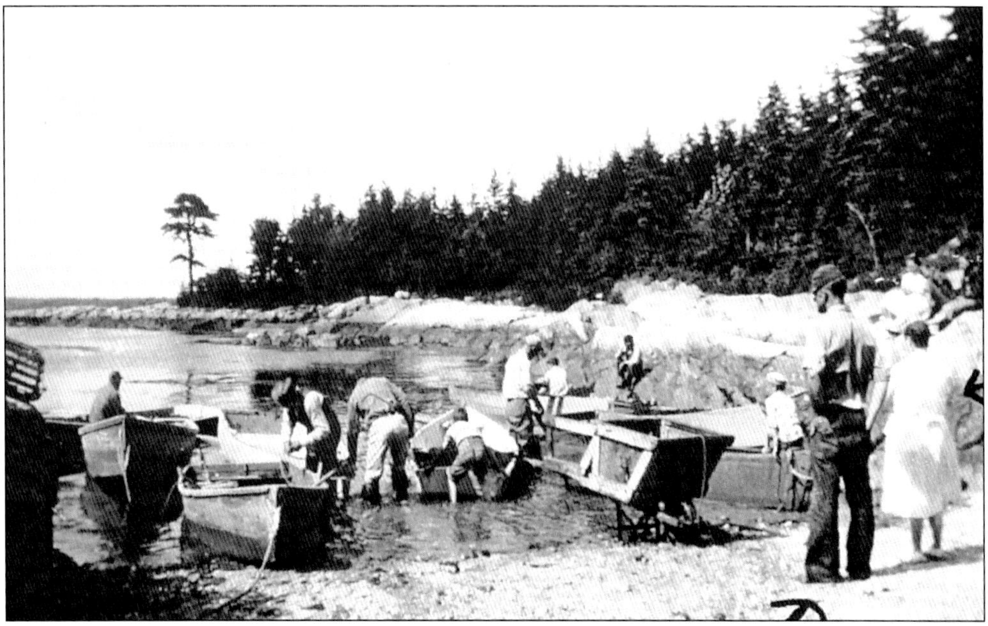

The harvesting of sea moss was once a big business in Phippsburg. Several fishermen are shown here bringing in sea moss for drying at Cat Cove in West Point, c. 1950. Watching from the beach are Robert Gilliam and Alice Atwood. The second fisherman from the left has been identified as Niles Wallace.

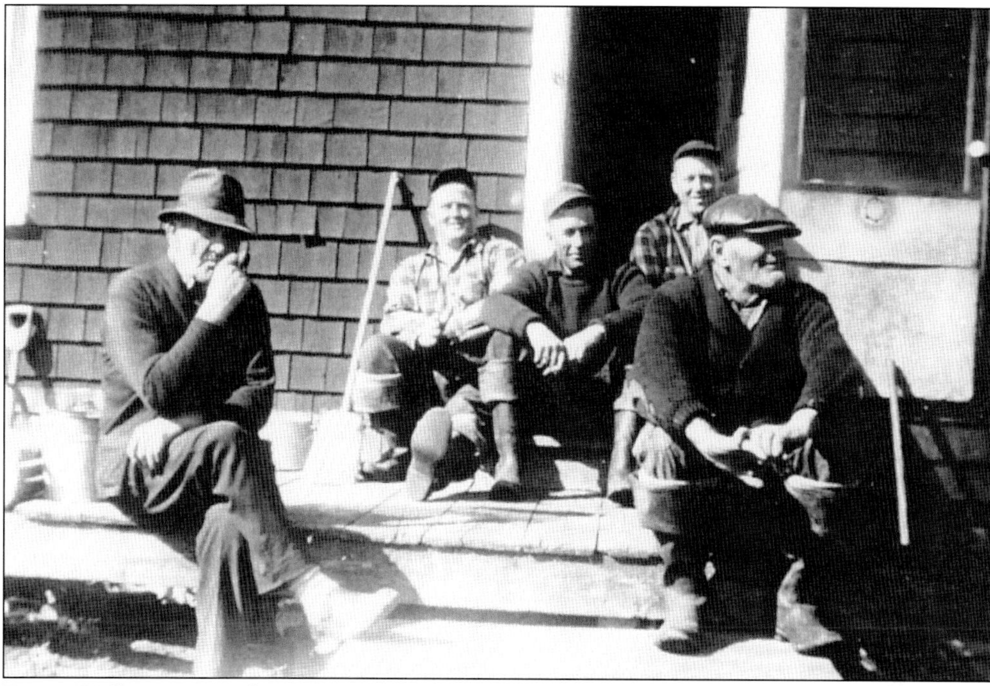

Emery Wallace, Howard Scott, Everett Wallace, Oscar Gilliam, and Amos Wallace sit on Golar Davis's porch in West Point talking, probably about fishing, *c*. 1945.

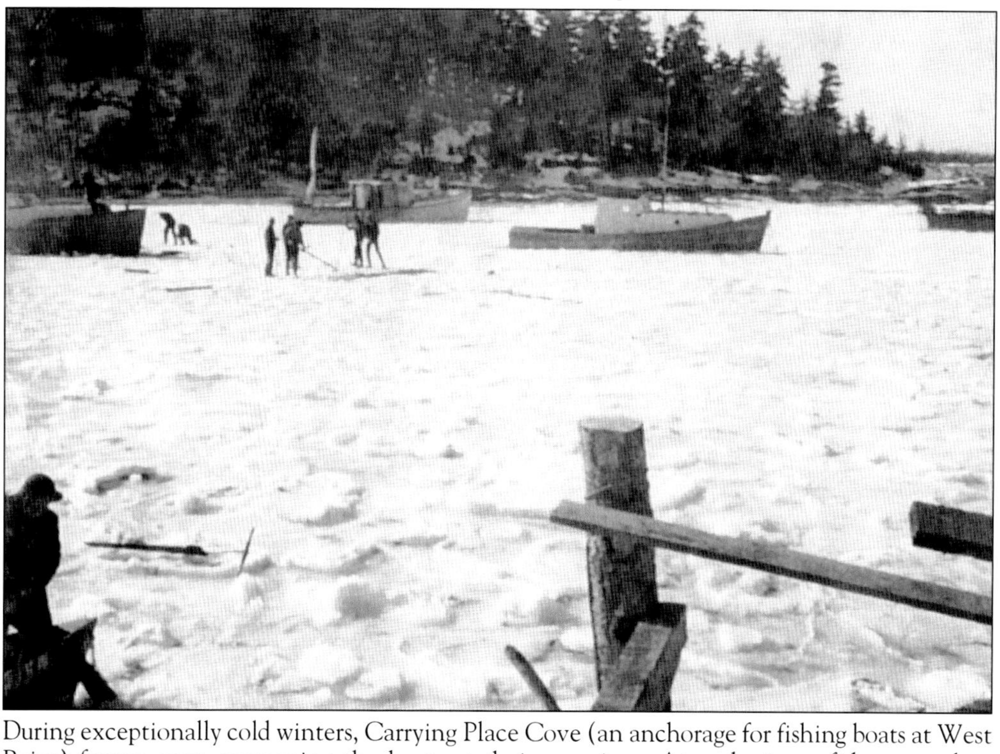

During exceptionally cold winters, Carrying Place Cove (an anchorage for fishing boats at West Point) freezes over, entrapping the boats at their moorings. At such times, fishermen clear channels in the ice, freeing the boats from their prisons.

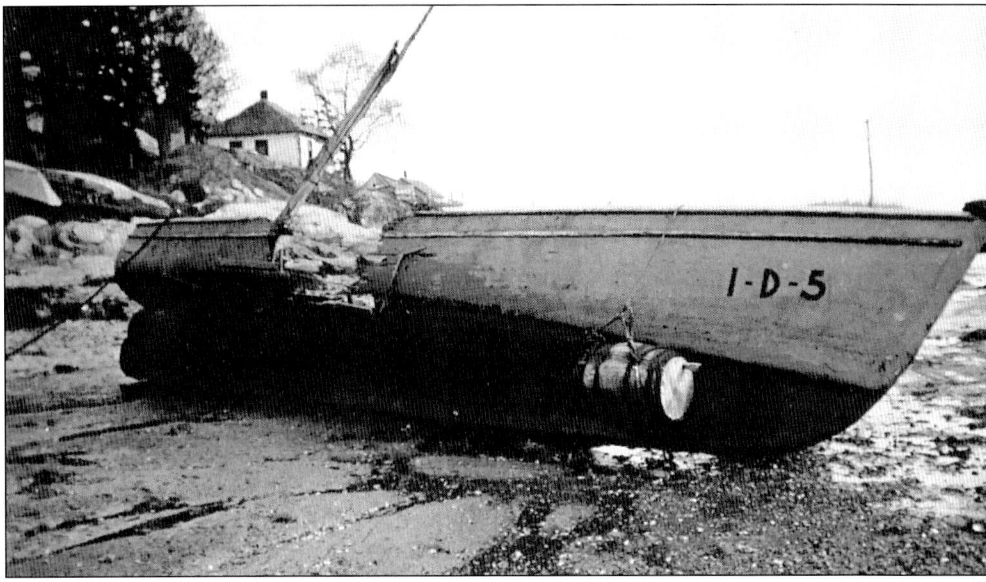

On May 24, 1944, Leroy Wyman's fishing boat got hit by a sardine carrier. Leroy escaped with his life, but without some of his toes.

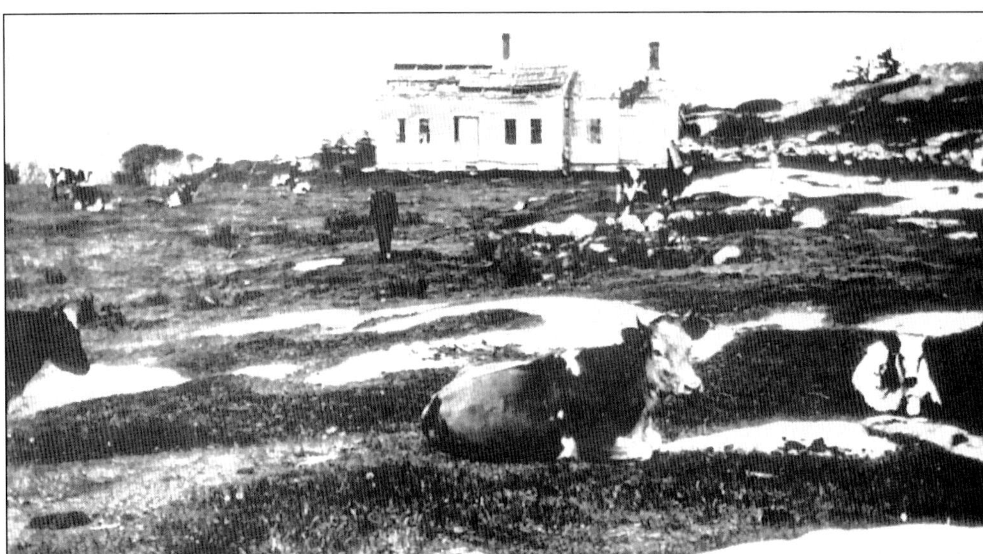
This herd of cows was pastured in 1921 on Morse's Mountain, earlier known as Mt. Ararat. The house in the background is believed to have once been the home of Albert Morse.

Marsh hay was at one time a very important resource. James Thompson used a scythe to cut marsh hay at Small Point about 1910.

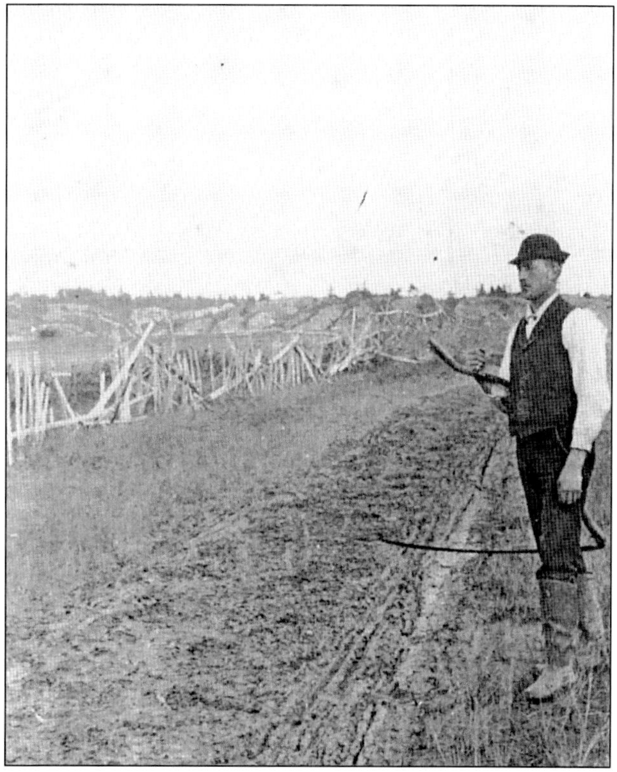

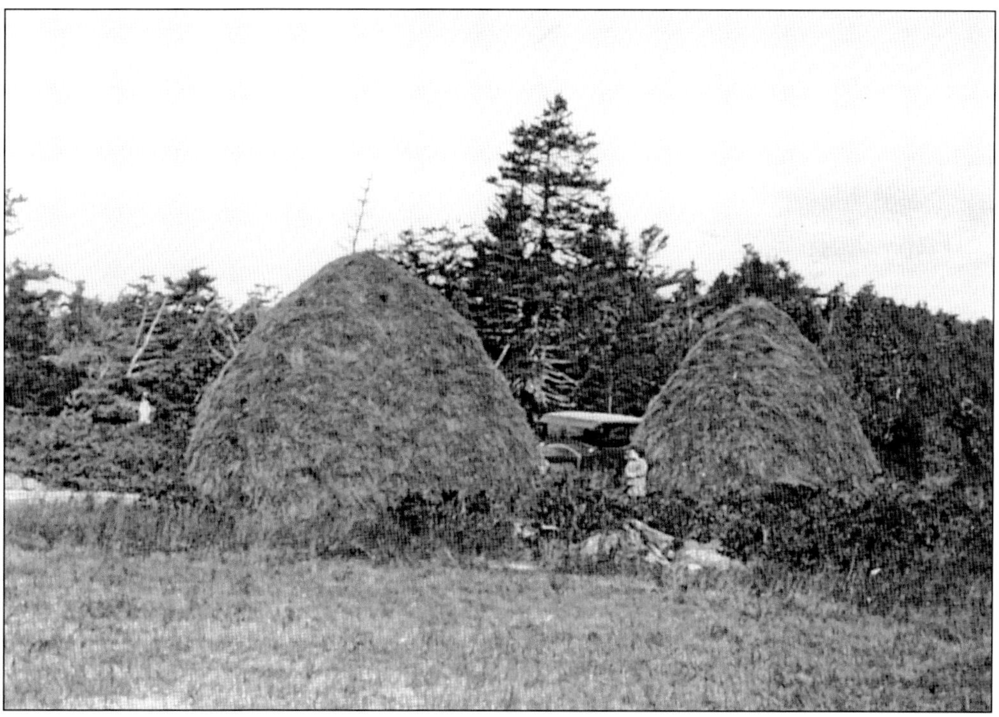

These piles of hay were cut on the salt marsh near Popham Beach in October 1926. The little girl between them is Ada Minott.

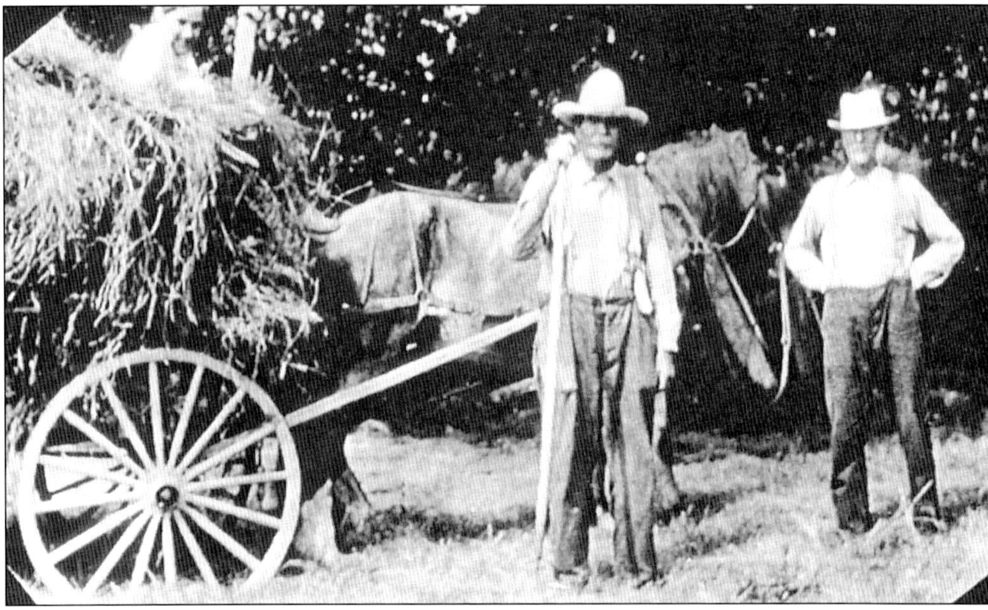

Getting in the hay c. 1935 near Cox's Head are Mr. McCollock and Nat Percy. An unidentified young lady rides in the hay rack.

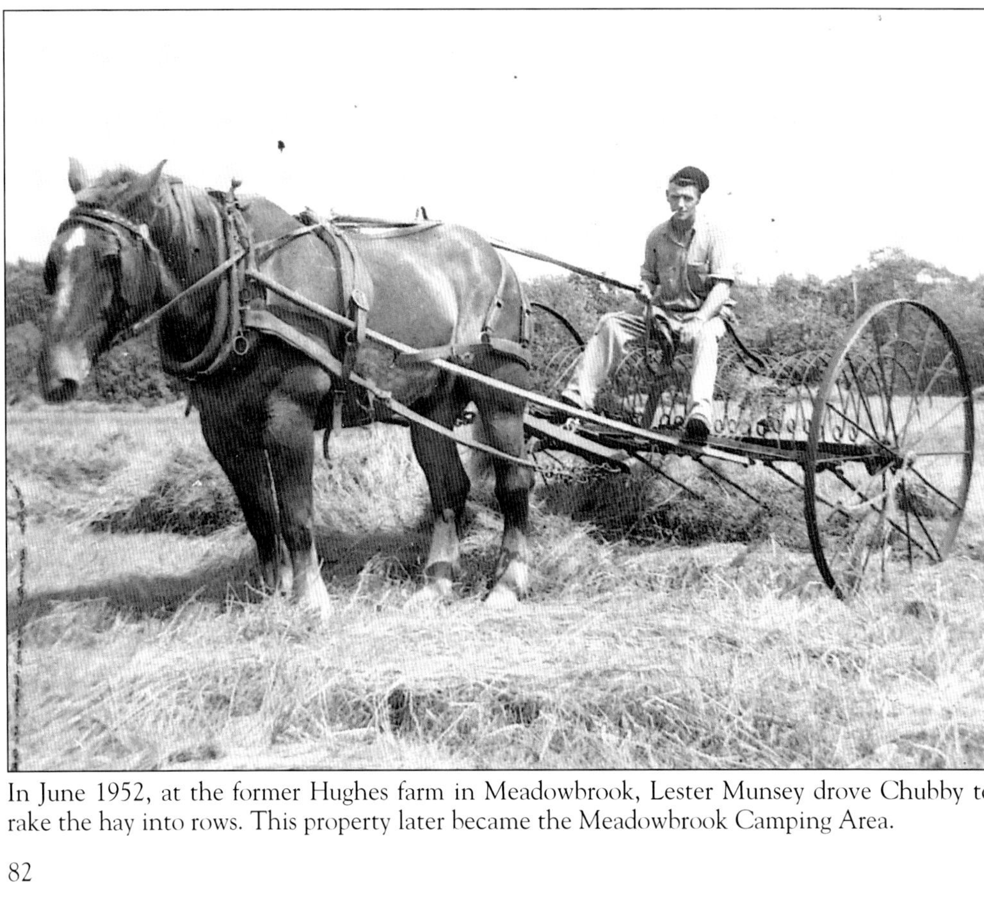

In June 1952, at the former Hughes farm in Meadowbrook, Lester Munsey drove Chubby to rake the hay into rows. This property later became the Meadowbrook Camping Area.

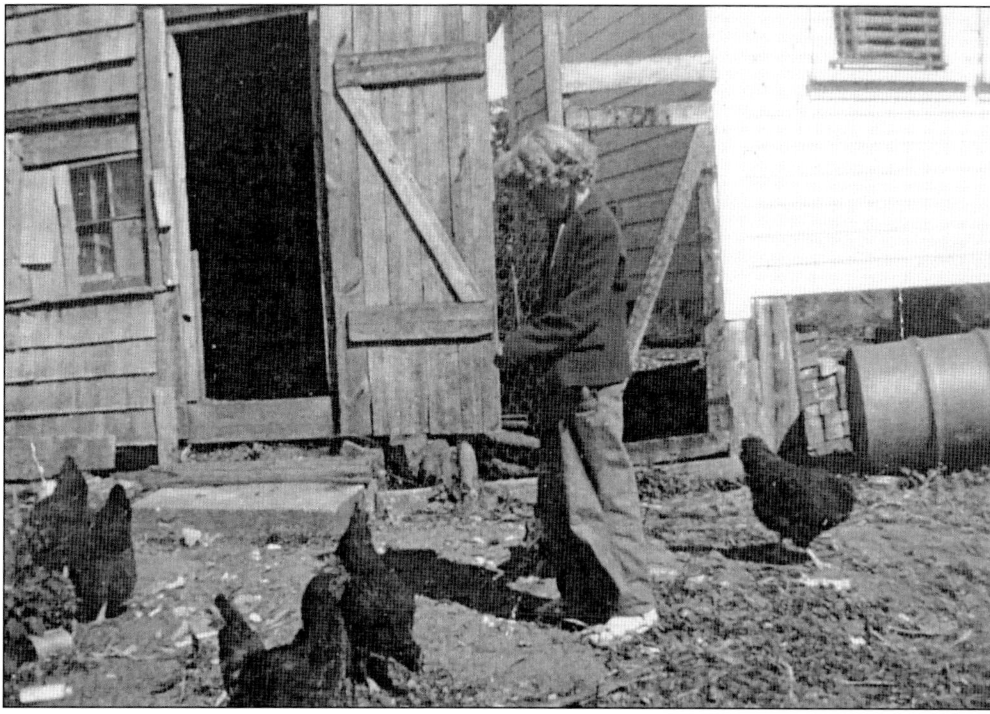

Carol Wyman feeds the hens at the Wyman homestead at Small Point in September 1950.

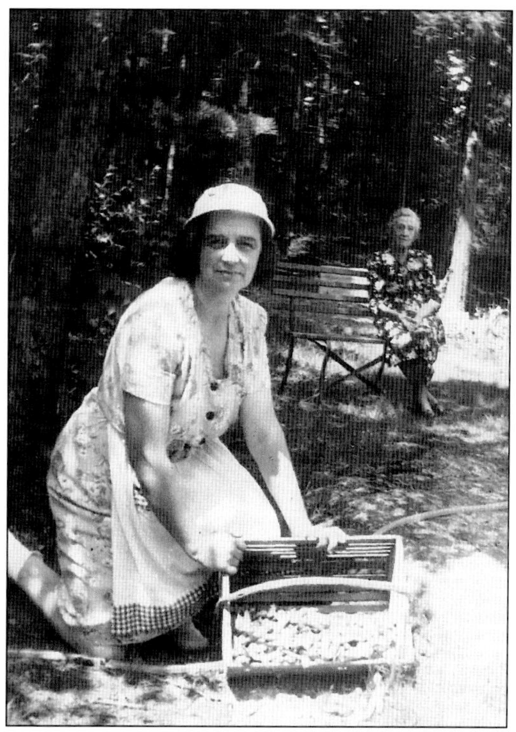

Gladys Dozois' clam hod held vegetables rather than clams. Here she proudly displays her crop of peas during the summer of 1954. Behind her on the bench is Julia Dozois.

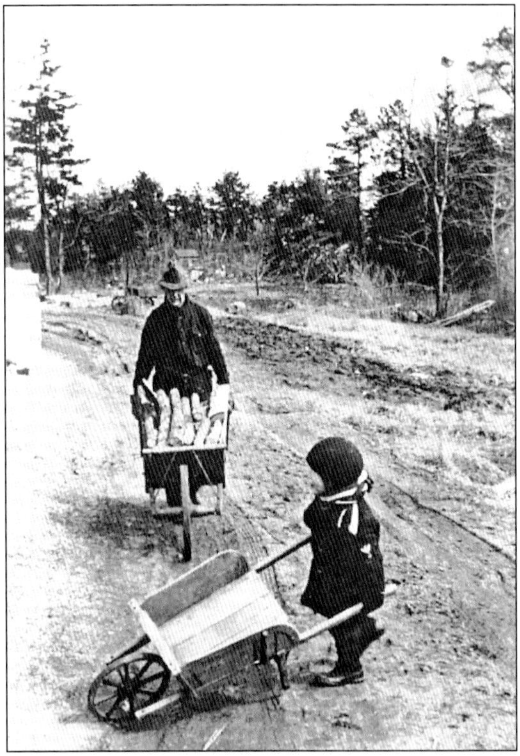

William H. Gilman is "assisted" by his two-year-old grandson, William S. Gilman, as he wheels wood home from his woodlot at Ashdale in 1936.

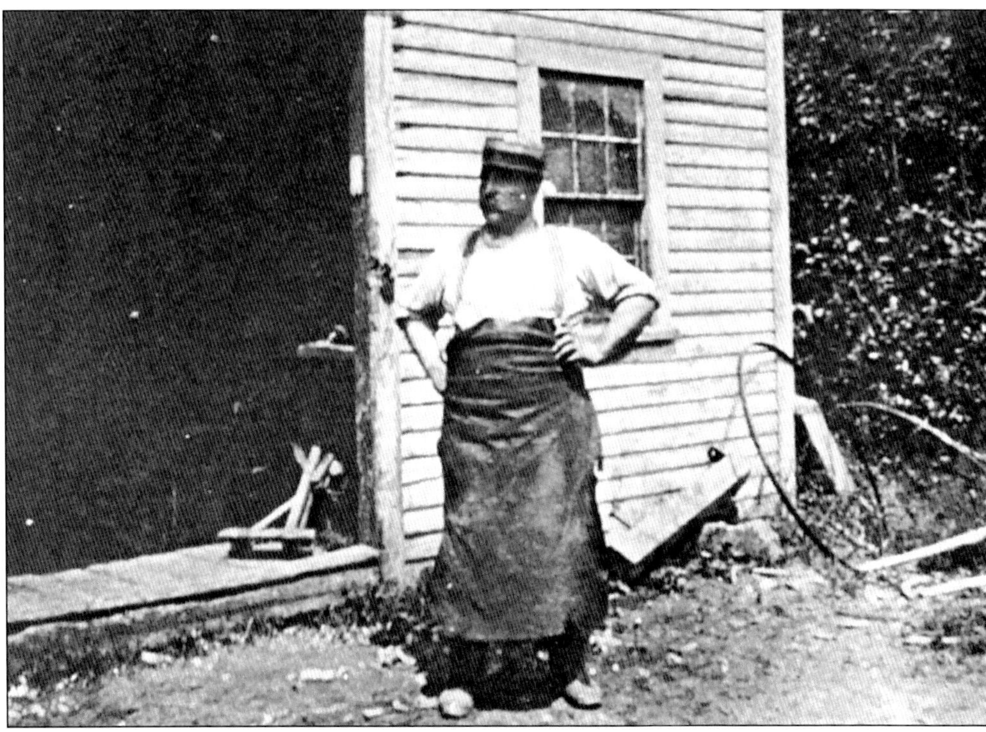

George "Cola" Pease was the village blacksmith. Wearing his long apron, he posed in front of what was probably his shop about 1910.

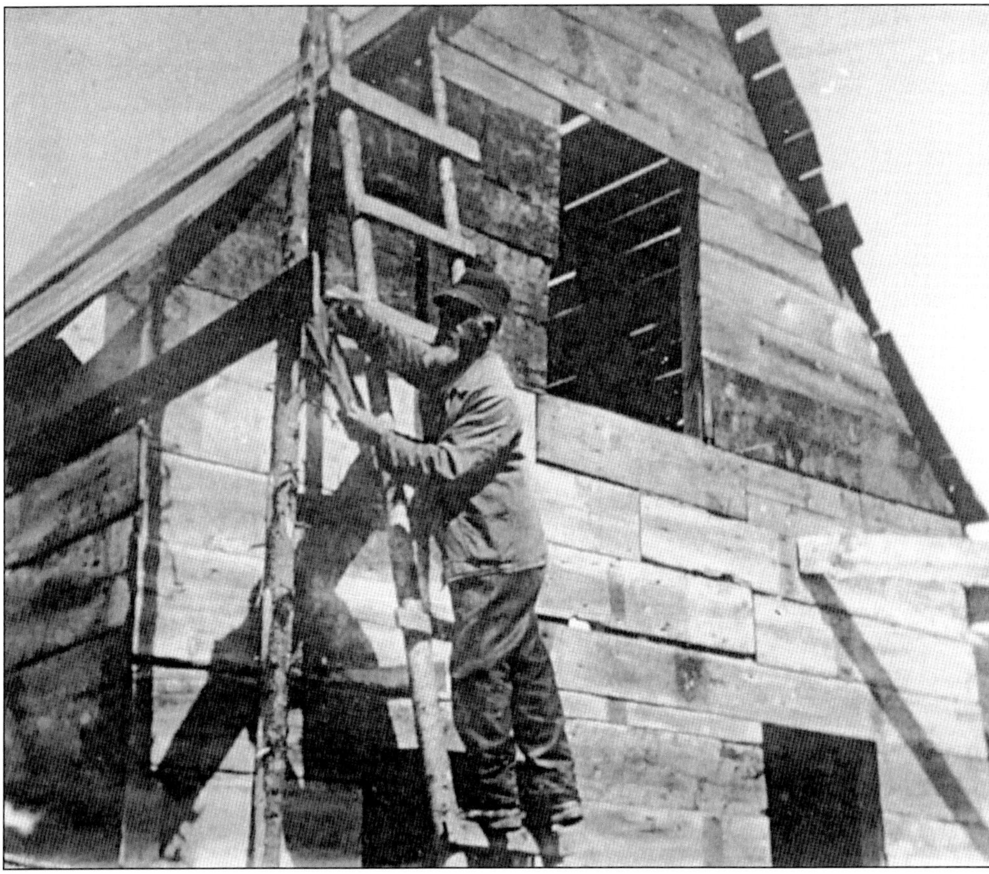

John Eason, as was common, had several occupations. He was a fisherman, an excellent mason, and a carpenter as well. Here he is shown building a home on Malaga Island.

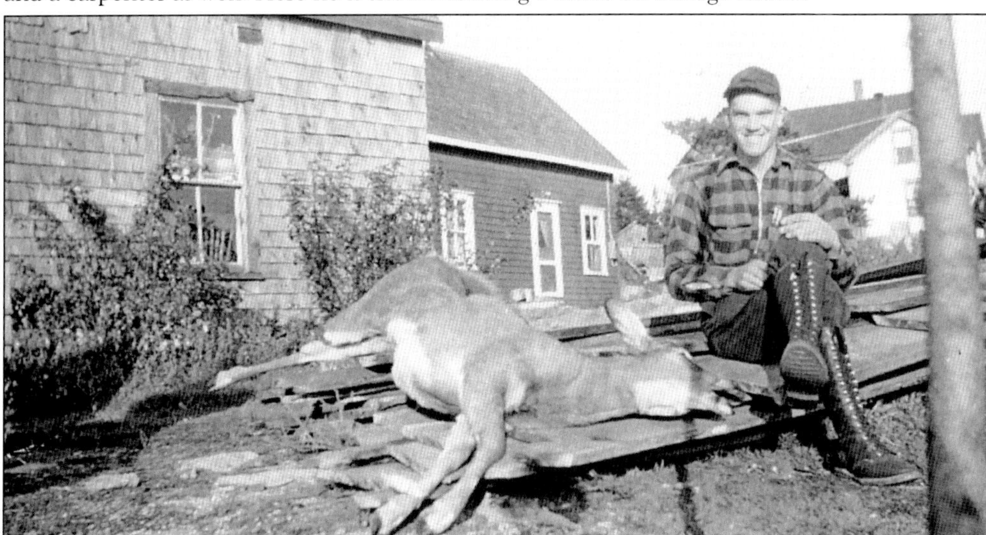

Venison fed families. Christopher Wallace of West Point proudly poses with a deer he shot in the fall of 1942.

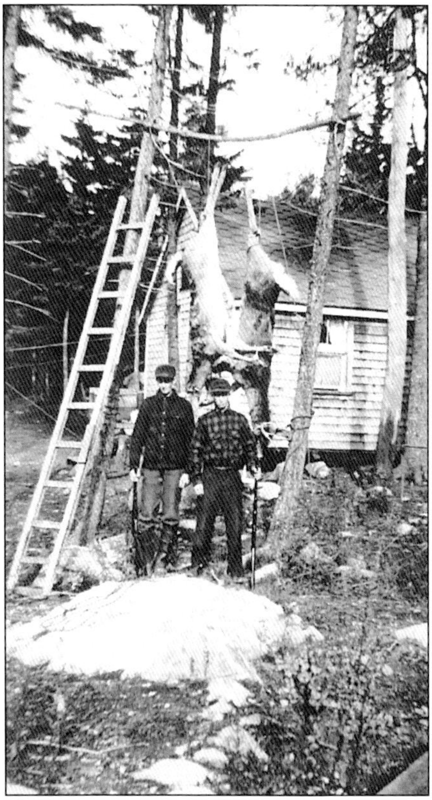

Brothers Bernard and Irving York each got a deer in November 1944. Alice and Irving Atwood's home is in the background.

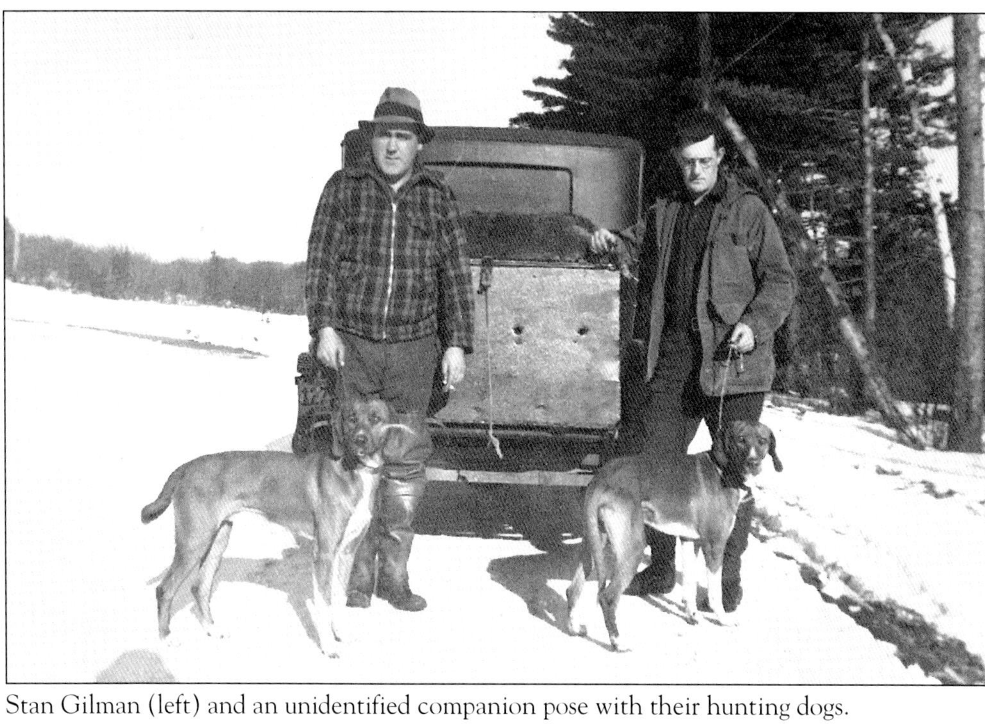

Stan Gilman (left) and an unidentified companion pose with their hunting dogs.

Five

VESSELS

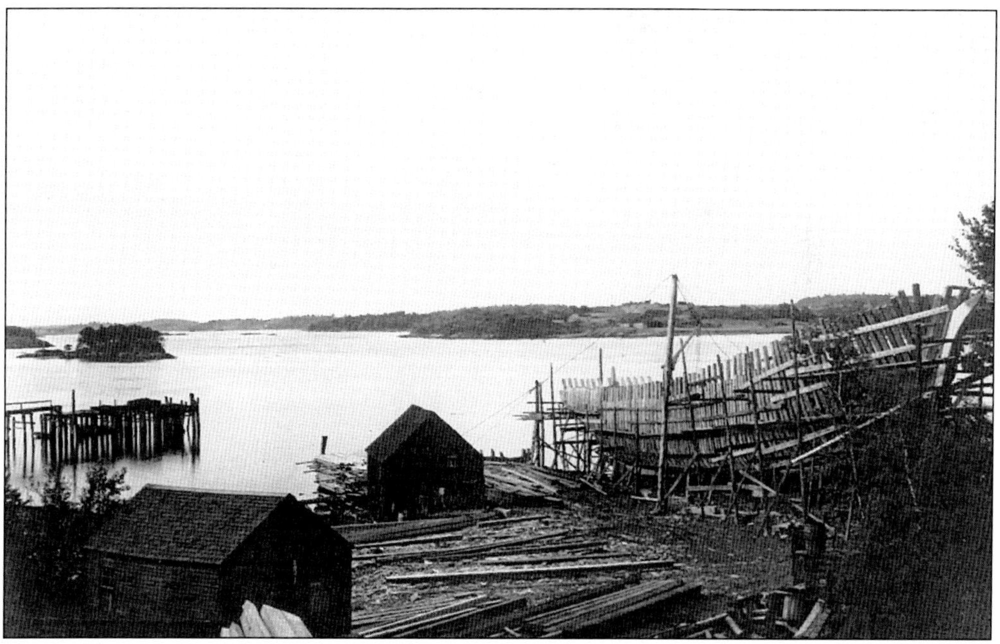

Shipbuilding has long been an important industry for the area. One of the major shipyards at Phippsburg Center was the Bowker Shipyard, shown here with a schooner under construction in the early 1900s. To the left can be seen one of two Minott wharves. The farm visible above the stern was across the river in Arrowsic.

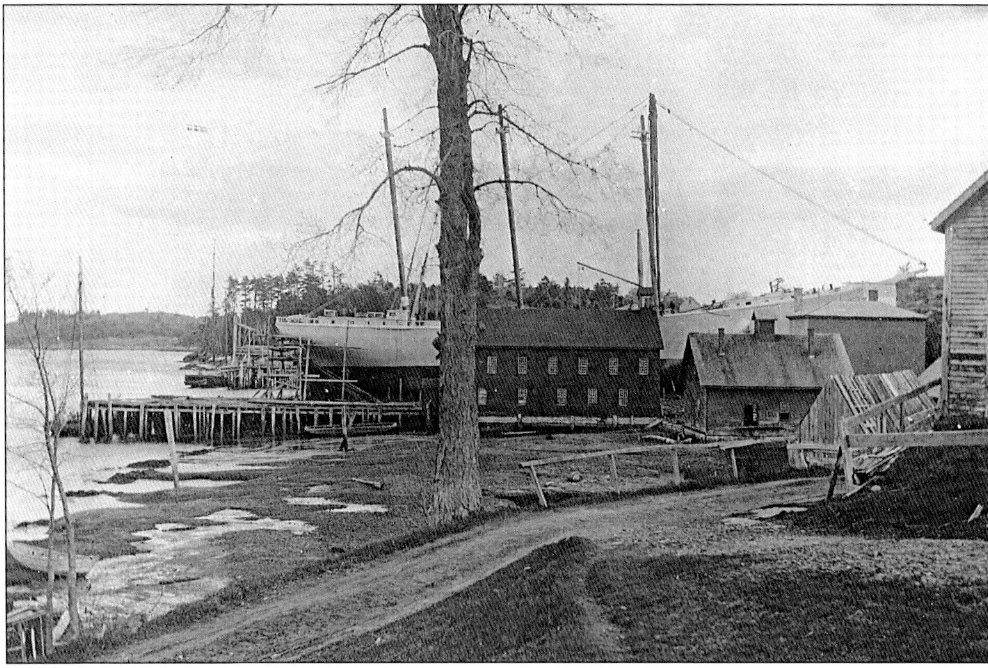

A picture of the Minott Shipyard taken from Church Lane shows the schooner *Ada F. Brown* under construction, with only three of her four masts in place. Her launch date was May 24, 1901. The joiner shop, blacksmith shop, and store are visible as well.

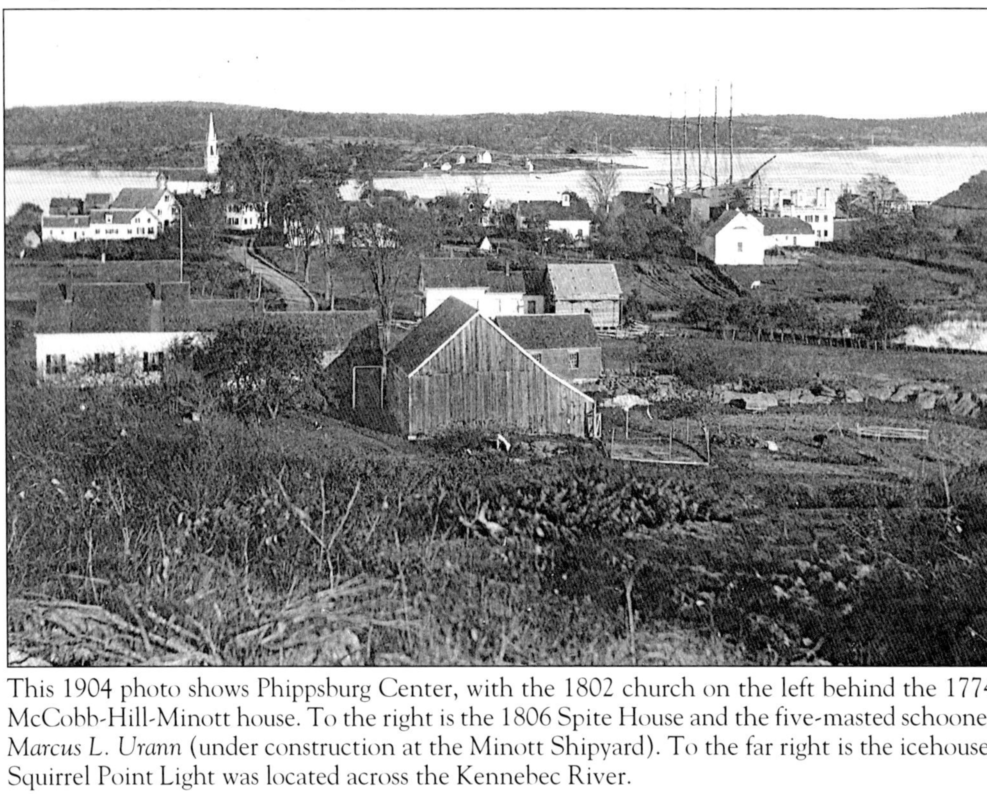

This 1904 photo shows Phippsburg Center, with the 1802 church on the left behind the 1774 McCobb-Hill-Minott house. To the right is the 1806 Spite House and the five-masted schooner *Marcus L. Urann* (under construction at the Minott Shipyard). To the far right is the icehouse. Squirrel Point Light was located across the Kennebec River.

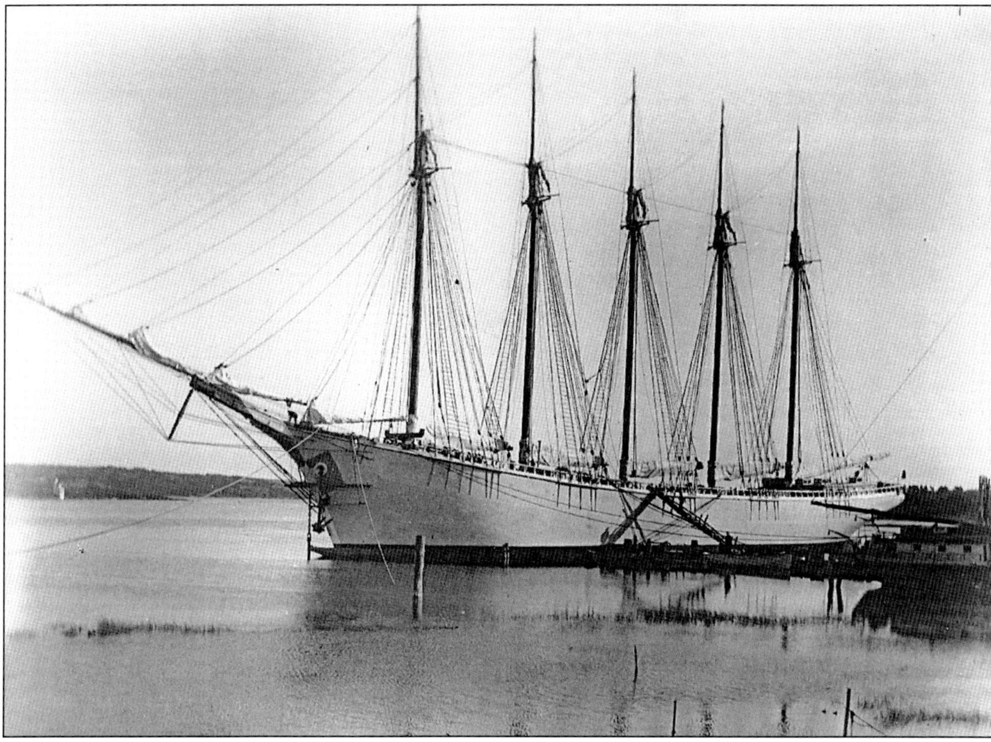

The *Marcus L. Urann*, at the dock after being launched on October 25, 1904, was the last new construction at the Minott Shipyard.

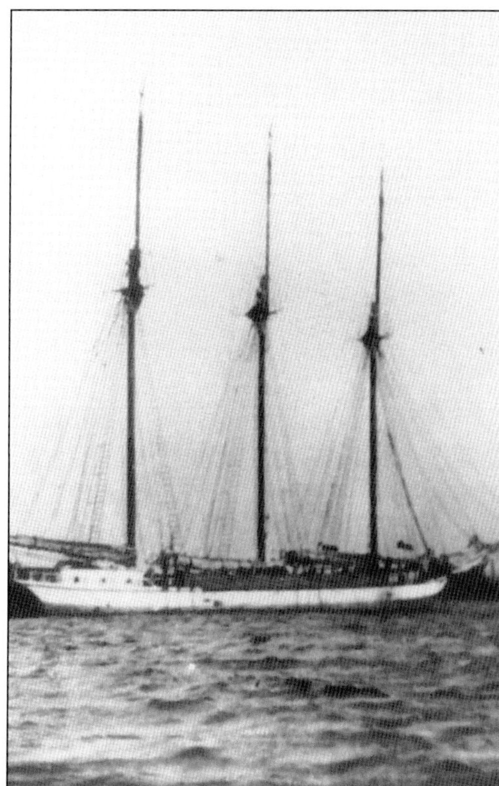

The three-masted schooner *Winnegance*, launched in 1890, was the last wooden vessel built by Richard Morse & Sons of Winnegance. After 38 years of service, she was abandoned at sea off Cape May in September 1928.

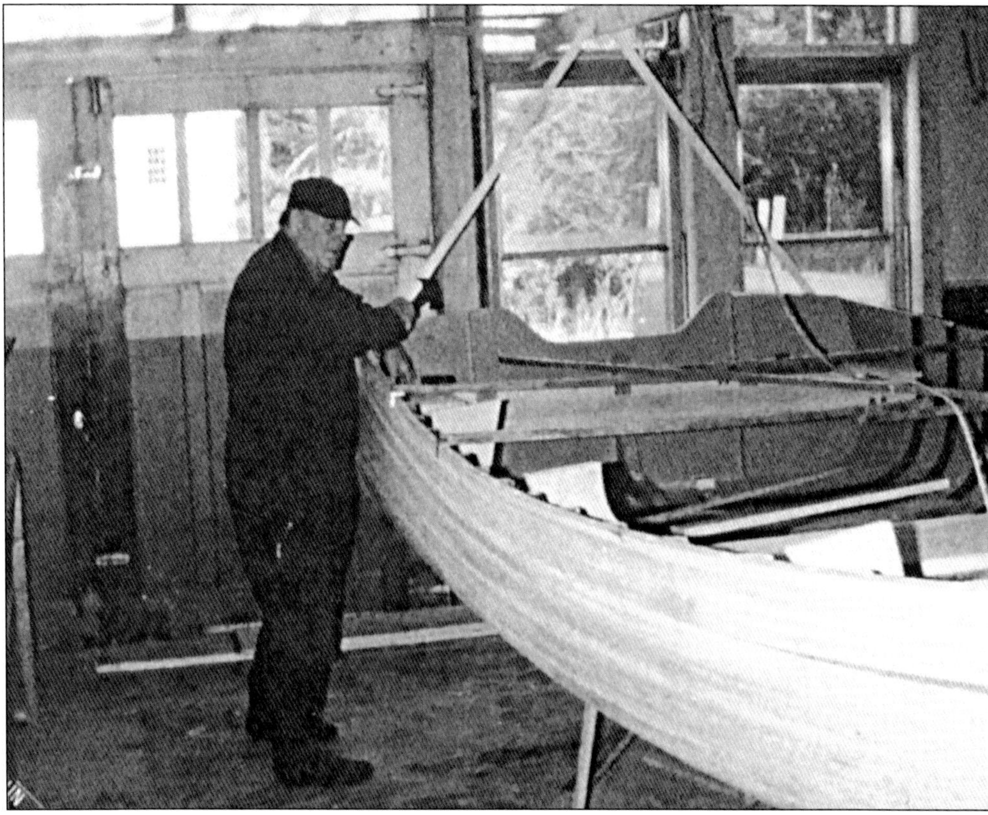

Although the construction of large sailing ships in the area ceased in the early 1900s, Phippsburg continued to produce skilled boatbuilders. Alton Wallace (1909–1995) began building his famous West Point Boats as a young man. He is shown here working on a boat in his boathouse, the old West Point School, near Pine Grove Community Church.

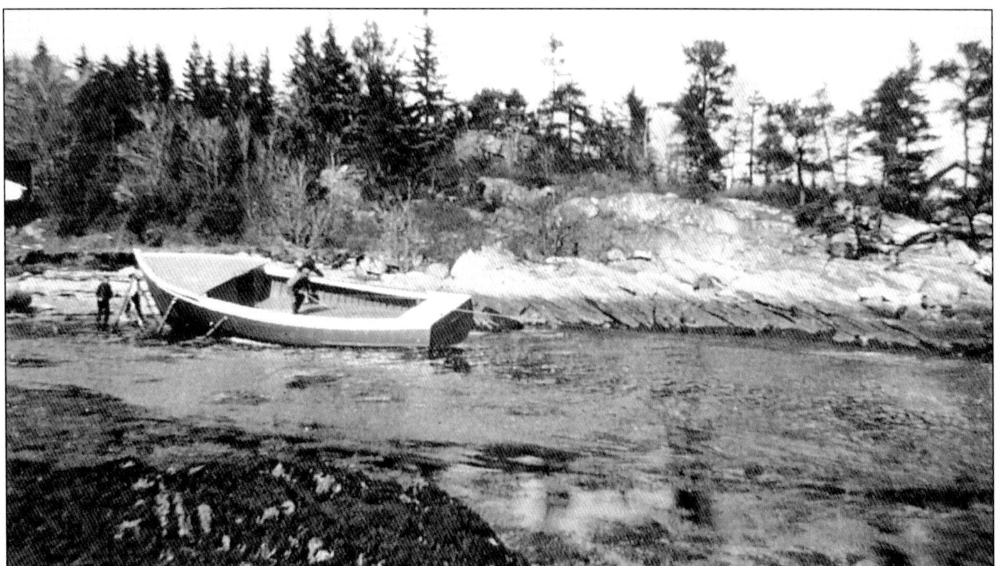

One of Bernard York's boats, built by Alton Wallace, was launched in May 1947 in Cat Cove.

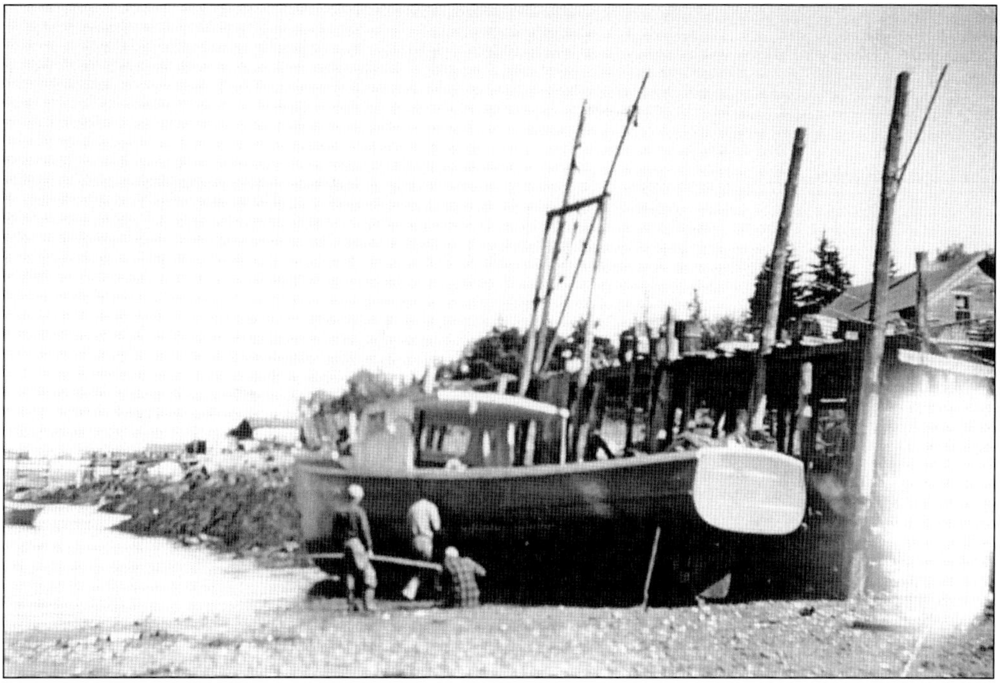

Another of Bernard York's boats, also built by Alton Wallace, has been pulled up beside Ally Wallace's wharf in West Point, probably to clean and repaint its hull.

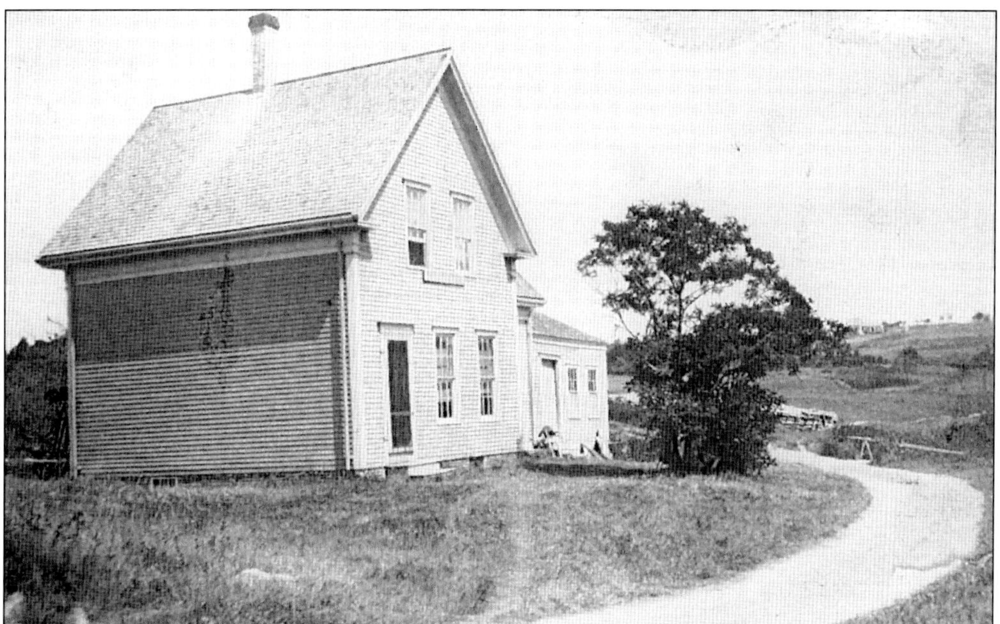

Early in the 20th century Eugene C. Perry built lobster and fishing boats near this house at Ridley's Landing in Sebasco. Beyond the Perry house, the fields of the Morrison farm, which sat on the hill beyond, were visible. Trees have completely taken over these fields now.

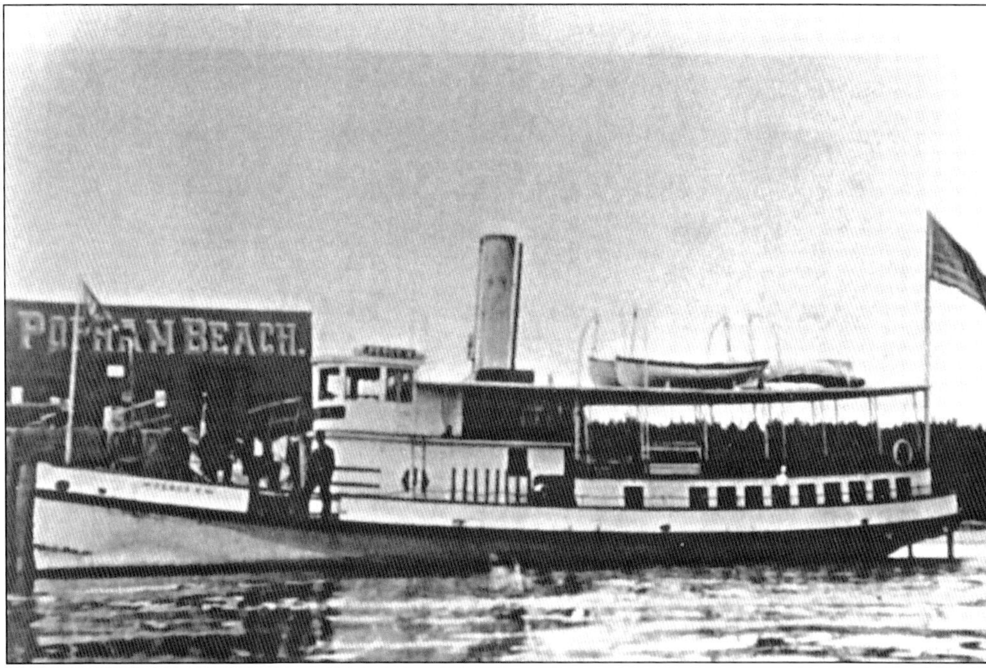

Steamboats were a familiar sight on the Kennebec River from the 1860s into the 1920s. Here the *Percy V*, built in 1883 for the Bath-Popham run, has pulled into the landing at Popham Beach.

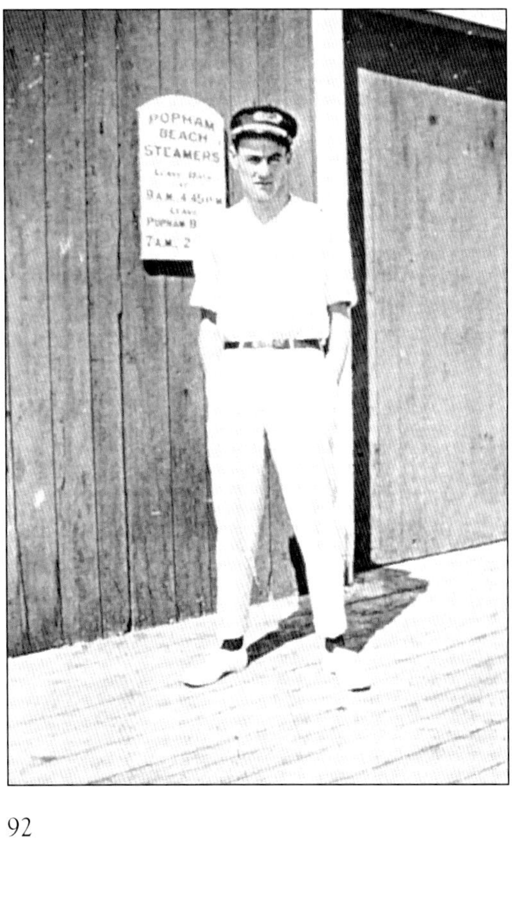

The Popham Beach steamers made regular runs between Popham Beach and Bath, as proclaimed by this *c.* 1920 signboard behind John Roscoe Stacey of Popham.

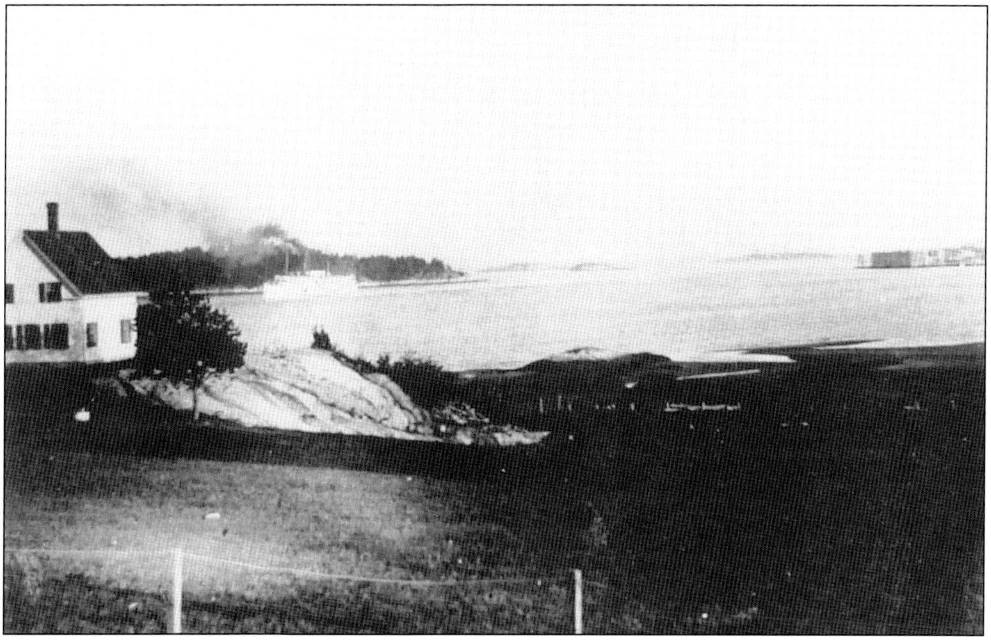

An Eastern Steamship Line vessel heads up the Kennebec River around 1900. To the left is the Thomas Perkins homestead.

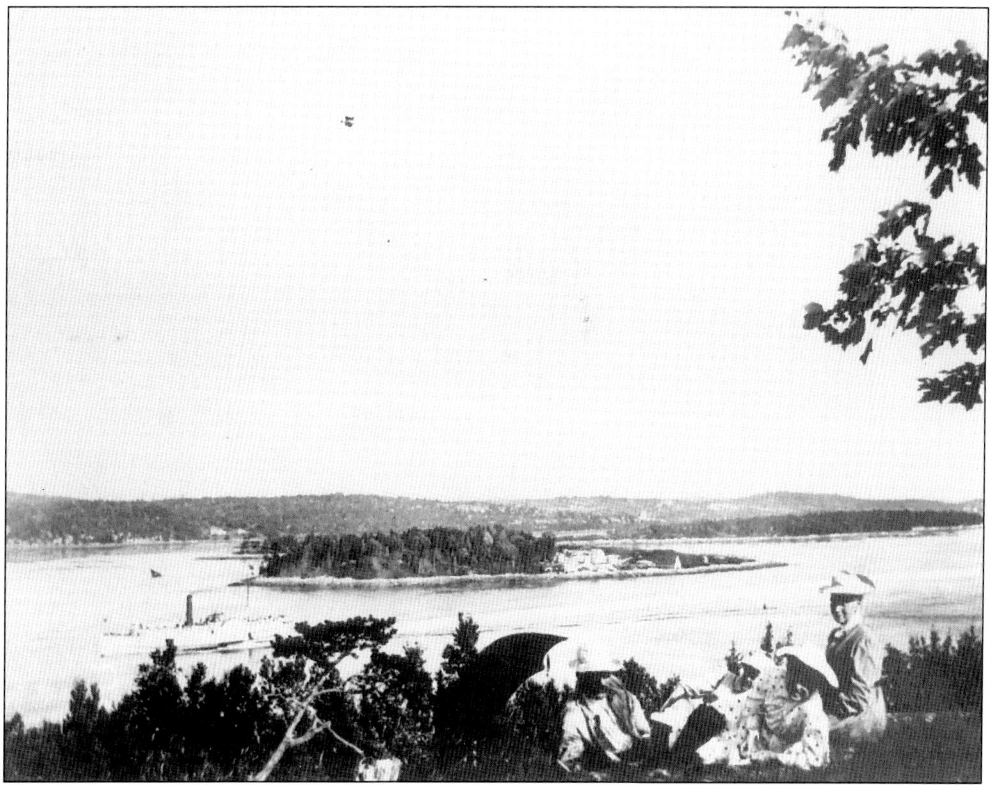

Another steamboat passes between Perkins Island Light and Parker Head Neck while a group of visitors relax at the height of land on the Neck.

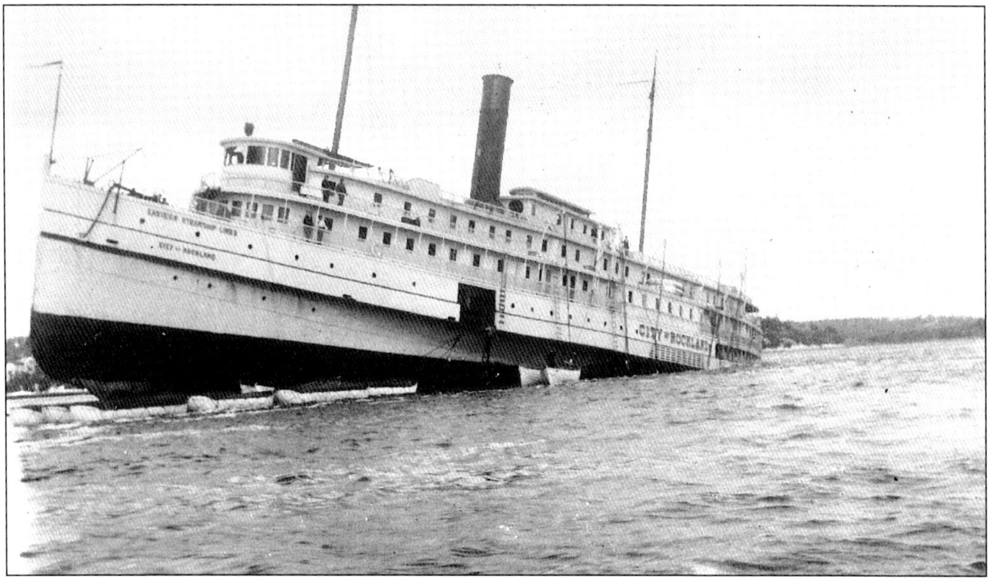

The *City of Rockland* of the Eastern Steamship Lines went aground on Dix's Island off Cox's Head in the fog on September 2, 1923. She was hauled to Boston for repairs, but never returned to service; instead, she was condemned and burned off Salem, MA.

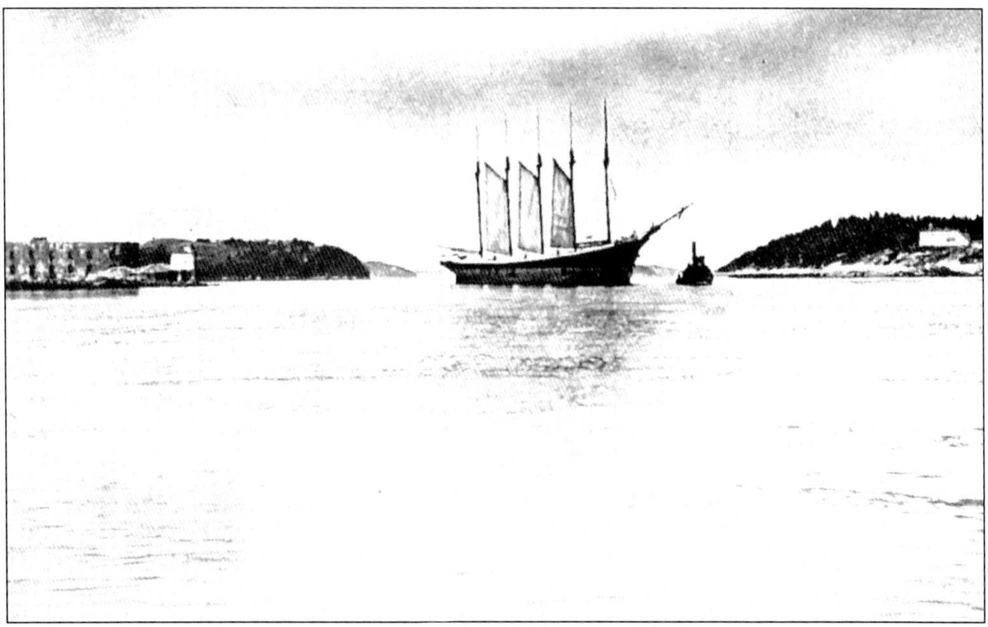

The Bath-built five-masted schooner *William C. Carnegie* is seen passing Fort Popham, going out of the Kennebec River. Gilbert Head is on the right and Cox's Head is on the left.

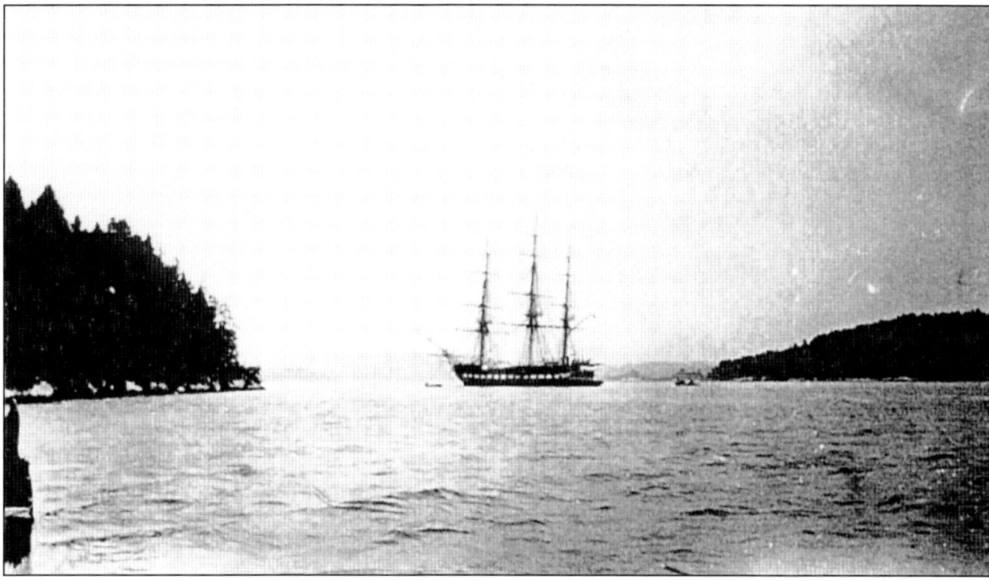

The USS *Constitution*, "Old Ironsides," was traveling up the Kennebec River past Cox's Head to visit Bath when this picture was taken in June 1931. A piling of the Cox's Head Landing is on the left.

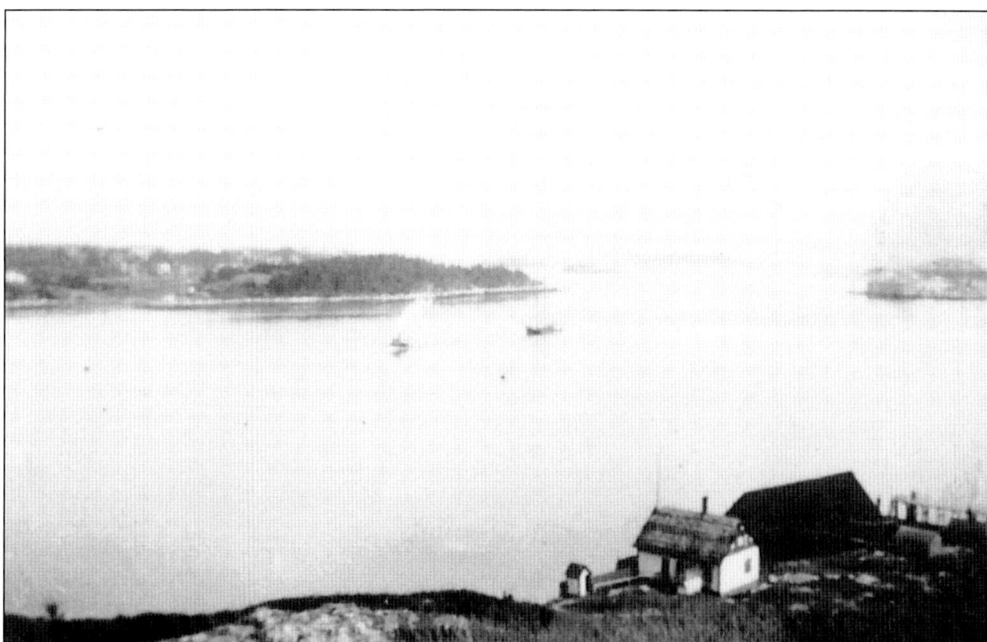

The photographer climbed atop Cox's Head to take this picture of a tug towing a two-masted schooner up the Kennebec River past the coaling station. The building with the striped roof is the telephone house. Note the privy out back.

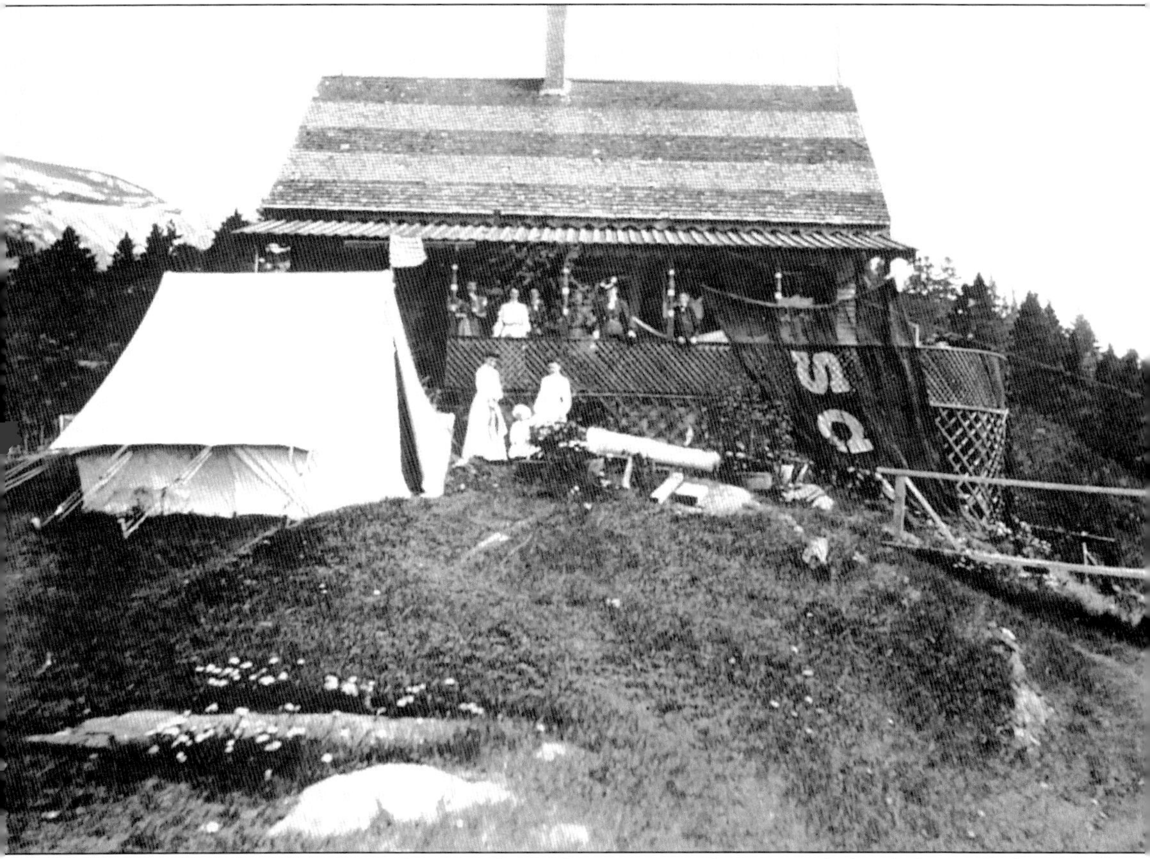

The telephone house, shown here in the early 1900s, stood on a rise behind the coal wharf at Green Point, Cox's Head. It was run by James Spinney and his wife, who got information from tugs going up river and telephoned it to their Bath office.

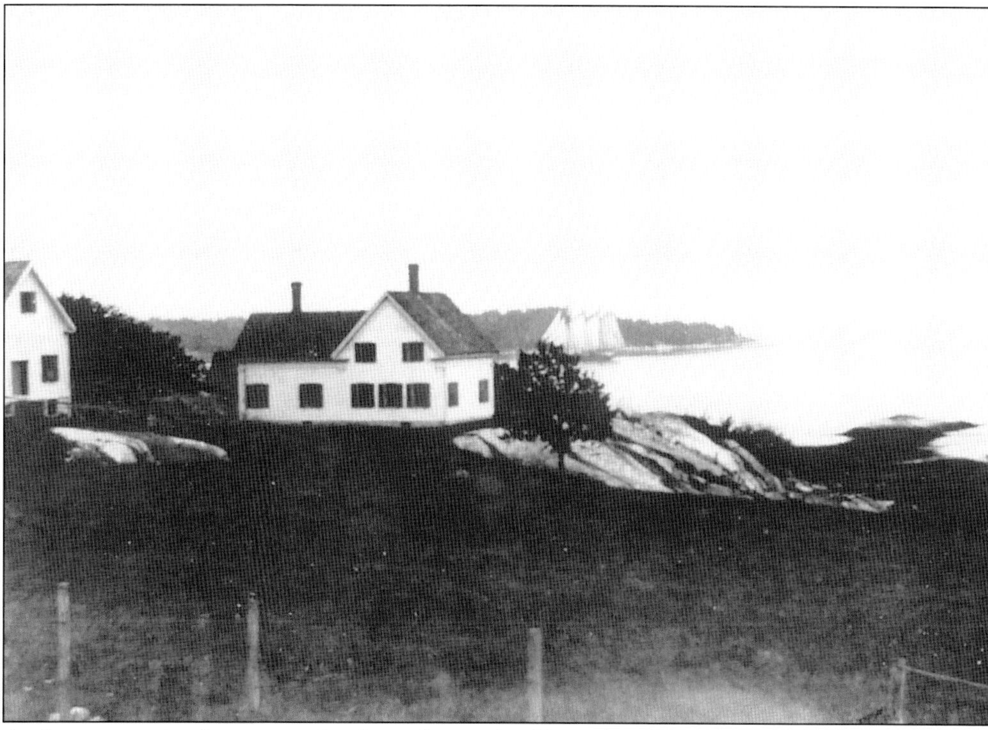

A three-masted schooner with jibs sails up the Kennebec River past the Thomas Perkins homestead at Cox's Head.

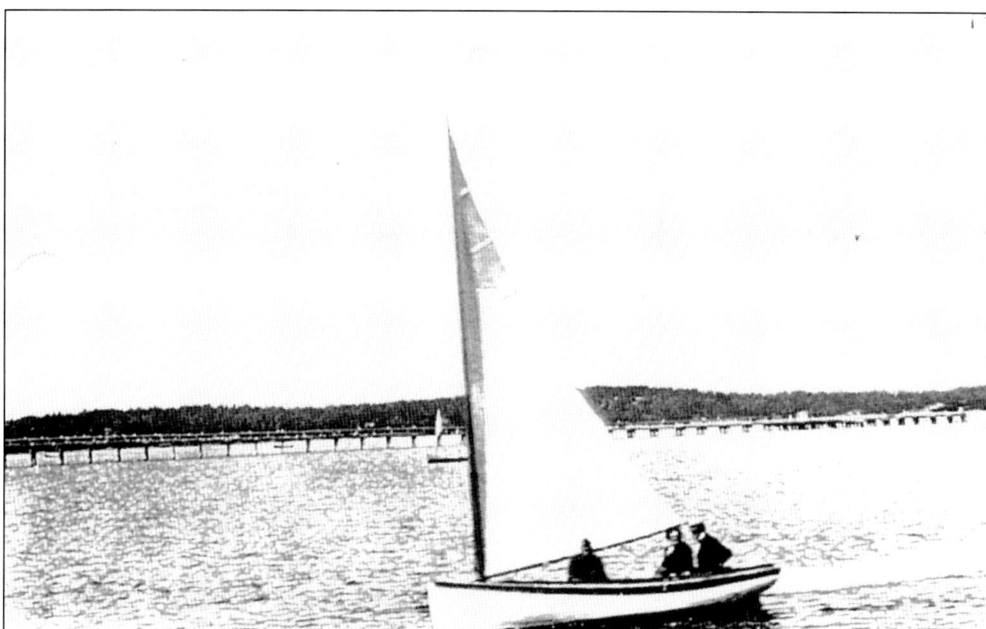

Three unidentified sailors cruise toward Popham Village in a catboat in 1926. Behind them is the Government Pier, part of Fort Baldwin, a World War I installation.

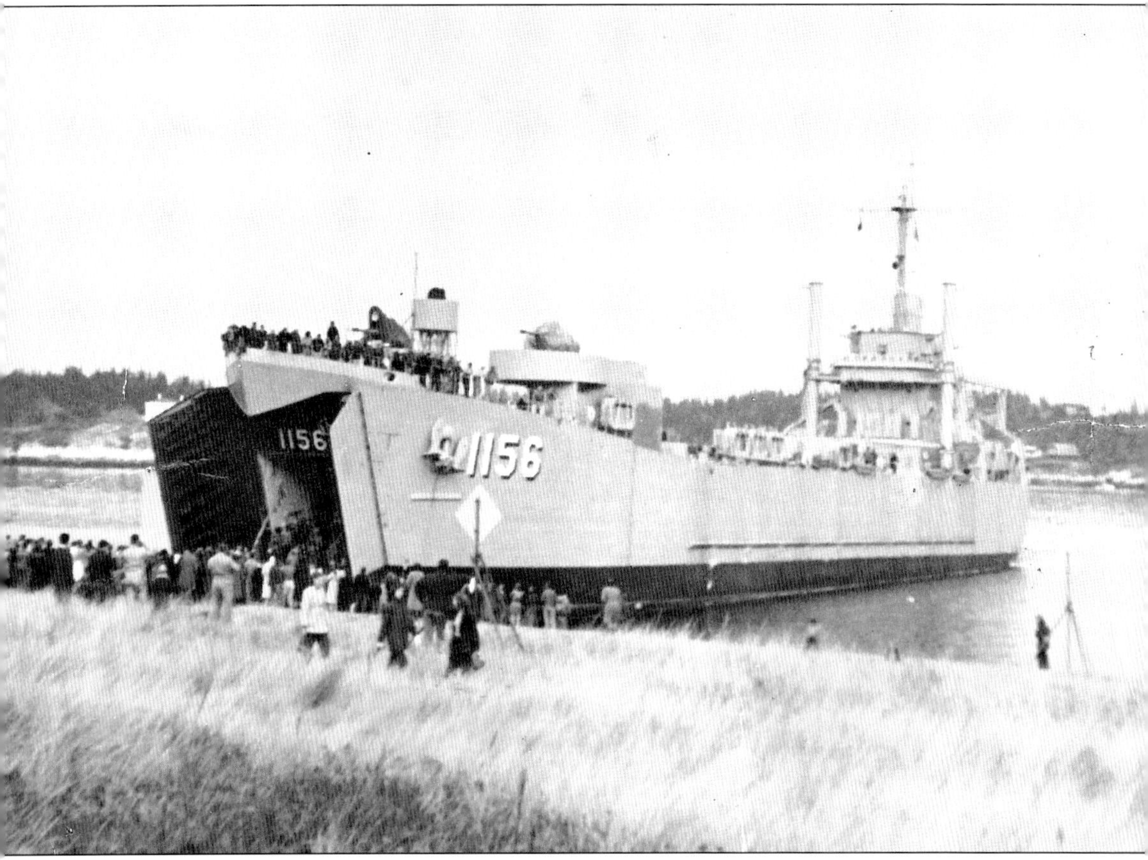

People from near and far flocked to the beach in Popham in the fall of 1952 to see the LST-1156, *Terrebone Parish*, when she landed there during trials. This "Landing Ship, Tank" was launched at Bath Iron Works in August of 1952 and was delivered to the U.S. Navy in November of that year. To the left is Gilbert Head, and to the right is Bay Point in Georgetown.

Six

Organizations and Activities

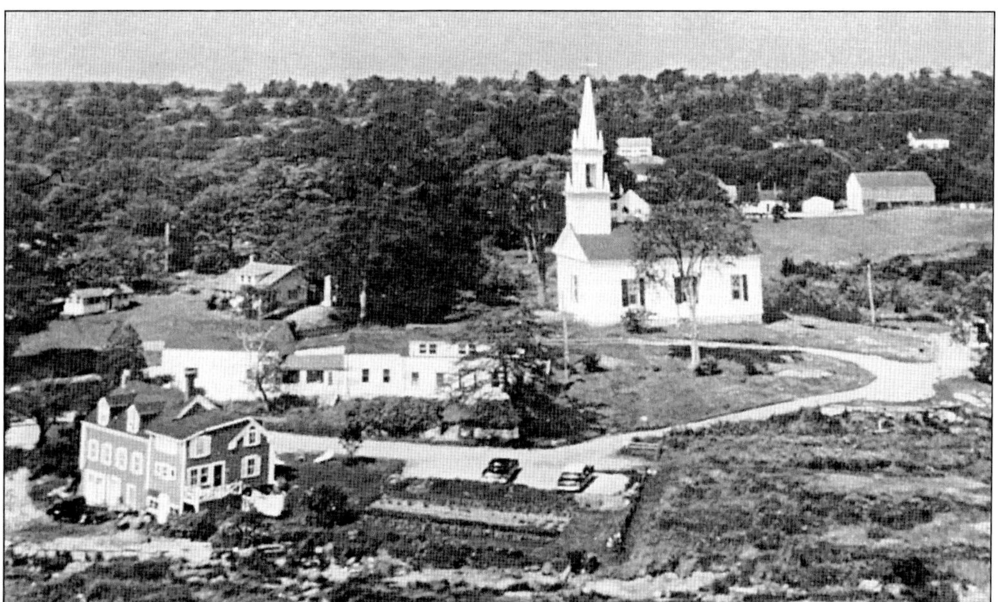

Kamp Keebec was a summer camp for boys run by Rev. Charles Stevens during the 1920s. This aerial view, taken in about 1965, shows Kamp Keebec's bungalow and dining hall in the clearing to the left of the Phippsburg Congregational Church.

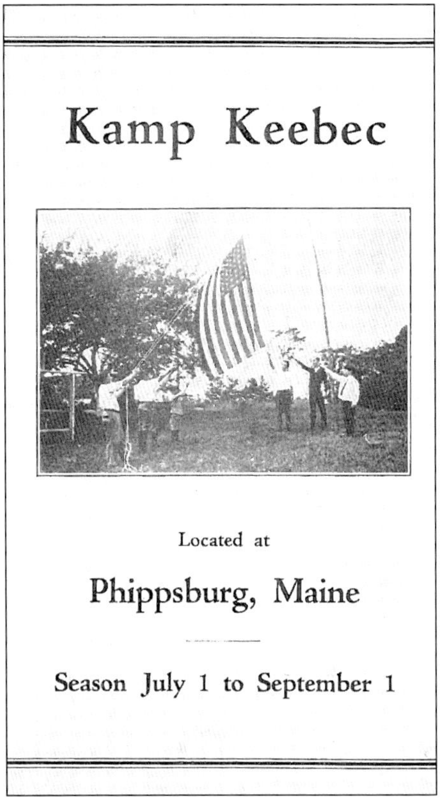

The brochure for Kamp Keebec described a full day for the campers, beginning with reveille at 7 a.m. and ending at 9 p.m. with taps. In between the boys were occupied with such things as camp duties, letter writing, swimming, boating, fishing, athletics, hikes, picnics, clam digging, and an evening program.

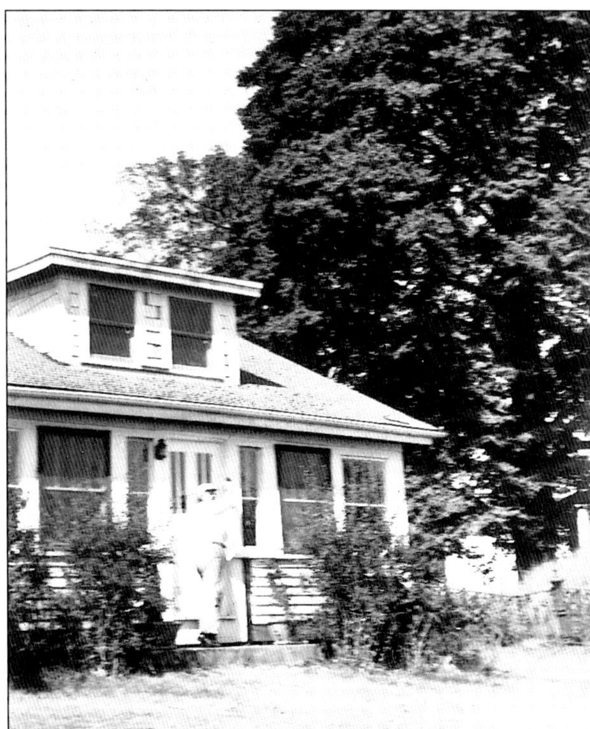

Rev. Charles Stevens works on the Kamp Keebec bungalow, which stood near the linden tree in front of the Phippsburg Congregational Church. The monument to its right marks the burial site of Mark Langdon Hill, Maine's first congressman from this district.

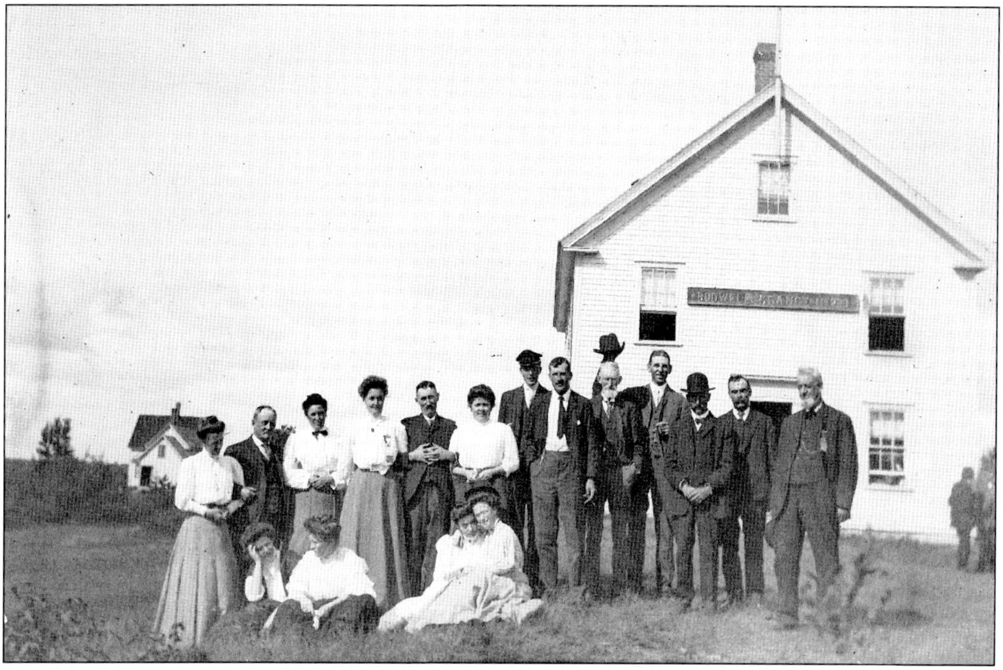

Unidentified Grangers are shown in front of the Bodwell Grange in Small Point. Though Bodwell Grange #289 was formed in 1887, it was not until 1911 that this grange hall was constructed.

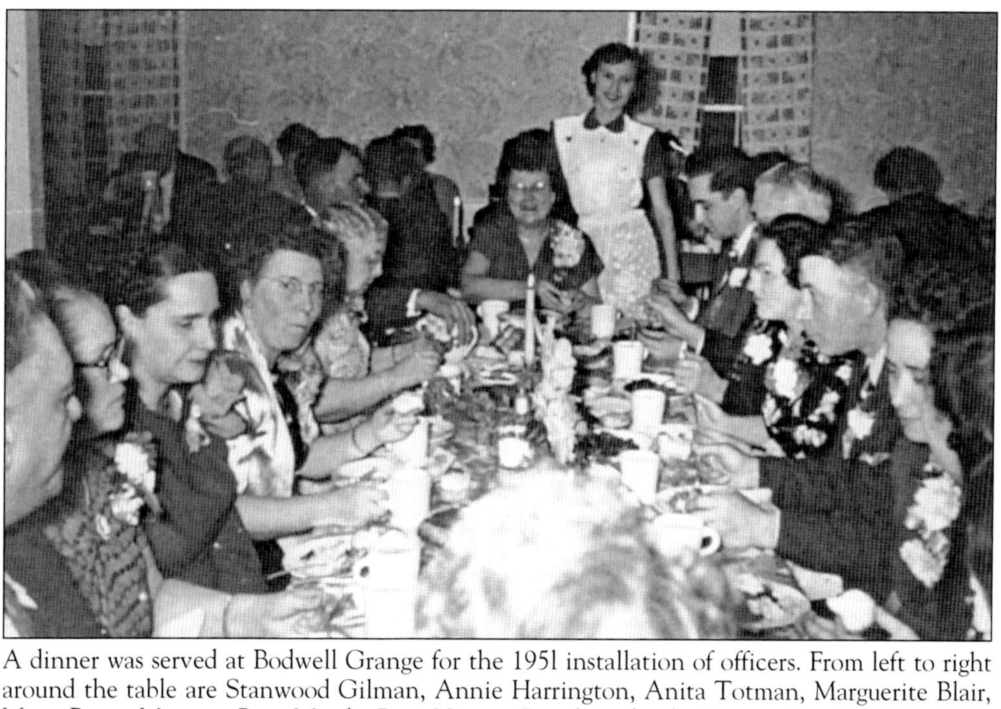

A dinner was served at Bodwell Grange for the 1951 installation of officers. From left to right around the table are Stanwood Gilman, Annie Harrington, Anita Totman, Marguerite Blair, Mary Pratt, Maurice Pye, Myrtle Pye, Norma Pye (standing), Rev. H. Macy Whitehead, Melvin Pratt, Helena Oliver, Winn Blair, Arlene Hamel, and two unidentified guests. Back to the camera, with only her head showing, is Margaret Gilman.

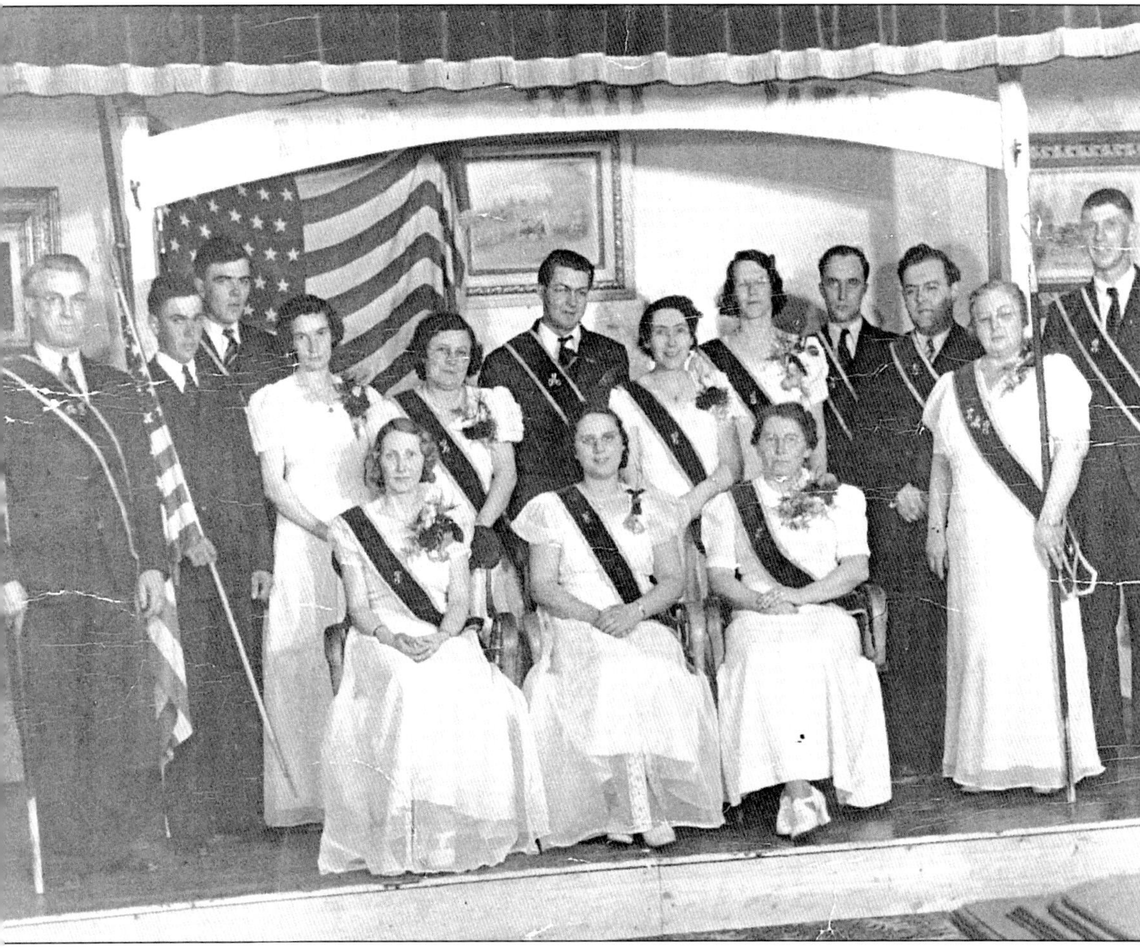

The February 1941 Degree Team at Bodwell Grange in Small Point included the following, from left to right: (seated) Marguerite Hilton, Flora; Anna Pratt, Ceres; and Marguerite Blair, Pomona; (standing) Melvin Pratt, Assistant Steward; Clyde Pye, Flagbearer; Clifford Pye, Gatekeeper; Frances Pye, Pianist; Myrtle Pye, Lecturer; Shirley Pratt, Master; F. Margaret Gilman, Secretary; Margaret D. Wyman, Chaplin; Heyen Hilton, Treasurer; Wesley Lemont, Overseer; Mary Pratt, Lady Assistant Steward; and Divinal Cornish, Steward.

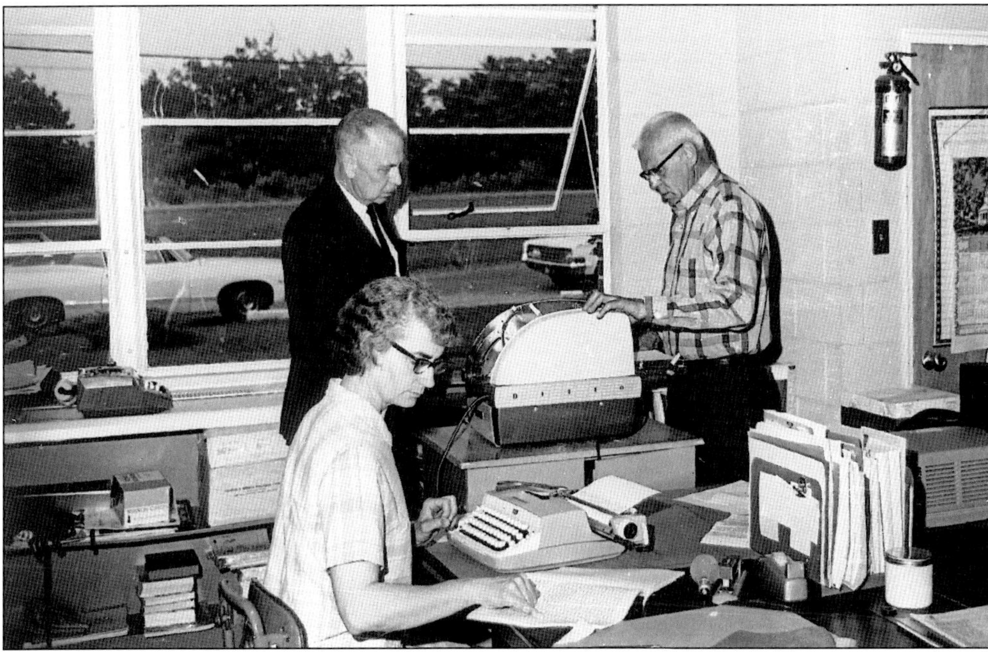

The Phippsburg *Observer*, a local newspaper sponsored by the PTA, was published in the Phippsburg Elementary School weekly during the school year from October 4, 1961, through June 16, 1978. All work was done by volunteers. Here Ada Haggett works at the typewriter while Newbold Varian and Tom Totman run the mimeograph machine.

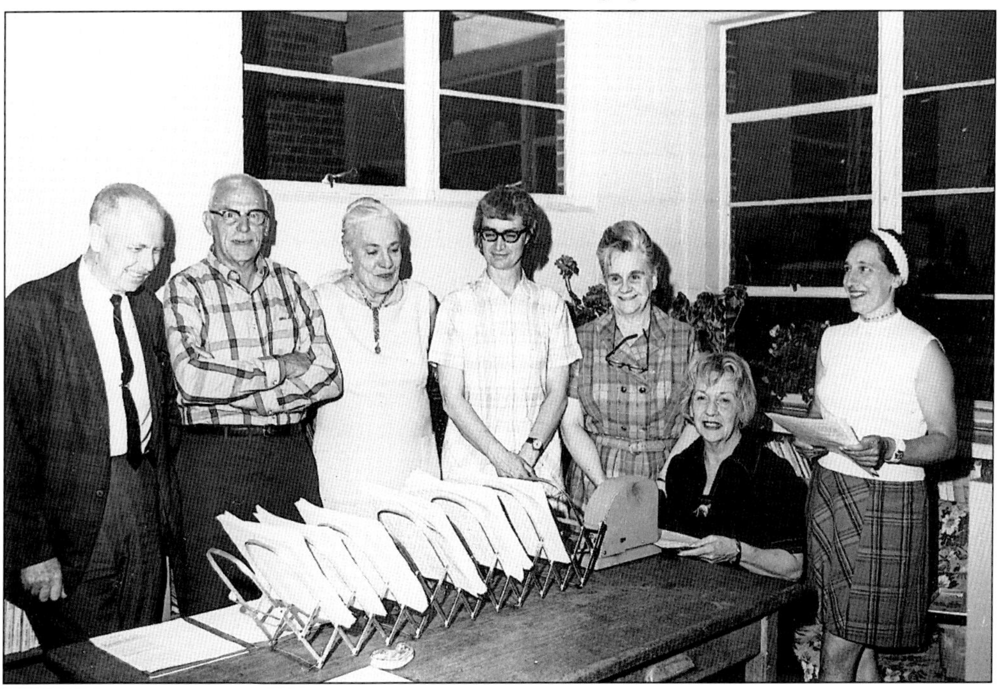

The volunteer staff of the Phippsburg *Observer* consisted of, from left to right, Newbold Varian, Thomas Totman, Dorothy Varian, Ada Haggett, Anita Totman, Editor-in-Chief Dorris Isaacson (seated), and Anda Bijhouwer.

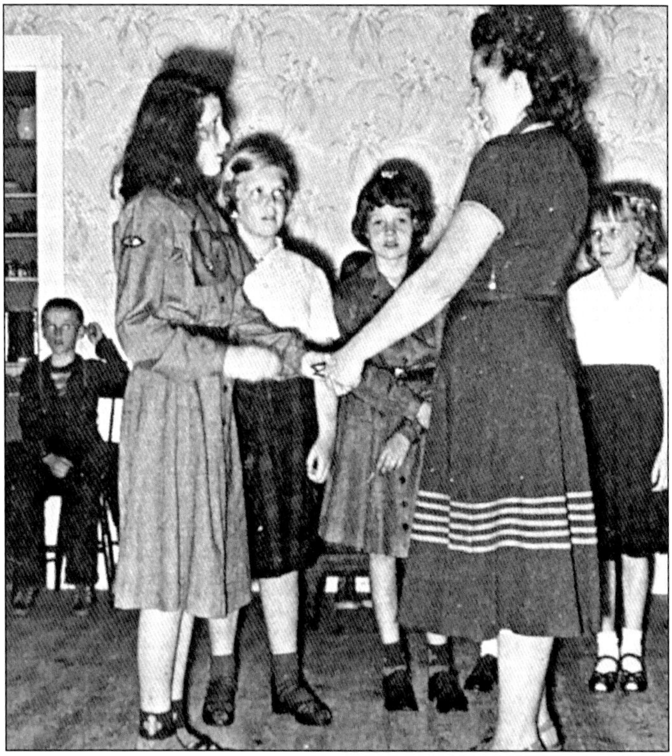

Gloria Eaton and Girl Scout Leader Arlene Hamel are shown in a Flying Up ceremony in 1951. Behind them are John Nortlund, Margaret Oliver, Diane Hamel, and Carol Wyman.

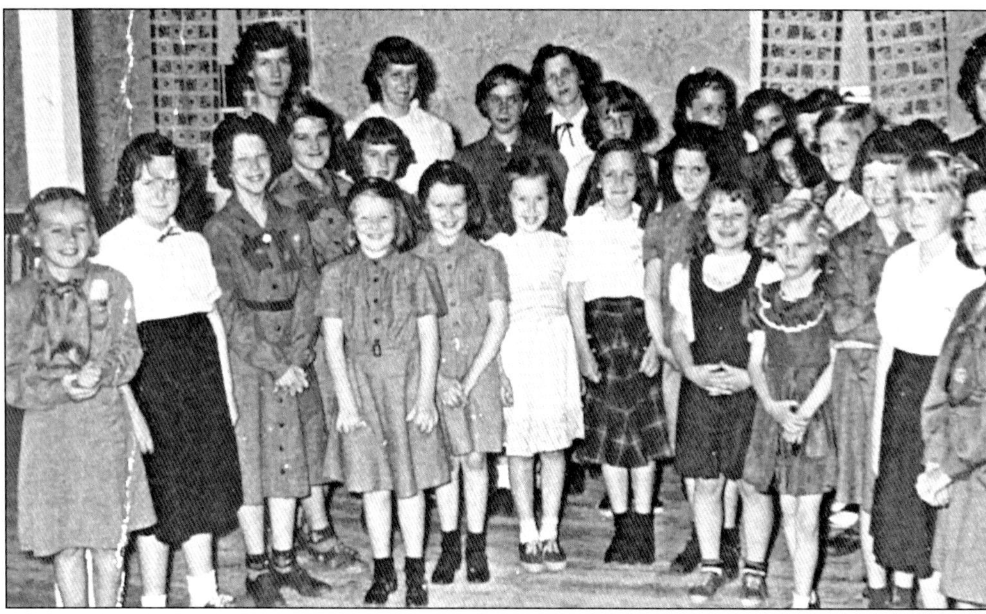

This 1951 Girl Scout Troop was sponsored by the Bodwell Grange. Pictured are, from left to right, as follows: (front row) Josephine Munsey, Joan Brewer, unknown, Edith Oliver, Phyllis Eaton, Martha Robinson, and Roberta Pye; (middle row) Ellen Blair, unknown, Irma Lee Gilman, Lona Moore, Natalie Wallace, unknown, Janet Wallace, unknown, Dianna Pye, unknown, Gloria Eaton, Margaret Oliver, Diane Hamel, Carol Wyman, and Fay Pye; (back row) Frances Pye, Vicki Blaisdell, Dorothy Pye, and Leader Arlene Hamel.

Girl Scouts Marlene Logan and Diane Hamel pose in their uniforms in August 1952.

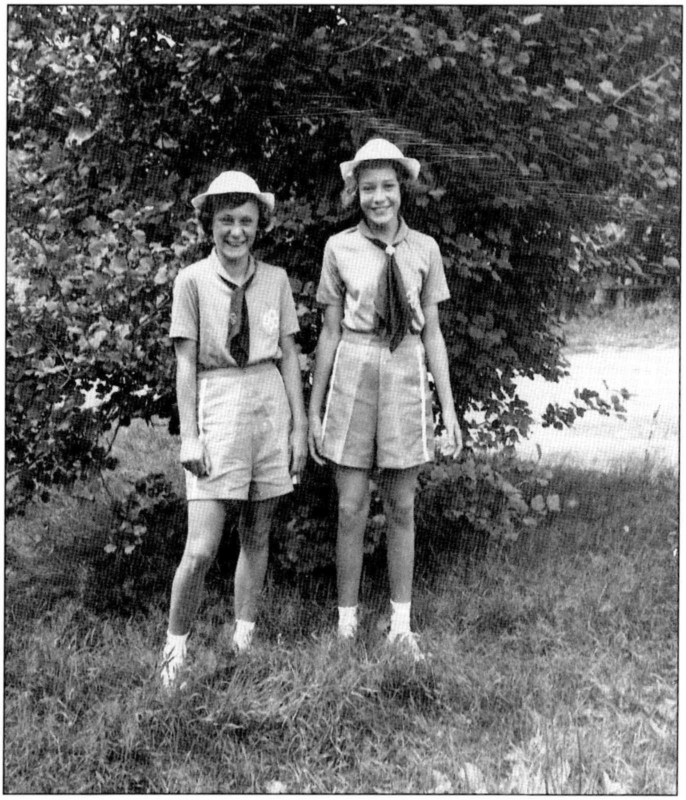

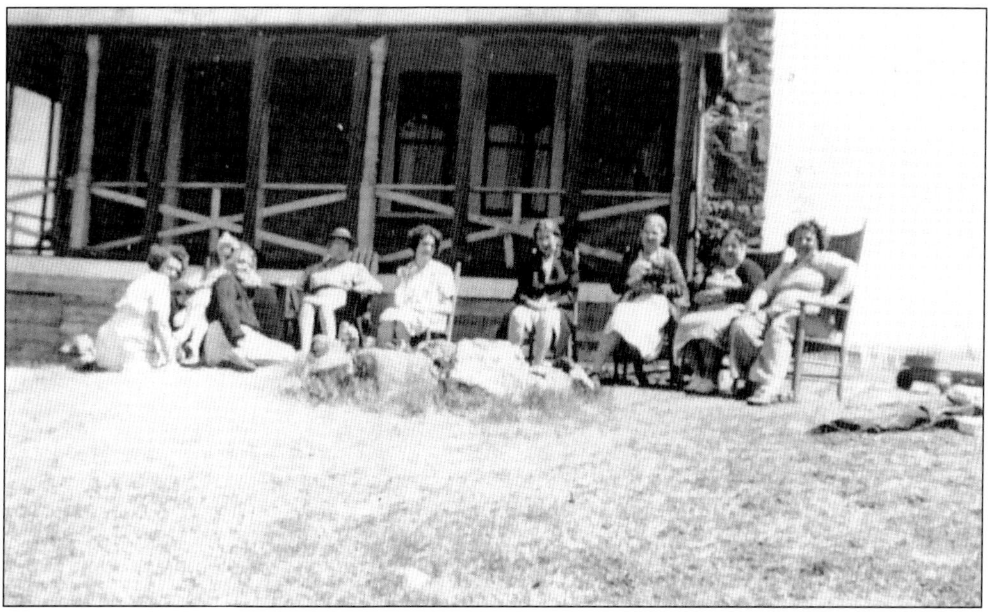

Members of the local Farm Bureau met in 1946 at Priscilla Thayer's cottage on Wyman Bay on the Kennebec, with Alice Lowell seated on the far right and Gladys Dozois fifth from the left. The little red wagon was used to haul supplies down the long lane from the "main" road.

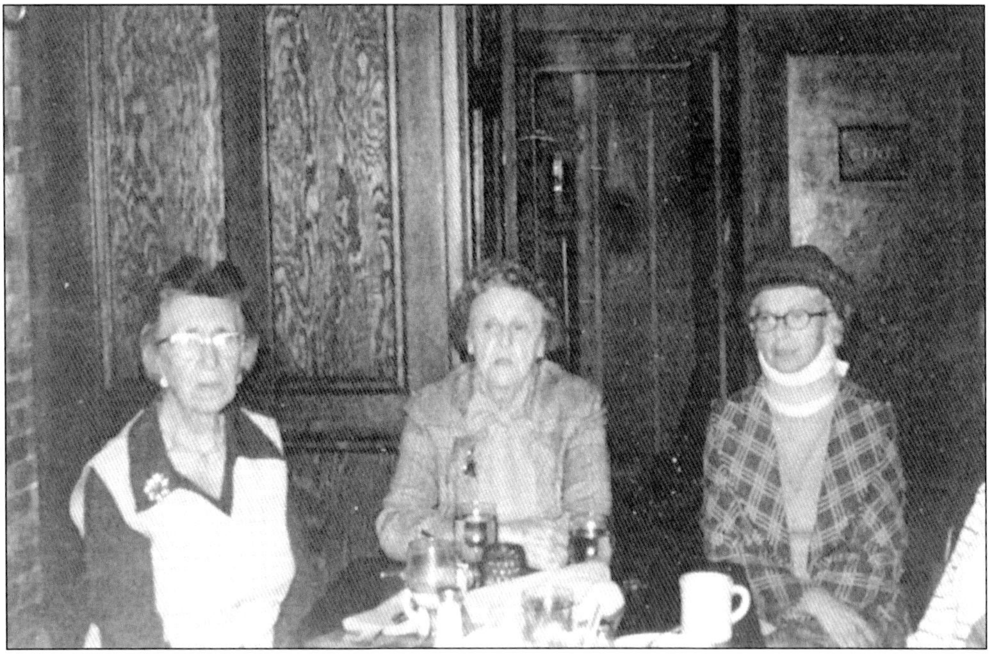

Members of the Unity Circle of Phippsburg enjoy an evening out after a year of hard work and a successful summer fair. Seated, from left to right, are Florence Oliver, Celeste Wallace, and Lou Harkins.

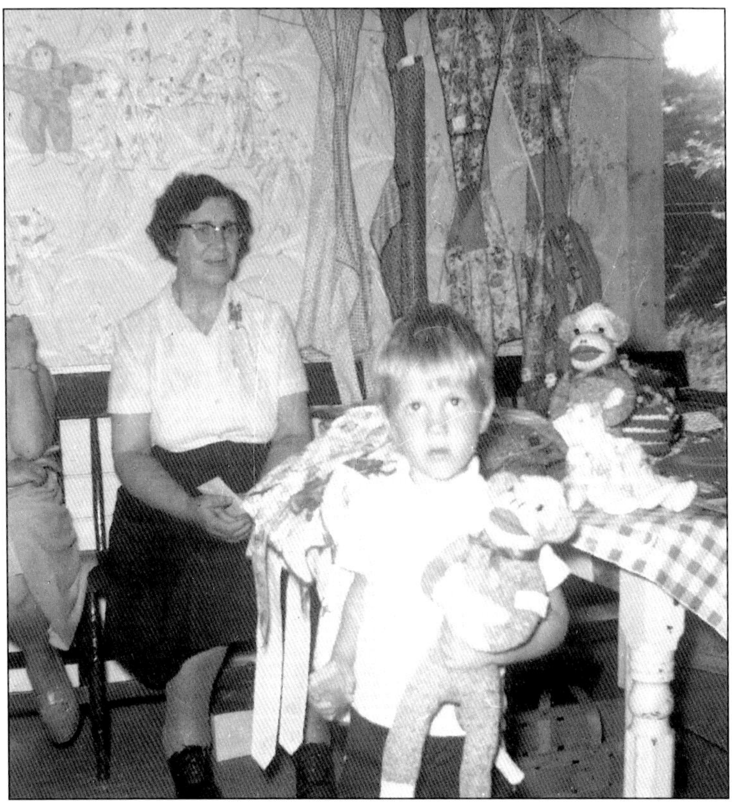

Florence Oliver often had a handicraft table at the local fairs. In August 1964, she was photographed by her table at the Bodwell Grange Fair while an unidentified youngster hugged one of her sock monkeys.

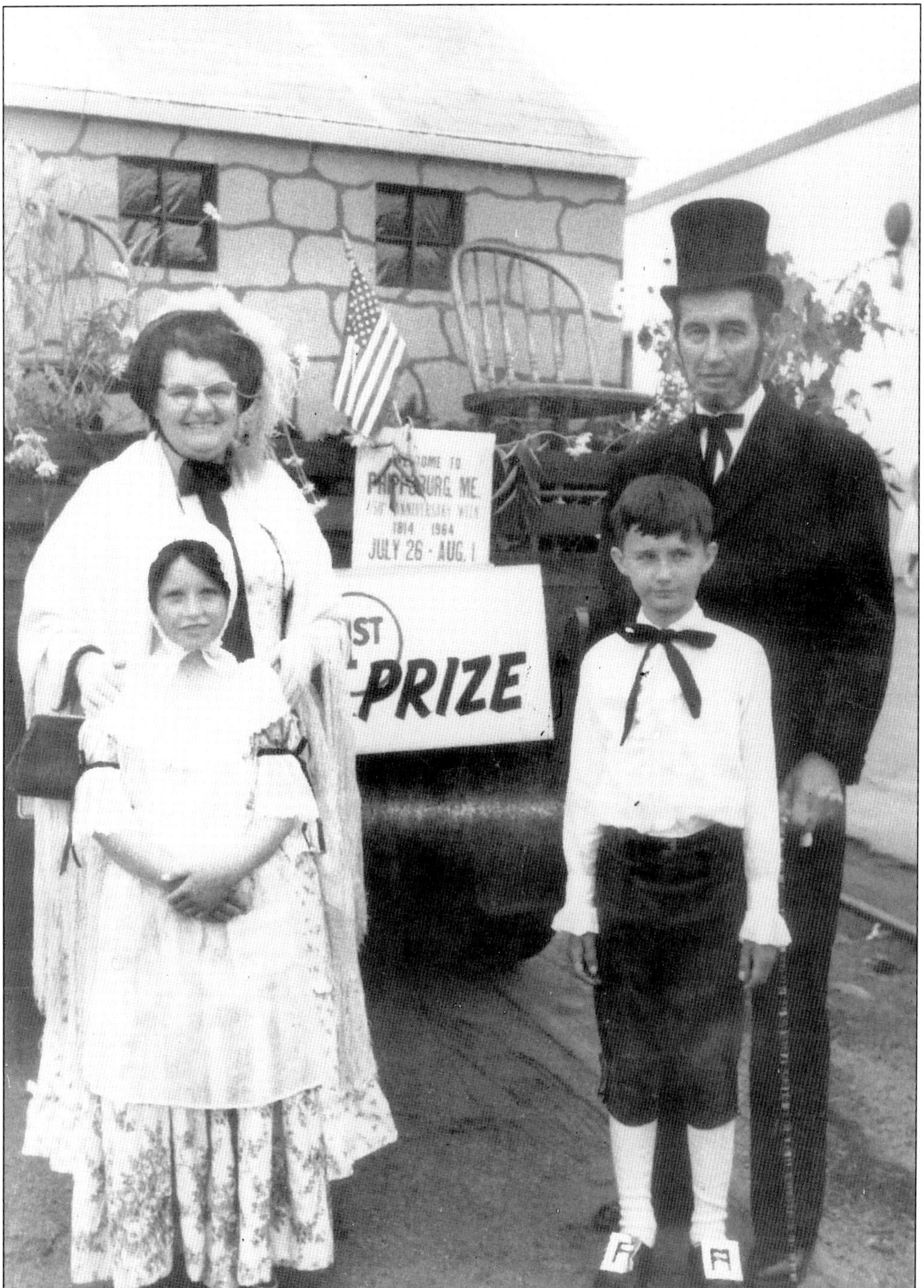

Abraham Lincoln (Selectman John "Hamie" McCourt) and Mrs. Lincoln (Town Clerk Alice Munsey) posed with the float that won first prize in Bath's 1964 Fourth of July Parade. The float, a replica of the Stone Schoolhouse, was in honor of Phippsburg's 150th anniversary. With Mr. and Mrs. Lincoln are Elizabeth and Clinton Richardson, Jr.

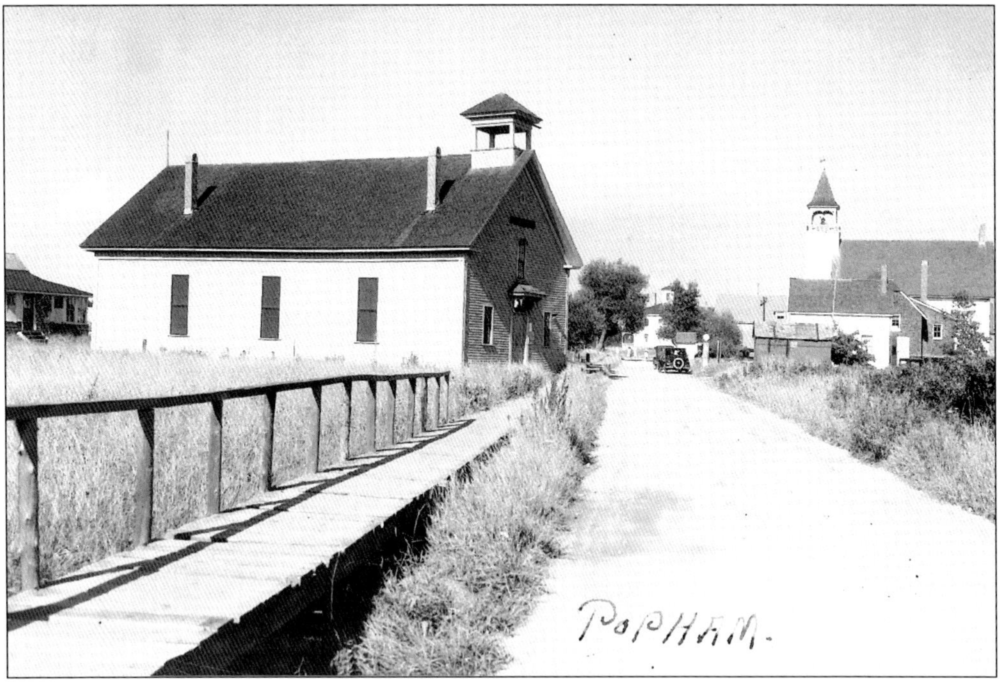

Society Hall in Popham was built after 1887 through the efforts of the Ladies Sewing Society and the local villagers. It was the social center of Popham and many dances, suppers, plays, and other community activities were held there. During both world wars the ladies turned the hall over to the Army for the use of the men at Fort Baldwin.

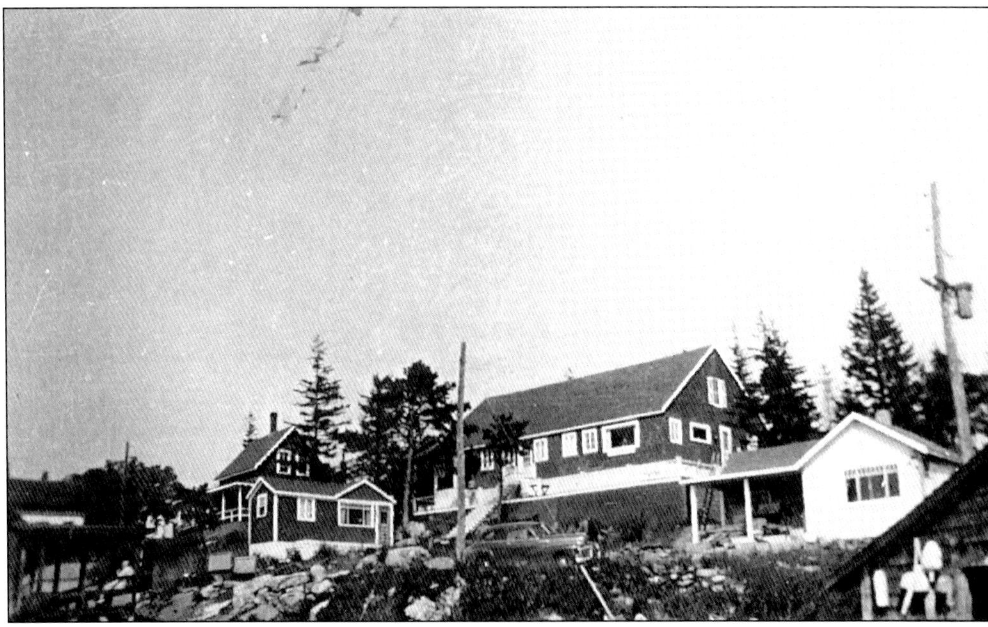

The long building sitting high above the road was once Herman Smith's dance hall in West Point, also known as the Sou'wester. Dances, masquerade balls, and other social events were held there from the 1920s into the 1940s. Local bands, as well as bands from surrounding towns, played at the Sou'wester.

Kit Totman, Fred Hutchins, and Leon Davis, shown here in the 1940s, often got together to play their fiddles.

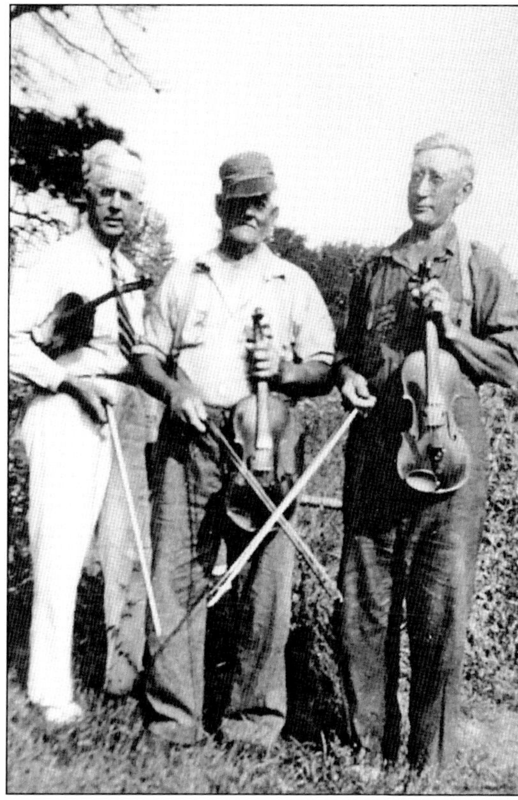

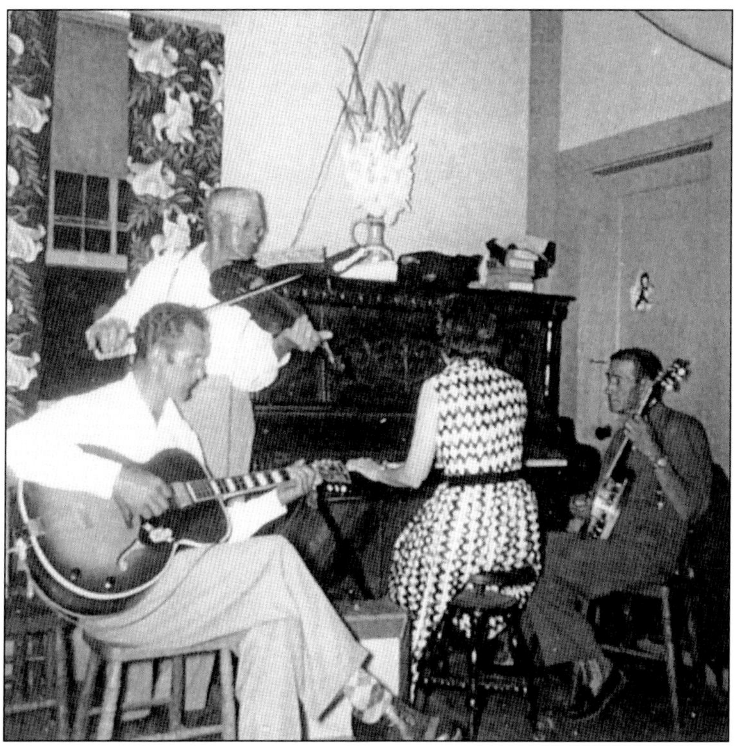

James "Sonny" Gilliam, Leon Davis, Annie Card, and Charles "Tweed" Anderson formed another musical group, playing largely for their own enjoyment.

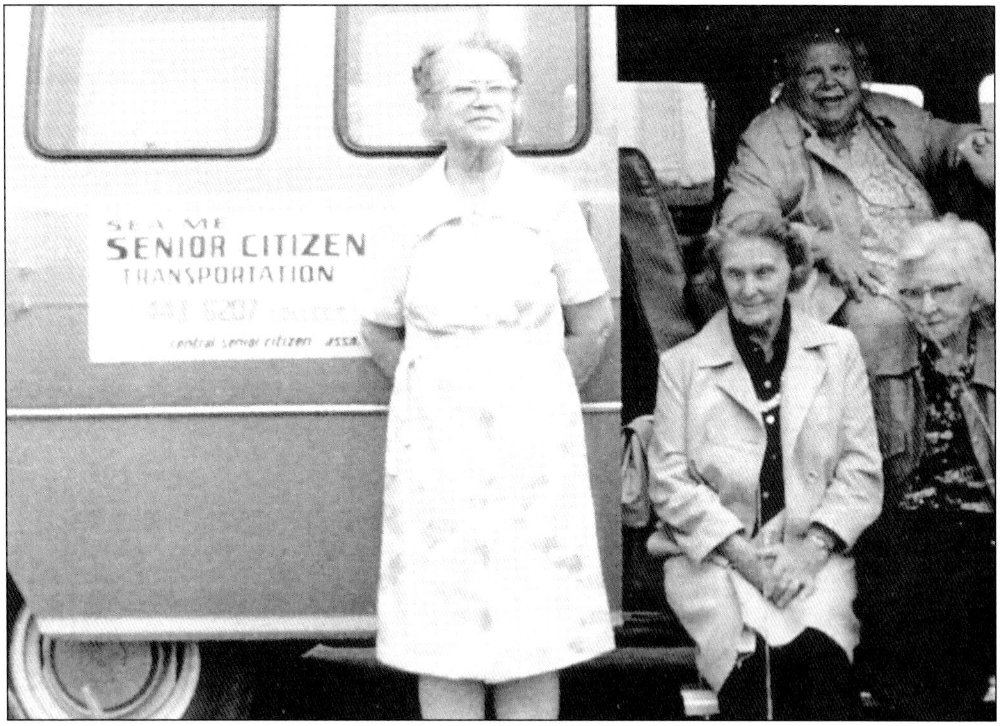

The SEA-ME bus was a great convenience for the senior citizens of the area. Annie Harrington is standing, Louise Hodgkins and Vera Rogers are sitting in the doorway, and Alice Lowell is inside the bus in this 1960s photograph.

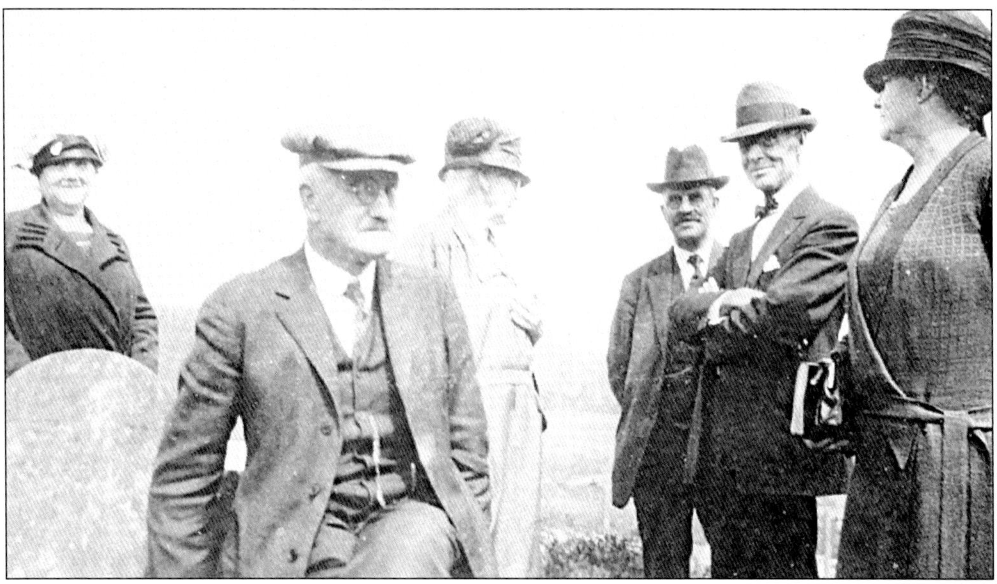

Members of the Dromore Burying Ground Association visited the Dromore cemetery north of Phippsburg Center, c. 1930. The lady behind the stone has not been identified. The others are, from left to right, Calvin W. Rogers (Bath and Florida), Mary Pelham Hill (Topsham), Charles V. Minott Jr. (Phippsburg), Elwell S. Crosby (Bath and Florida), and Mrs. Henry W. Butler (Bath).

Seven

Resorts

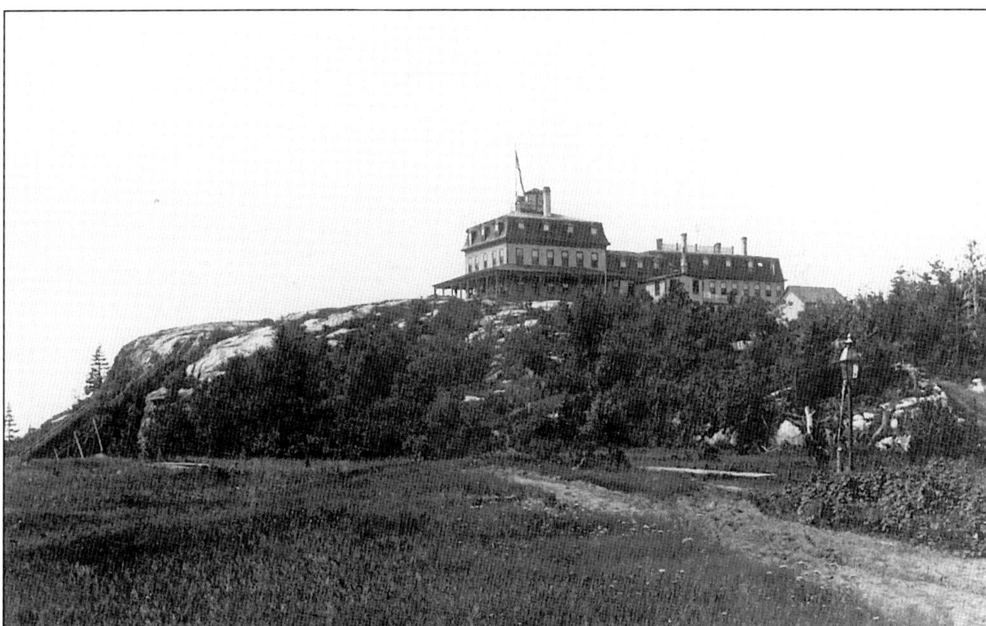

Popham Beach, with its sandy beaches and steamboat service, developed into the first major resort area in town. Hotel Rockledge at Popham Beach (earlier known as the Ocean View House) added an elegant tone to the social life of this resort area at the turn of the century. This impressive 100-room hotel, with its grand view of the ocean, is shown here c. 1892, about eleven years after it was built. It was destroyed by fire in 1915.

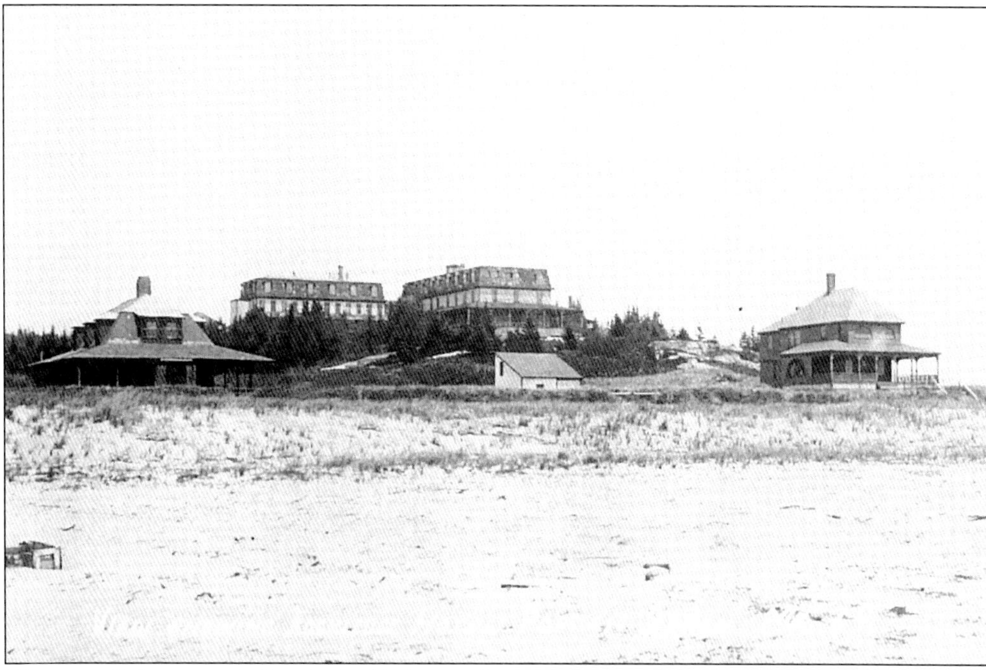

This *c.* 1900 view of Hotel Rockledge includes a couple of the more imposing cottages on Popham Beach.

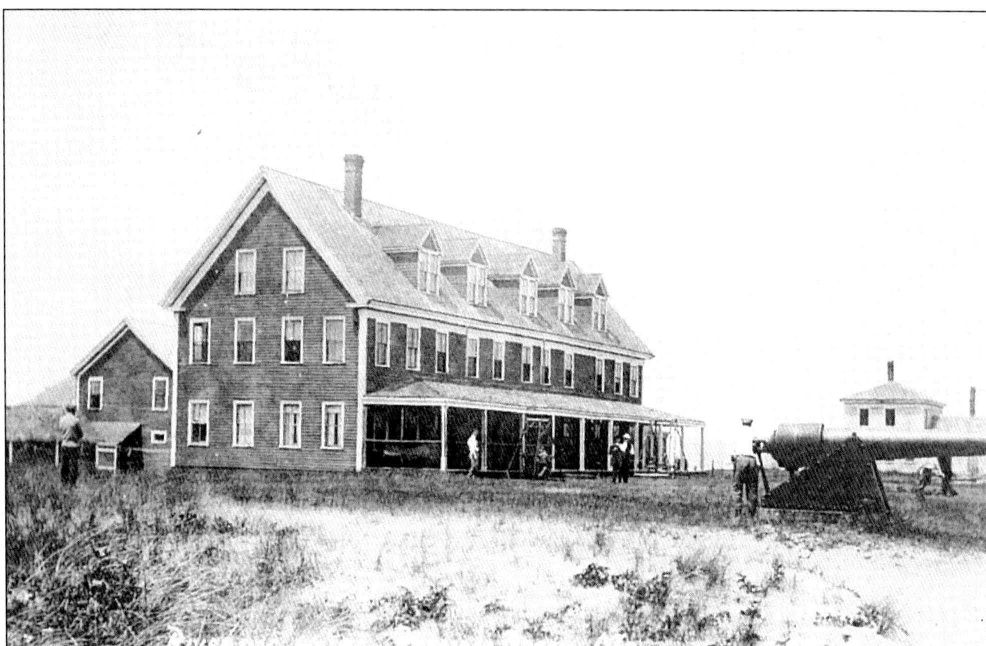

The Riverside Hotel, located on the beach between the Popham Life Saving Station and Fort Popham, was known as the Eureka House when it was built in 1878.

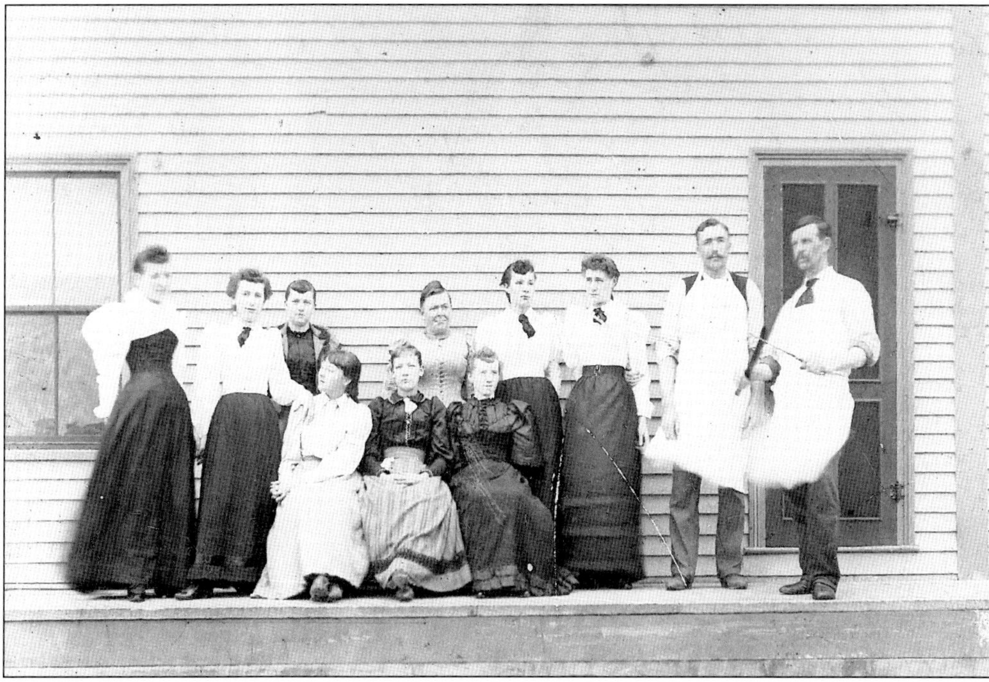

The staff of the Riverside Hotel in Popham is pictured here around 1895. Seated on the left is Emma Pearl Stacey, daughter of the hotel's owner. In 1899 she became Popham Chapel's first bride, when she married Dr. A.F. Williams.

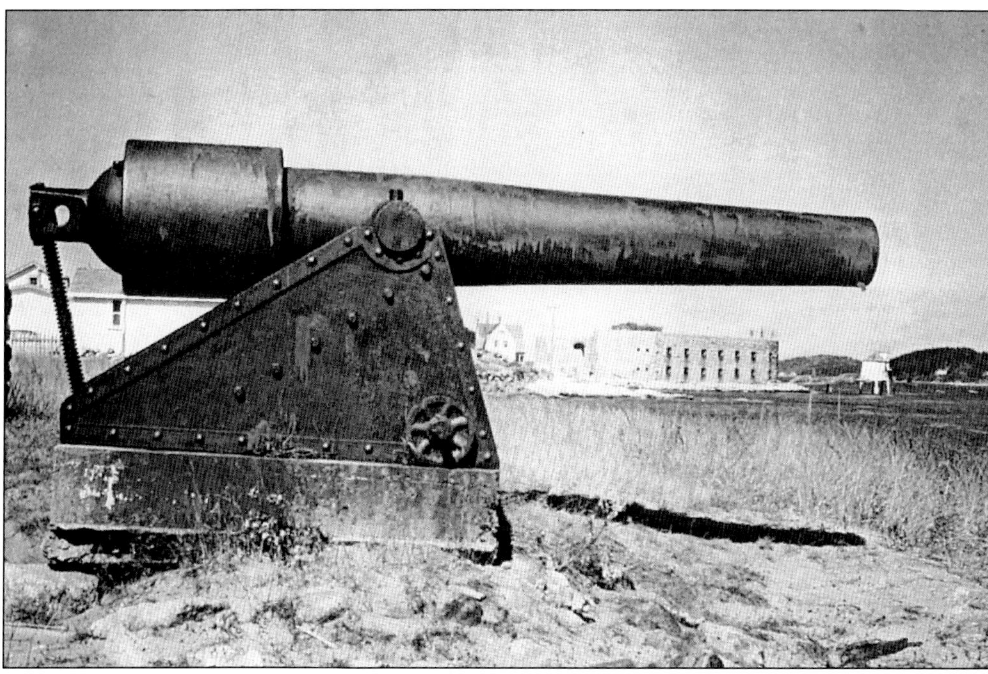

This cannon was installed in front of the Riverside Hotel by owner John Stacey in 1906. The Riverside Hotel is long gone, but the old Civil War cannon remains, pointing out to sea. Under the barrel of the gun can be seen Fort Popham, where the cannon was originally housed.

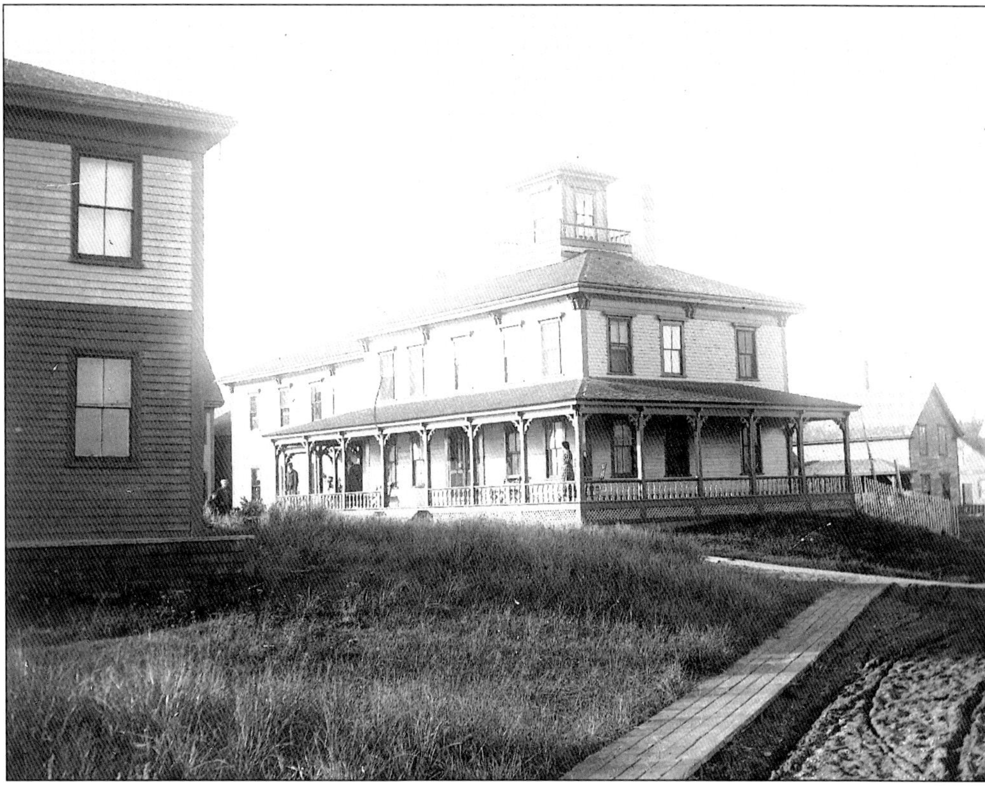

The Stacey house at Popham was built in 1885. It was the home of John Stacey, owner and operator of the nearby Riverside Hotel.

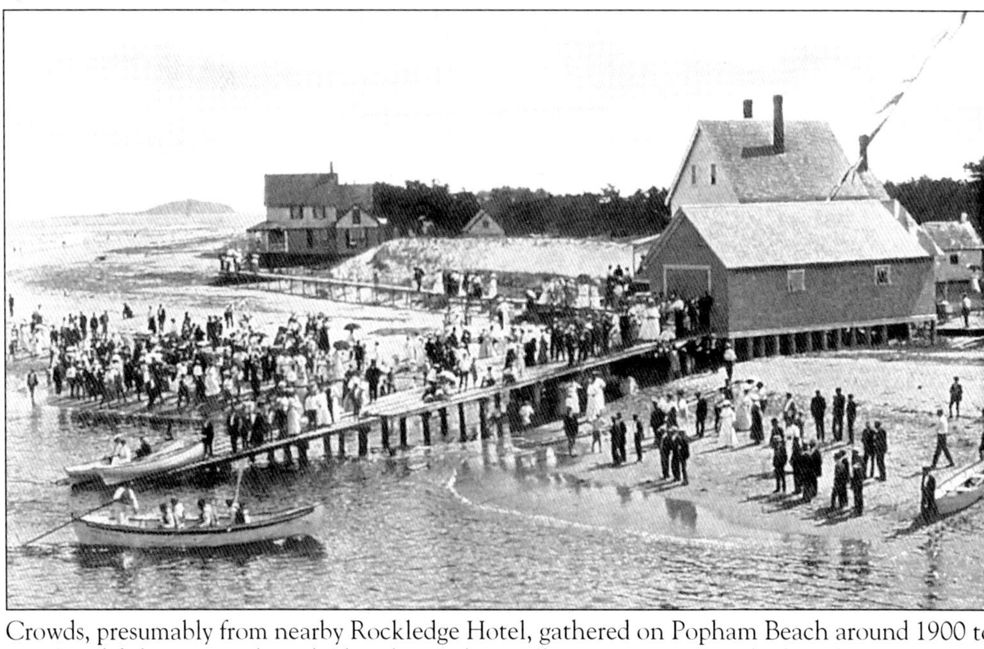

Crowds, presumably from nearby Rockledge Hotel, gathered on Popham Beach around 1900 to watch as life boats were launched at the Popham Life Saving Station. The boardwalk along the beach was also popular.

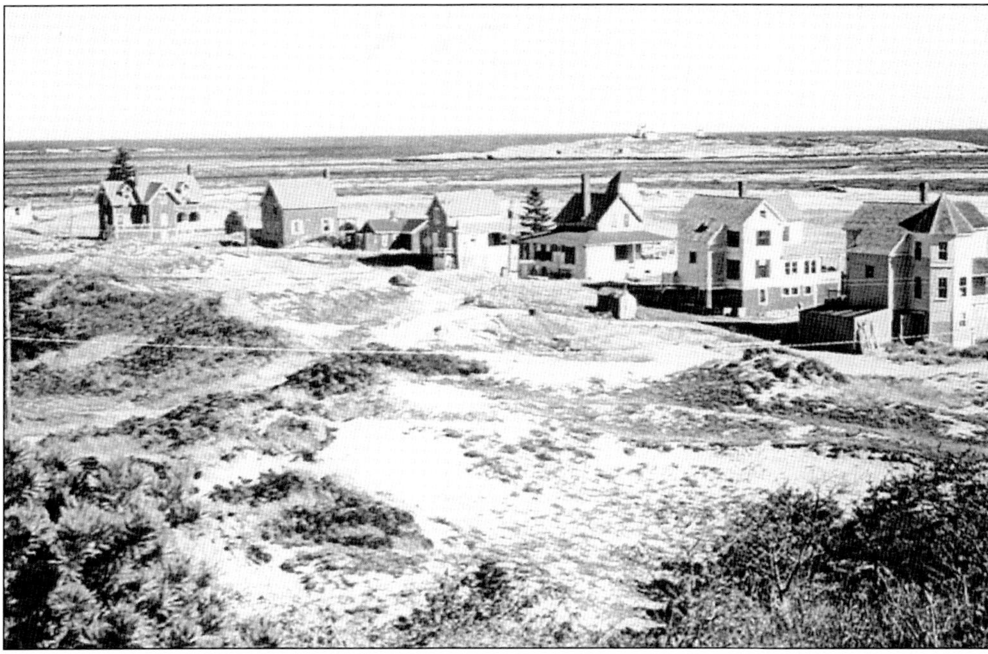

Erosion has claimed some of these Victorian-style cottages on the dunes at Popham Beach. Those on the point are gone, but the four on the right are still standing. The view is from the site of the old Rockledge Hotel.

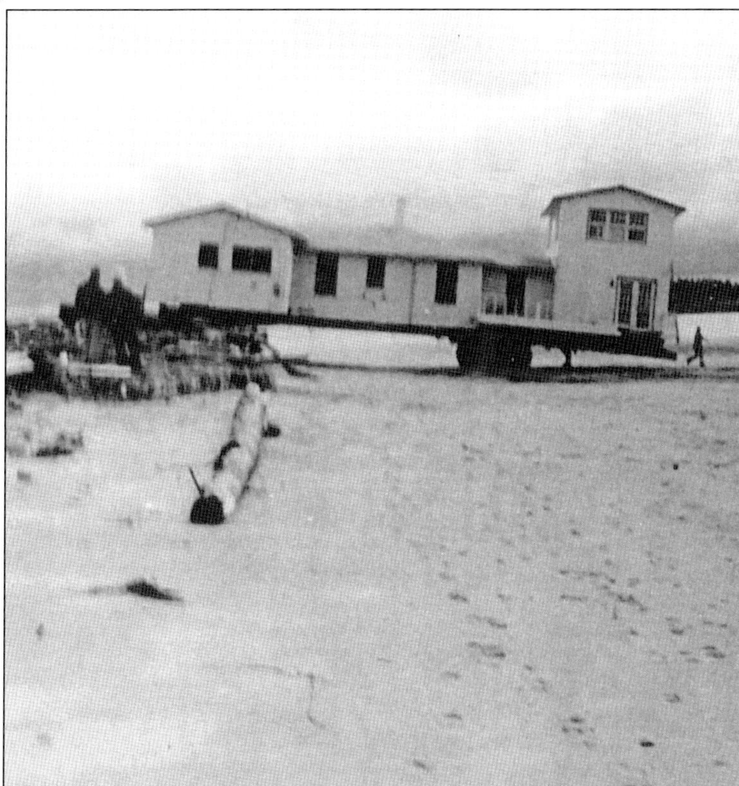

The Stimson cottage was moved back from its site on the point at Popham Beach, thus saving it from the fate of its neighbors, which were washed away in the winter of 1976.

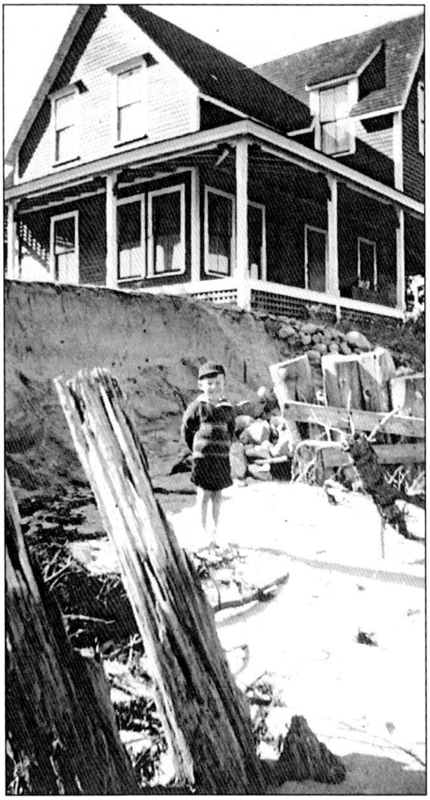

Erosion at Popham Beach is nothing new. In November 1938, this cottage stood very close to the sea after a storm washed out the beach. The little fellow smiling for the camera is William S. Gilman.

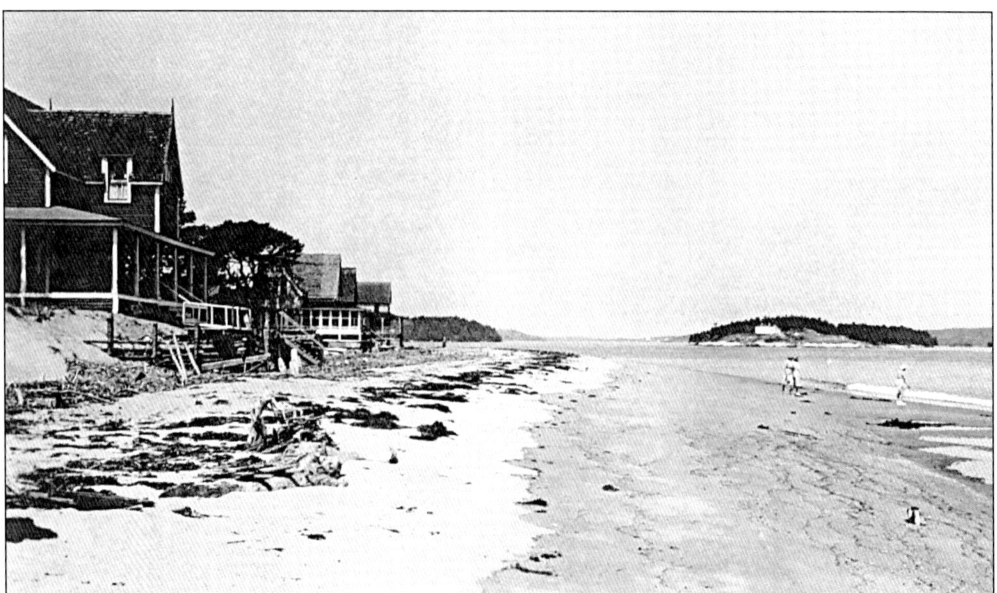

This row of cottages on Popham Beach sat at the water's edge c. 1940. They have either been moved or have been destroyed. In the background on the right is Gilbert Head, while Cox's Head is on the left.

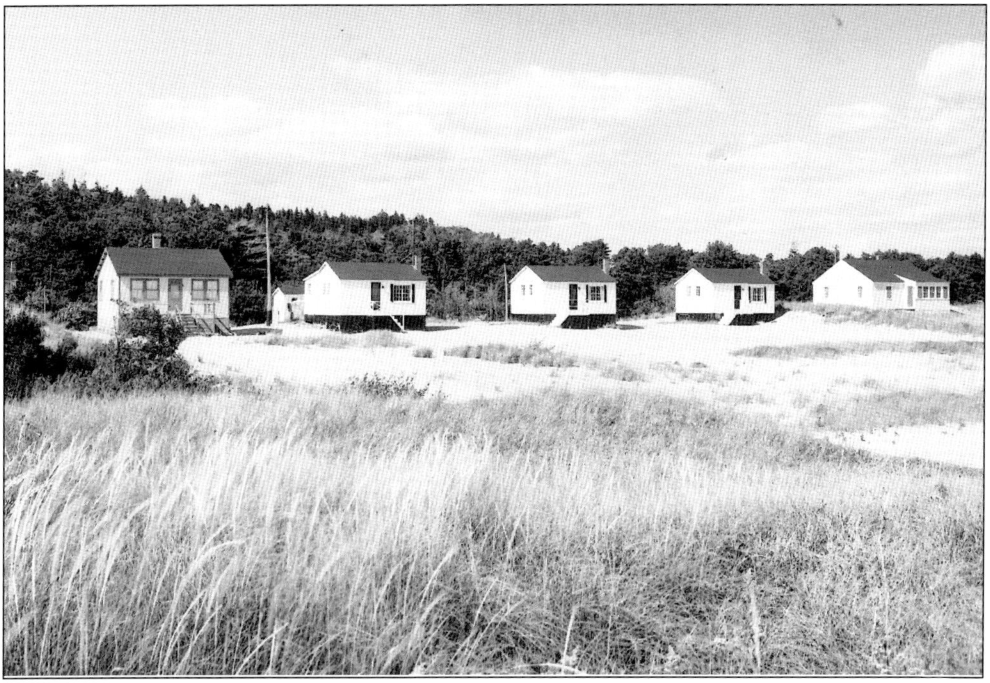

Markham's Cottages on the South Shore at Popham were built about 1950, but those that were not moved elsewhere were claimed by the sea during the winter of 1976.

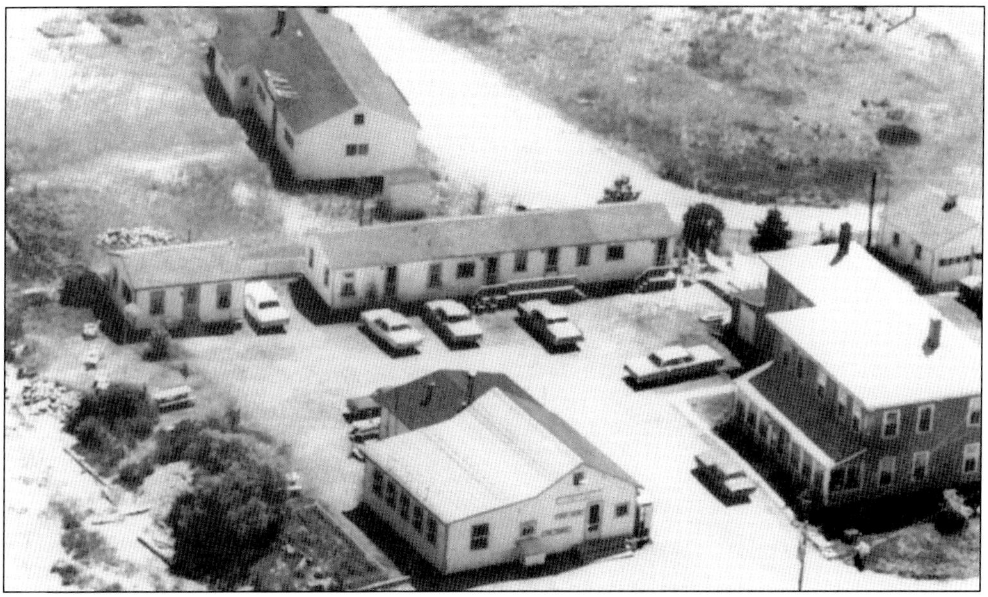

Spinney's store, restaurant, cottages, and guest house (formerly the Stacey house, built in 1885) are shown here in a *c.* 1950s aerial photo. Behind the cottages was Taylor's store, built near the site of the Riverside Hotel.

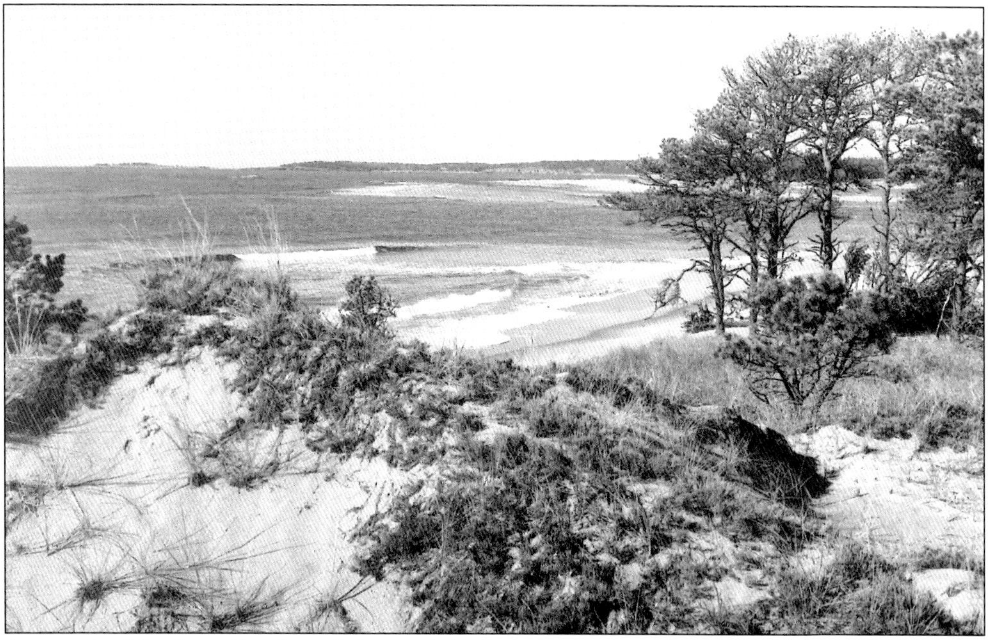

A stretch of Popham Beach and the sand dunes near Morse's River are pictured on a postcard of Popham Beach State Park. This land, which was originally given to the town in 1949 by the heirs of Charles V. Minott Jr. for use as a recreational area, later became a state park.

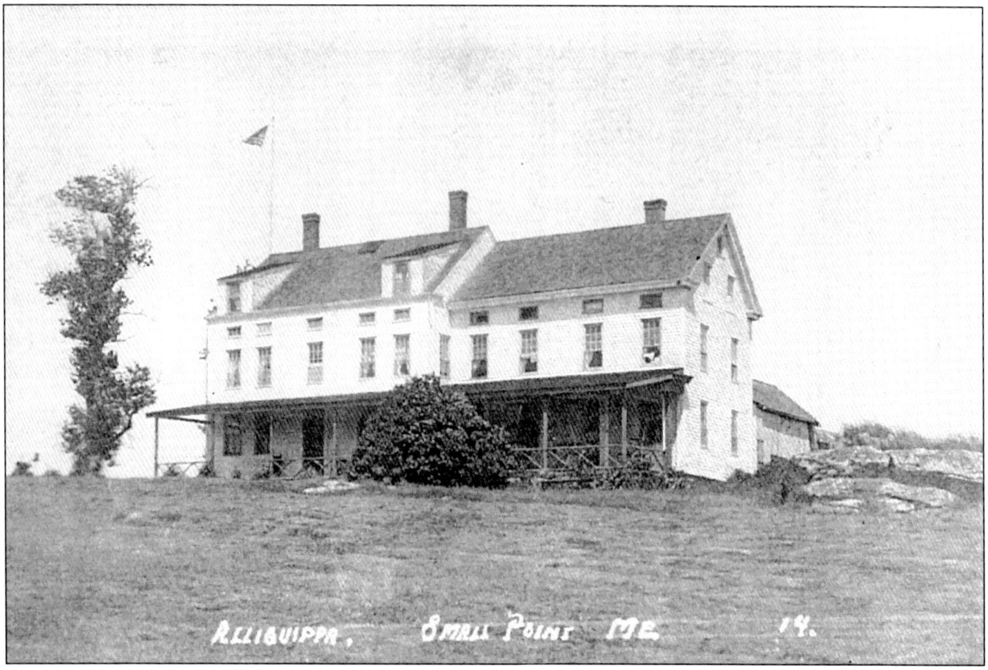

The Alliquippa Hotel, built in 1836, sat near the entrance to the inner harbor at Small Point. It was one of the town's earliest hostelries.

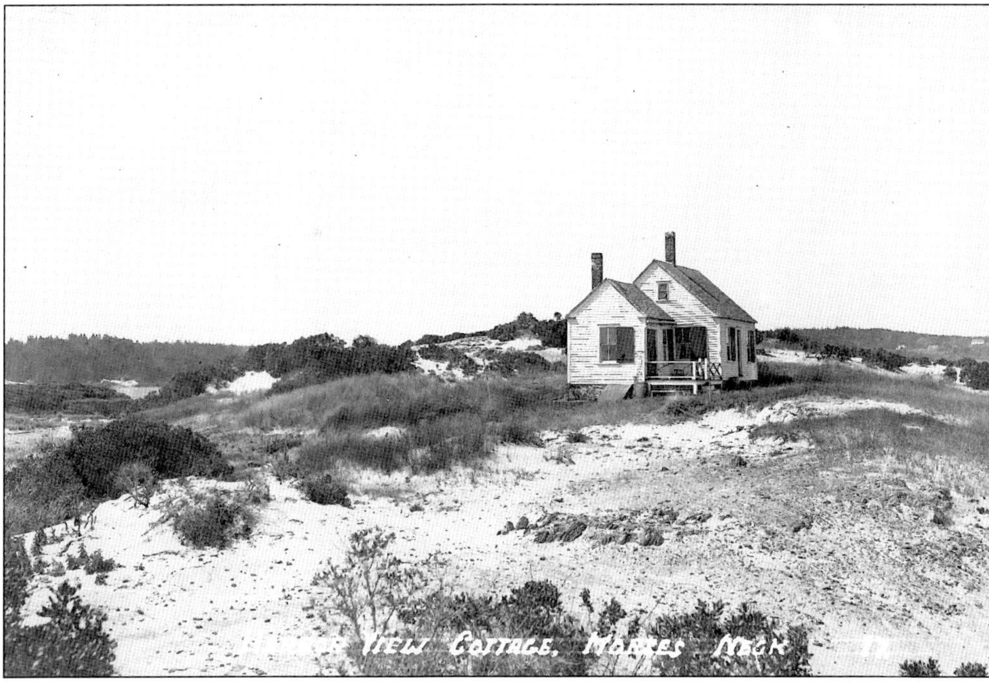

Harbor View Cottage once sat on the dunes at the end of Morse's Neck, now Hermit Island.

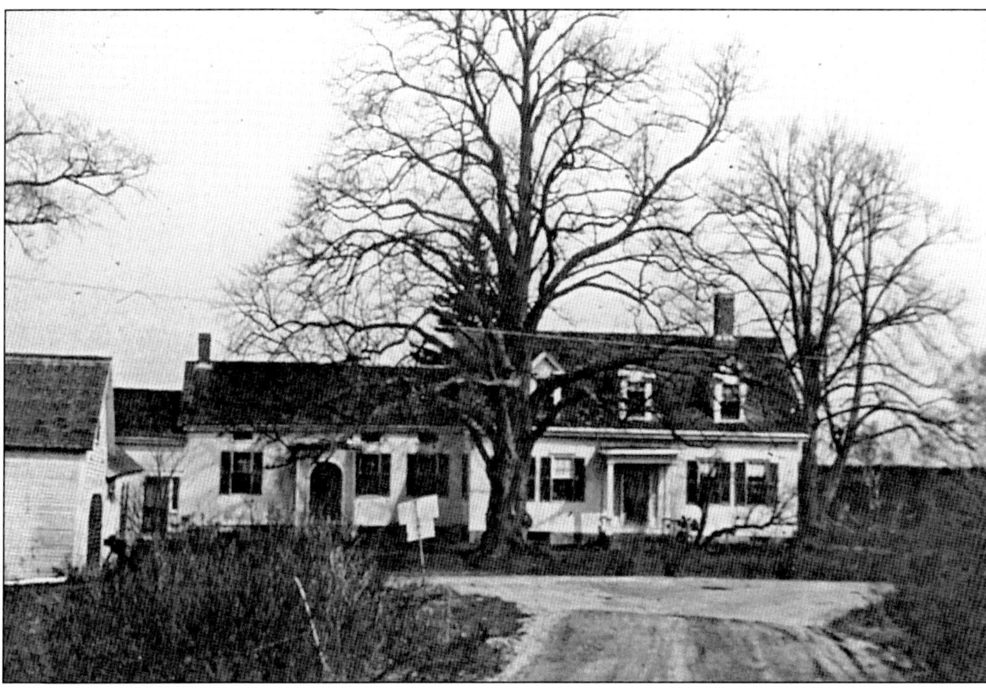

Spinney's Inn at Small Point, built in 1828, was a boarding house at the turn of the century. The English linden trees in front of the inn were planted by the building's original owner, Captain Abner Lowell.

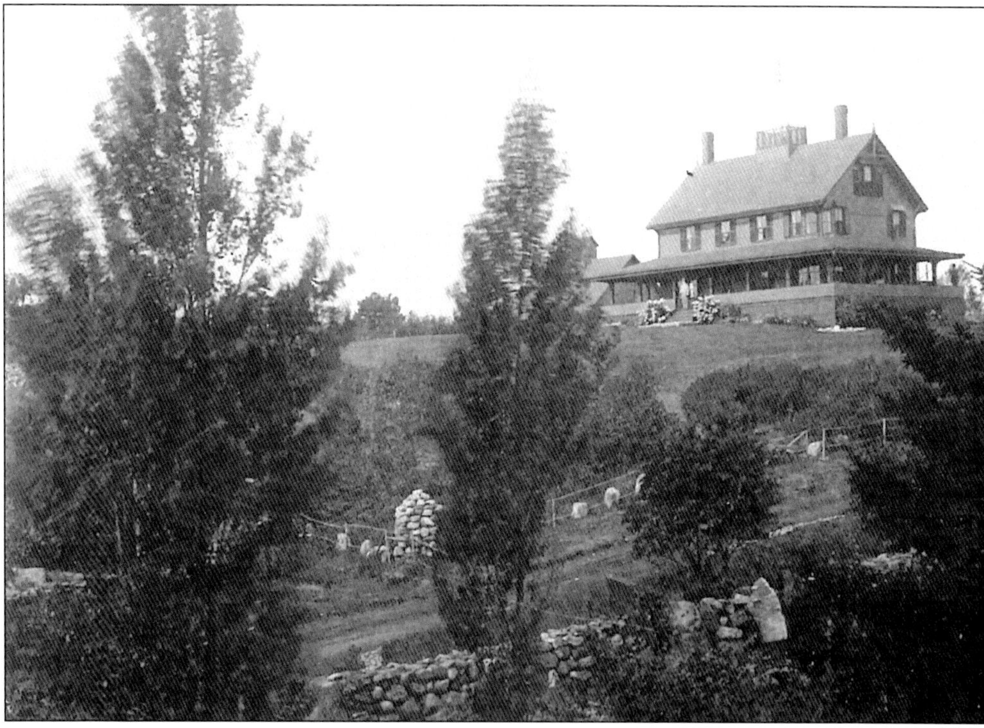

The Watson-McLanathan house at Small Point, thought to have been built around 1860, was called "Sea Winnocks," meaning "A View of the Sea." It later became the summer home of Chase Mellon and then of the Vandervoorts.

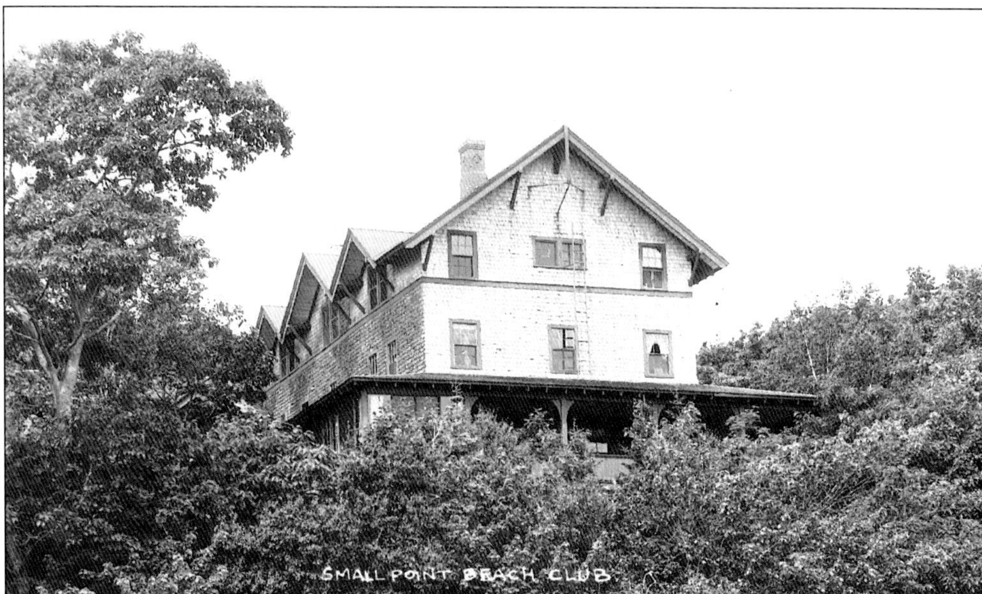

Members of the Small Point Beach Club entertained their guests at the building they called the Club, built in 1897. The first floor included a reception hall, library, dining room, and kitchen, while 17 bedrooms and 4 baths occupied the upper floors. Each bedroom is said to have a view of the sea.

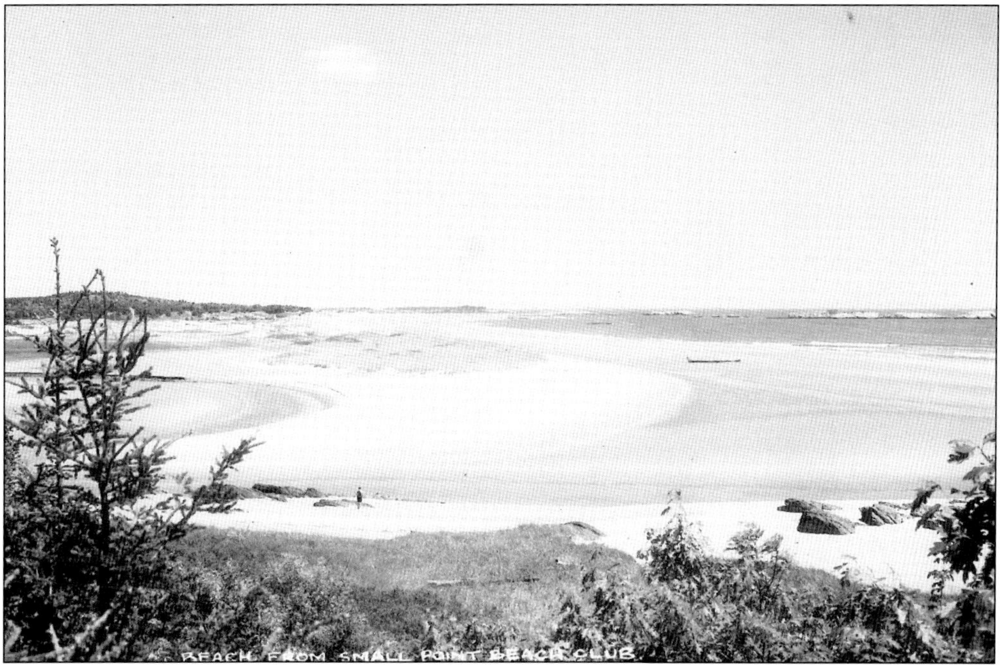

In this *c.* 1940 photograph, taken from the Small Point Club porch, a long stretch of Seawall Beach, sand dunes, and the mouth of Sprague River are all visible, in addition to the wreck of the schooner *E.F. Willard* (in the sand near the center of the image).

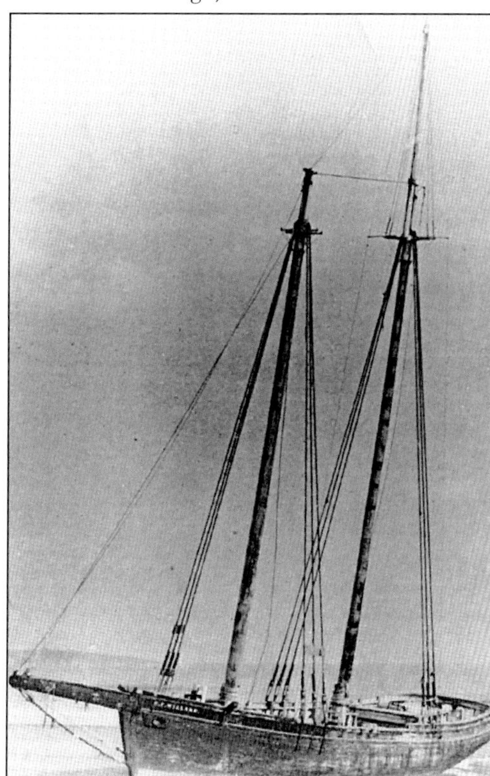

The schooner *E.F. Willard* went aground on Seawall Beach in 1895. Although it did not crash against rocks, it sank firmly into the sand. Over the years the weather and waves took their toll, but its remains were still visible well into the 1990s.

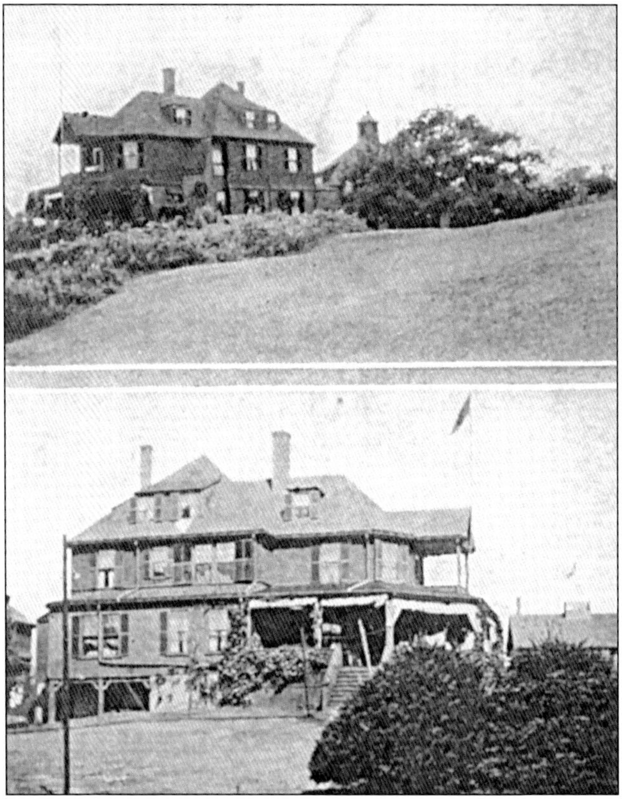

The Manley cottage was built in 1888 for Joseph H. Manley, one of the founders of the Small Point Club. This Queen Anne cottage was designed by George M. Coombs, an architect from Lewiston.

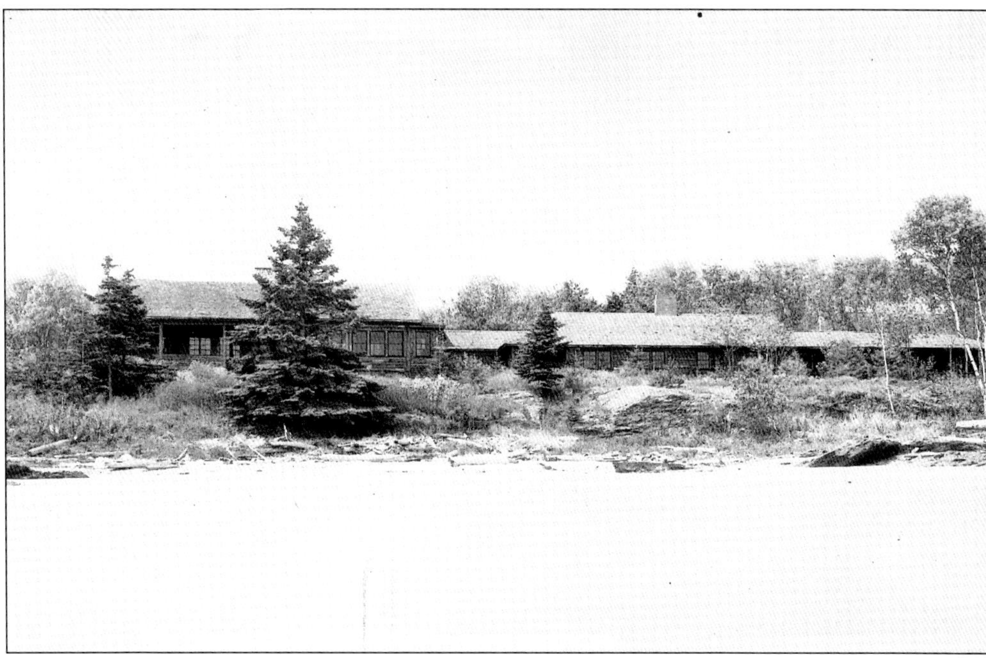

The Dearborn cottage at Small Point was built in 1912. Until the 1950s it was sided with slabs, giving it the appearance of being made of logs. At the time of its construction, it was said to be the largest and most expensive camp in the area, probably in the state.

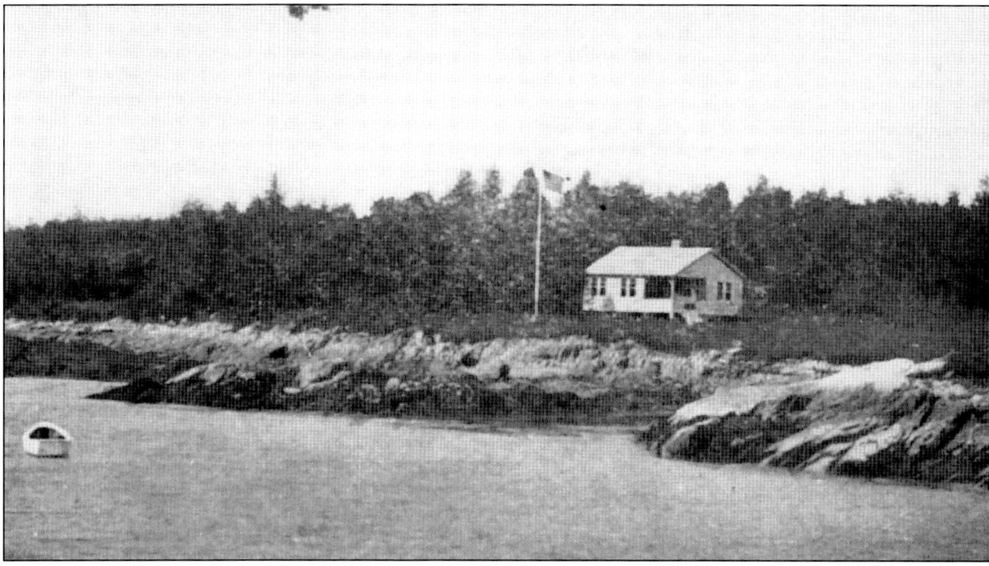

A majority of the summer homes in town were more modest than those built around the Small Point Club. The summer home of Dr. and Mrs. A.F. Williams, built in 1914 at Sebasco, was called "Miramichi," meaning "Happy Retreat." Mrs. Williams individually selected pretty stones from the shore to be used in building the fireplace.

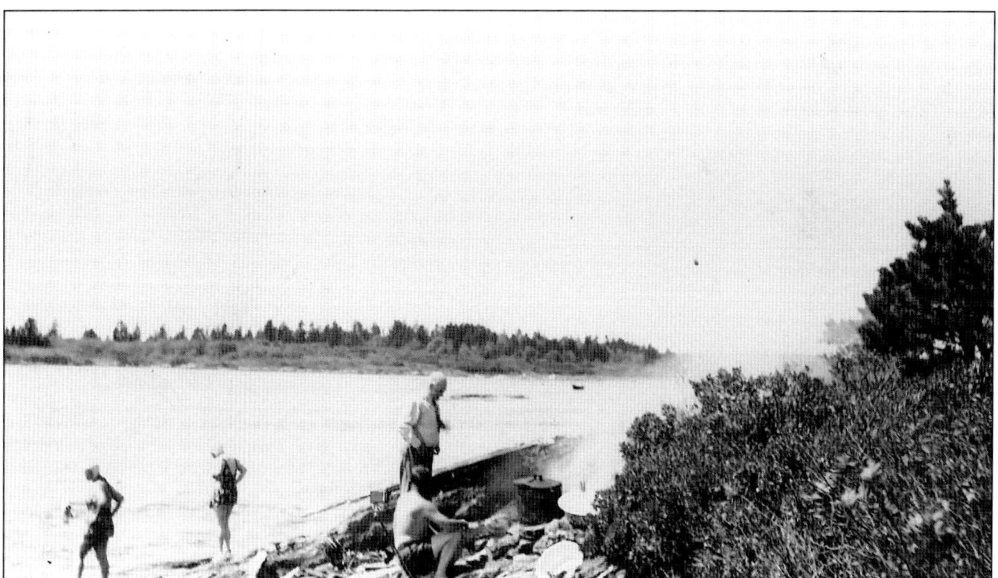

The Williams family enjoyed frequent guests, and a gathering of bathers and pot-watchers are shown here in front of their camp in 1941. Horse Island, with young trees taking over former pastureland, can be seen beyond.

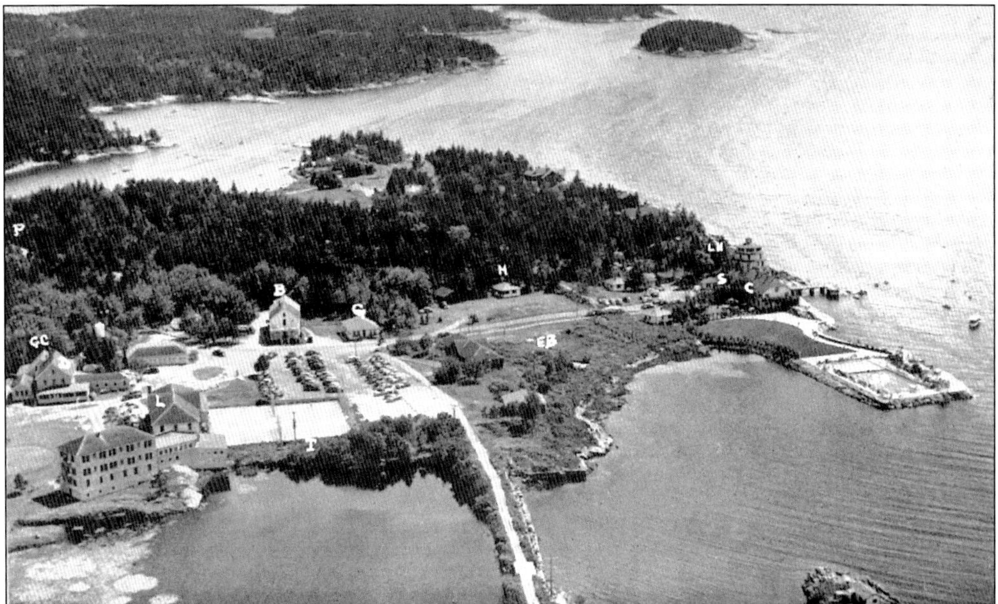

SEBASCO LODGE AND COTTAGES SEBASCO ESTATES, MAINE

This postcard of the Sebasco Lodge and Cottages was labeled with the following caption: "L - Lodge, D - Dining Room, GC - Golf Club House, T - Tennis Courts, B - Beauty Shop, G - Gift and Photo Shops, EB - Early Bird, C - Clipper, SP - Swimming Pool, H - Non-Housekeeping Cottage, S - Snack Bar, P - Playhouse, LH - Lighthouse." The body of water to the left of the causeway is Wattah Lake, formerly Cornelius Pond. On the point beyond the lodge is another resort, Rock Gardens Inn. Both resorts were started around the turn of the century.

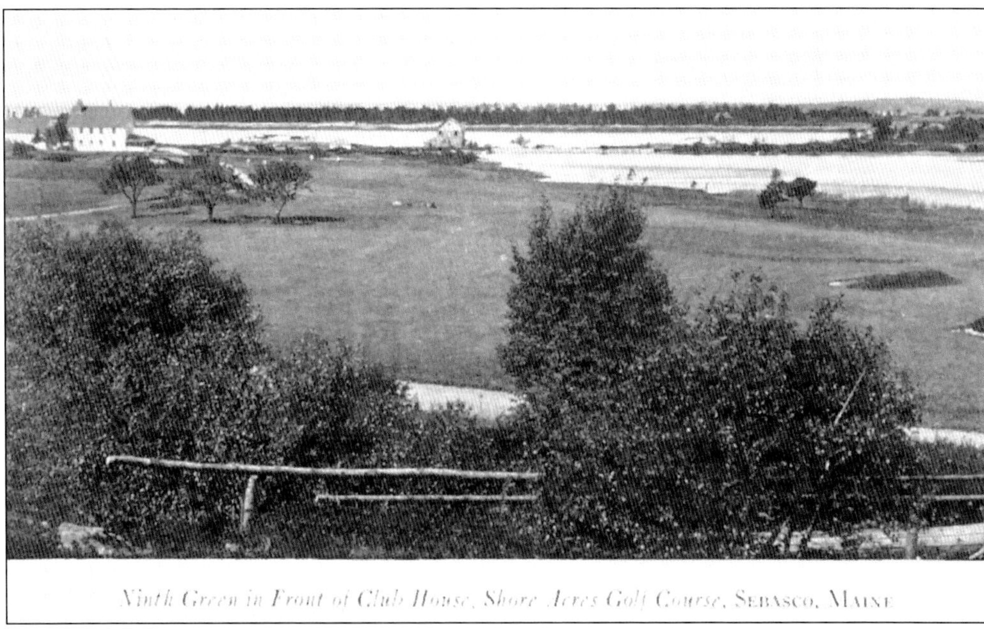

Ninth Green in Front of Club House, Shore Acres Golf Course, SEBASCO, MAINE

This *c.* 1925 photograph of the Shore Acres Golf Course (later Sebasco Lodge) shows the ninth hole, with the store and post office on the left, the ice house in the center, and Wattah Lake (formerly Cornelius Pond) on the right.

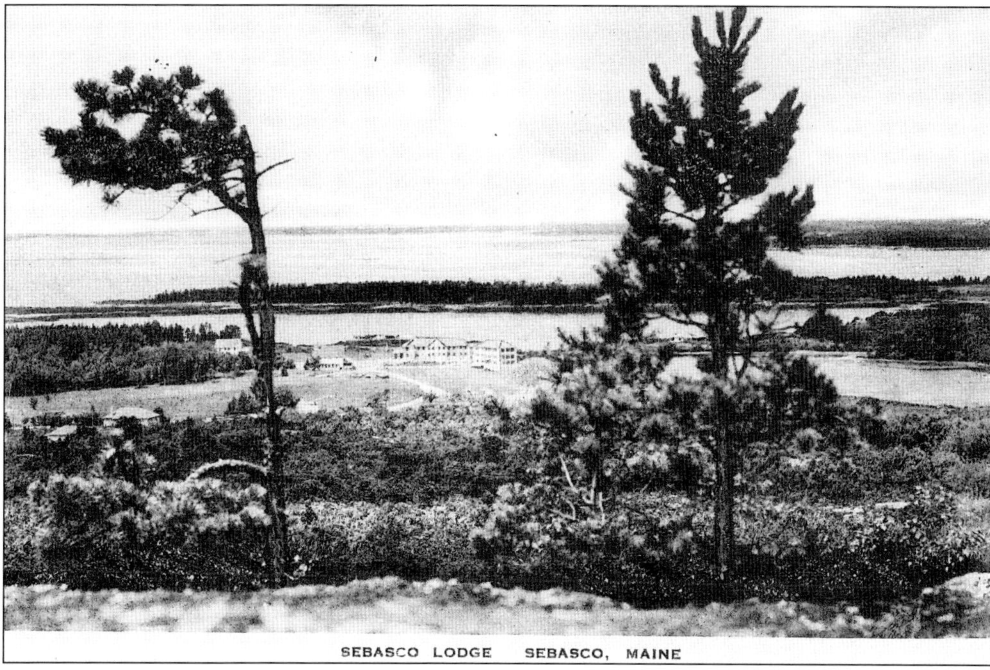

In the 1930s, a modern hotel was added to the resort at Sebasco Estates, as seen in this view from Merritt Mountain.

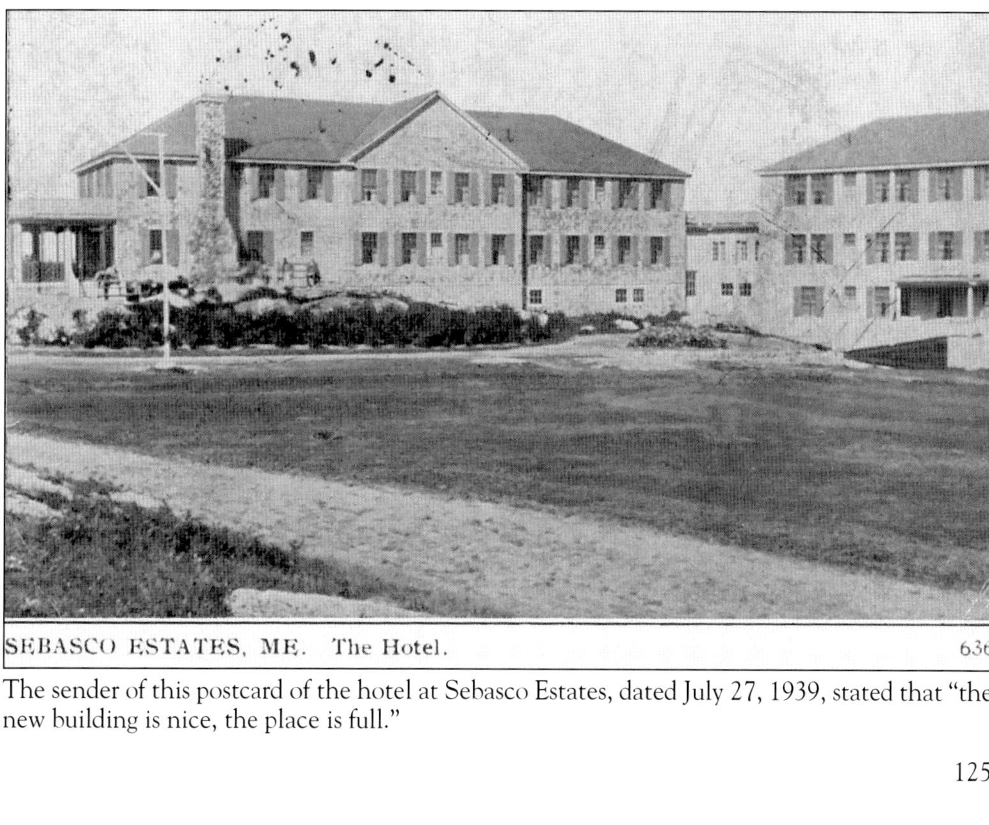

The sender of this postcard of the hotel at Sebasco Estates, dated July 27, 1939, stated that "the new building is nice, the place is full."

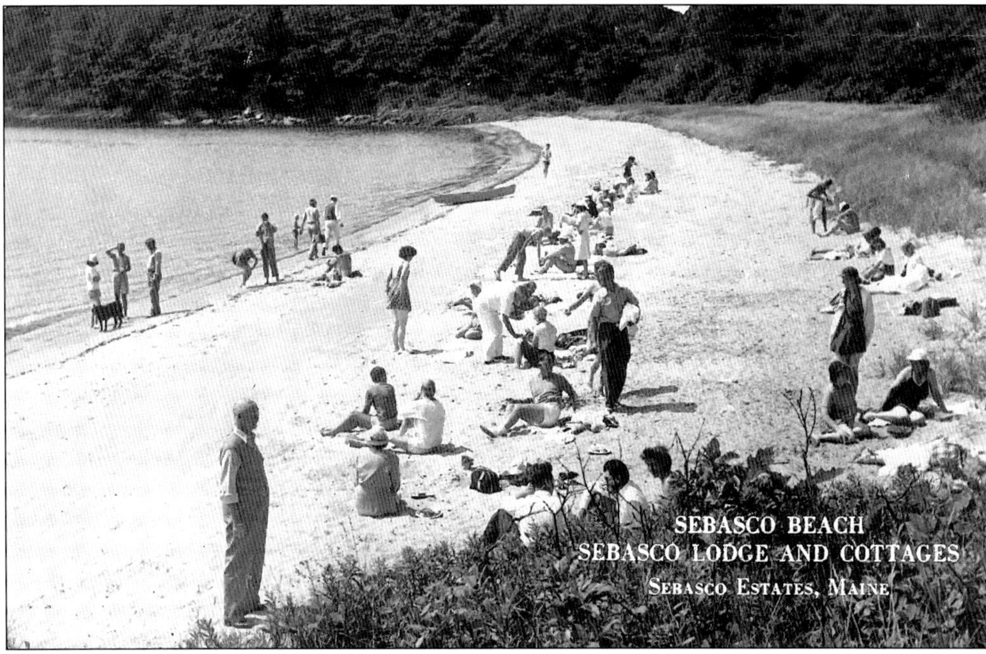

Guests from the Sebasco Lodge and Cottages are shown c. 1945 enjoying the sun at the lodge's beach, Sebasco Beach, off the West Point Road.

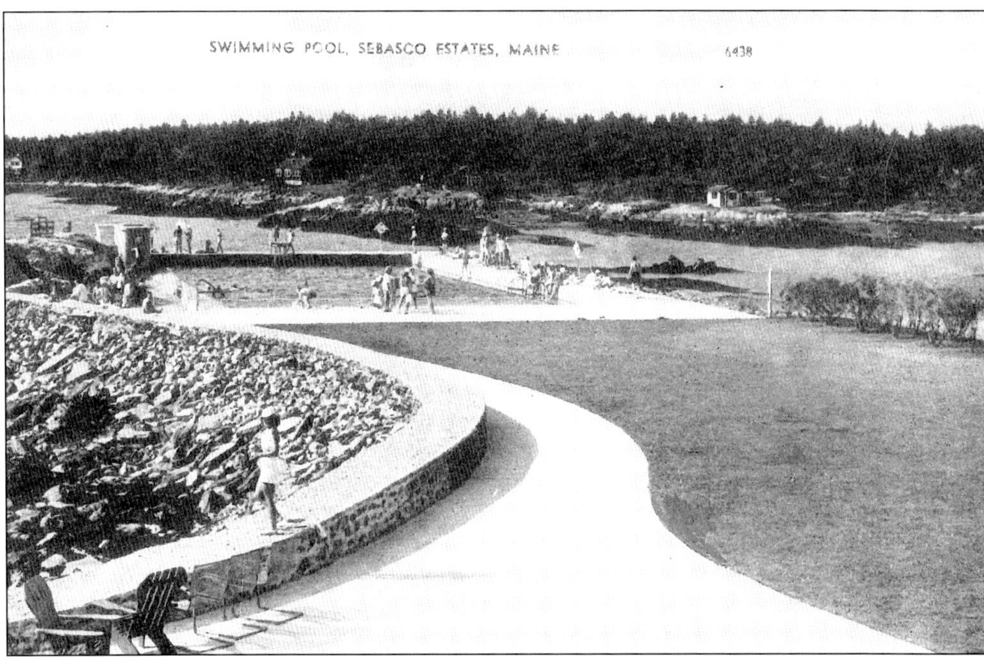

For those guests who preferred a swimming pool, this salt water pool was added to the facilities at the Sebasco Lodge.

Unidentified bathers play in the water in Atkin's Bay near Punch Rock in 1923.

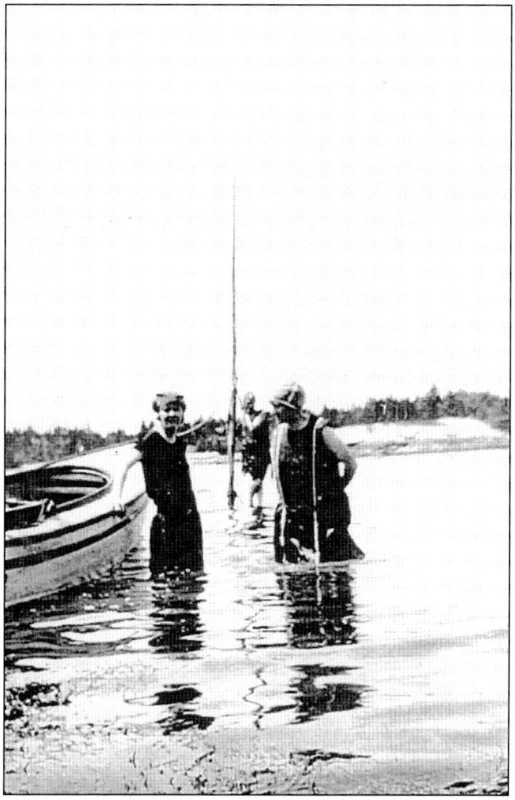

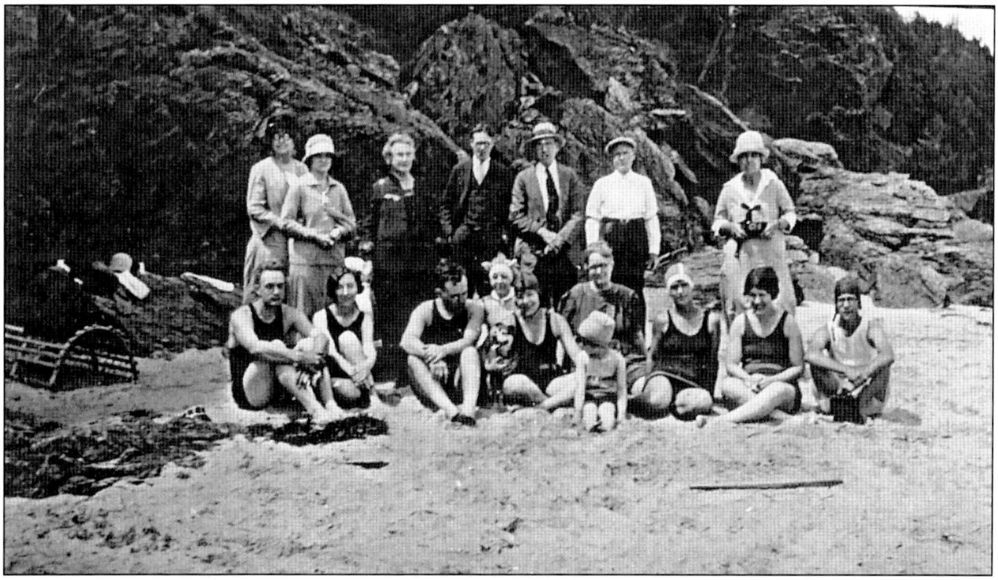

A group from Phippsburg Center picnicked at Small Point Beach in 1927. They are, from left to right, as follows: (sitting in the very front) Ada Minott; (front row) Frank and Susie Leach, unknown, Bertha Wyman, Marilla Williams, Rose Wyman, Margaret Minott, unknown, and Pauline Wyman; (back row) Alice M. Minott, Georgia Leach, Mrs. Sprague, Golder Leach, Hite Wyman, John Leach, and Abbie Minott—with her camera.

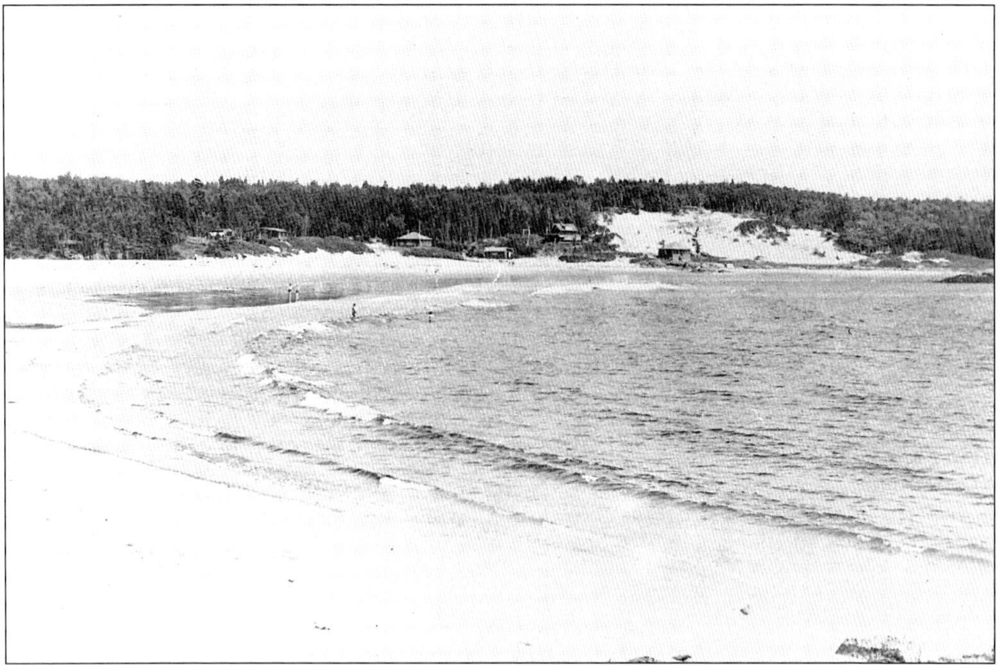

Head Beach, on the west side of Small Point, is all that separates the Atlantic Ocean from The Branch. It has long been a popular bathing beach for the people of Phippsburg. By about 1940, a few cottages had been built near the east end of the beach.

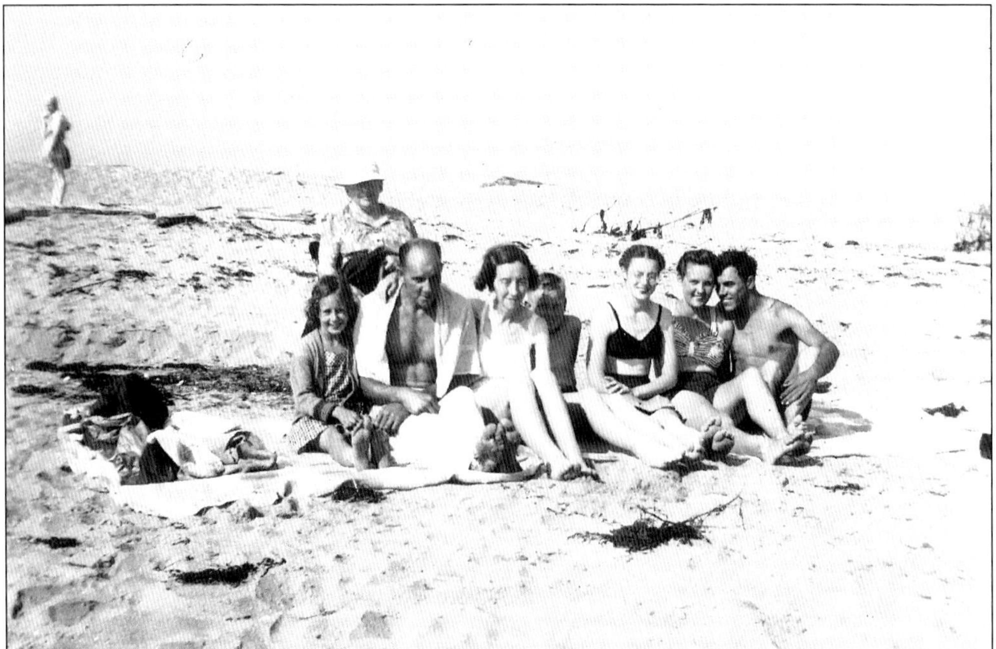

This group gathered at Head Beach for a cool swim in the late 1940s. Lillian Barbour (in the hat) is in the back. The others are, from left to right, Laura Libby, Lyman Barbour, Susie Barbour, Eldon Scott, Lillian Smith, Gladys Scott, and Sam Gomez.